Young Adult Nonfiction

Young Adult Nonfiction

A Readers' Advisory and Collection Development Guide

Elizabeth Fraser

LIBRARIES
UNLIMITED®

An Imprint of ABC-CLIO, LLC

Santa Barbara, California • Denver, Colorado

Library of Congress Cataloging-in-Publication Data

Names: Fraser, Elizabeth, 1970- author.
Title: Young adult nonfiction : a readers' advisory and collection development guide / Elizabeth Fraser.
Description: Santa Barbara, California : Libraries Unlimited, [2020] | Includes bibliographical references and index.
Identifiers: LCCN 2019040778 (print) | LCCN 2019040779 (ebook) | ISBN 9781440869792 (paperback) | ISBN 9781440869808 (ebook)
Subjects: LCSH: Young adult literature—Bibliography. | Teenagers—Books and reading—United States. | Readers' advisory services—United States. | Libraries and teenagers—United States.
Classification: LCC Z1037.A1 F73 2020 (print) | LCC Z1037.A1 (ebook) | DDC 016.8088/99283—dc23
LC record available at https://lccn.loc.gov/2019040778
LC ebook record available at https://lccn.loc.gov/2019040779

ISBN: 978-1-4408-6979-2 (paperback)
      978-1-4408-6980-8 (ebook)

24 23 22 21 20   1 2 3 4 5

This book is also available as an eBook.

Libraries Unlimited
An Imprint of ABC-CLIO, LLC

ABC-CLIO, LLC
147 Castilian Drive
Santa Barbara, California 93117
www.abc-clio.com

This book is printed on acid-free paper ∞
Manufactured in the United States of America

Contents

Part 3: Nonfiction Subject Interests

Introduction

Purpose, Scope, and Selection Criteria

The last decade has seen the continued publishing of titles that recognize young adults between the ages of 12 and 18 as a respected and valued audience, alongside the development of titles that recognize them as having their own voice, interests, and agenda. Libraries are able to have current, appealing collections of young adult nonfiction because publishers and authors persist in creating titles that young adults want to read; these provide both popular reading and fulfill educational requirements. In summarizing the small year-over-year increase in print sales figures for print units in 2018, *Publishers Weekly* noted that young adult nonfiction, along with its adult counterpart, helped to account for the overall gain.

As is pointed out by Kathleen T. Horning in her invaluable book on the art of examining children's books, *From Cover to Cover: Evaluating and Reviewing Children's Books*, the various subgenres of nonfiction may be evaluated using the same criteria: accuracy, organization, illustrations, design, prose, and documentation. Each of the titles included in this volume has been judged to meet each of these criteria.

It may be assumed that the goal of a reader's advisory guide is to help offer suggestions to a reader looking either for something new to read or for something similar to a title or subject for which they already have an affinity. This book is intended to act in that capacity, as well as offering practical suggestions and serving as a starting point for librarians, teacher-librarians, or others who find themselves put in the position of purchasing or replacing the young adult nonfiction collection for their library.

This is a guide primarily intended to offer choices for recreational reading, and as such does not include dictionaries, encyclopedias, or reference books used solely for homework. Using a broad definition of nonfiction as meaning works that are not fiction, genres and formats that are highly appealing to young adults have been included, including graphic nonfiction, poetry, and a wide variety of how-to and craft books.

The titles included in this book have been published since 2012, with exception of a small number of classic titles that remain mainstays of curricula and public library shelves. These titles, which meet the same criteria as the other books in the guide in addition to giving depth to a collection, have been included as "Now Try" titles to give librarians an option to pair titles when offering books to readers.

Organization and Features

The main part of this book is made up of 11 chapters, each of which includes a definition of the genre or literature type, a description of the subgenres and themes within it, and annotations for each title. The author has reviewed each individual title. Where a series has been included, readers will find either annotations for individual titles within a series or the series itself.

The book divides nonfiction categories into three sections, notably: "Nonfiction Genres," "Life Stories," and "Nonfiction Subject Interests." The first part focuses on two exciting and fast-paced genres, "True Adventure" (chapter 1) and "True Crime" (chapter 2). Part 2, "Life Stories," includes both "Memoirs and Autobiographies" (chapter 3) and "Biography" (chapter 4). "Nonfiction Subject Interests," comprising the remaining chapters, includes subject interests that are both popular in publishing and relevant in school and public libraries, including "History" (chapter 5), "Science, Math, and the Environment" (chapter 6) and "Sports" (chapter 7).

Chapter 8, "All about You," contains titles of interest to teens developing their own identities. This chapter covers a wide variety of subjects, such as personal growth, health and wellness, relationships and sex, mental health, and career directions. Chapter 9, "How To," contains a wide range of books for both genders, varying from general crafts to cooking, fashion, technology, drawing, and survival skills. Chapter 10, "The Arts," examines visual and performing arts, music, film, and literature. Chapter 11, "Social Justice and the World," includes areas that have become much more prevalent in the last several years, as teenagers have become much more certain about the world and their place in it. Some of the topics in this area include the media and consumer culture, activism and awareness, social concerns, and religions.

"Consider Starting with . . ." and Fiction Read-Alike Sections

Two additional sections are provided at the end of each chapter. The first, "Consider Starting with . . . ," lists a selected number of popular, highly accessible titles from the chapter. These have been chosen as a starting point for people who would like more information about or who are unfamiliar with any particular genre. They may also be considered as suggestions for display, or booklists. The titles listed in the "Fiction Read-Alikes" sections offer additional possibilities for readers interested in particular genres, themes, or subjects, and may be used to help guide readers who feel more comfortable with either fiction or nonfiction sections to find a topic in which they will be interested.

The Entries

The entries in each category are arranged alphabetically by the authors' last names. Exceptions to this are books in a series that have been written by more than one author, which are listed under the series title. Each entry includes the book's author, title, original date of publication, and number of pages. Each annotated book has also been assigned a suggested reading level:

M   middle school (grades 6–8)

J   junior high school (grades 7–9)

H   high school (grades 10–12)

The following symbols also appear on the entries:

🎗   title has won award(s)

A/YA   books that both teens and adults will enjoy

GN   graphic nonfiction

The annotations are intended to provide enough information about the content and style of the book to help a reader or librarian answer a reader's advisory question. Awards won are indicated at the end of annotations, using the following acronyms or short forms:

ALA	Association for Library Services to Children Notable Books for Children
Alex	Alex Award
BG-HB	Boston Globe–Horn Book Award or Honor
CSK	Coretta Scott King Award or Honor
AENYA	YALSA Award for Excellence in Nonfiction for Young Adults or Honor
GGNT	Great Graphic Novel for Teens
ILA	International Literacy Association Teachers' Choice List
NBA	National Book Award
Newbery	John Newbery Medal Honor
Norma Fleck	Norma Fleck Award or Honor
OP	Orbis Pictus Nonfiction Award or Honor
PP	YALSA Popular Paperbacks for Young Adults
Printz	Michael L. Printz Award or Honor
Pura Belpré	Pura Belpré Book Award or Honor
QP	YALSA Quick Picks
Sibert	Robert F. Sibert Informational Book Award or Honor

Selecting Nonfiction for a Young Adult Collection

All decisions for collection development will ultimately be guided by the overall budget. A budget is generally spent over a fiscal year or by a designated time, and selection may either be done by one person, using tools such as catalogs, review journals, recommended titles from blogs, awards, recommendations from publishers, and profiles from vendors, or by a group of people working in concert to choose materials that will serve the needs of their community.

Knowing the community for whom books are being purchased means the person or people doing the collection development may choose books that will fulfill that community's needs. This allows teenagers to find books that will give them something in which they are interested, in a format that reads like fiction or one that is more easily digestible. Angela Carstensen's *The Readers' Advisory Guide to Teen Literature* divides teen nonfiction into task books, which provide practical information about doing something from repairing a car to making a smokey eye, and nontask books. These are the bread and butter of nonfiction, and make up the majority of the titles included in this volume, as they do in most library collections. Teens read these books not only for enjoyment but also because they provide a rich reading experience, through narratives that enlighten in a number of areas, including character, place, experience, and language.

Applying the details about the book provided in the catalog copy to the purchaser's knowledge of the community will help in deciding whether or not to purchase a title. From deciding whether to buy hardcovers or replace worn books with paperbacks, looking at the number of copies, deciding on the desired cataloging and processing, and considering the percentage of each Dewey number in a collection, working with a vendor may be a desirable solution. An ARP (Automatic Release Plan) may be an alternative choice in which a vendor provides materials for a library or system. A plan follows a budget, may include processing and records, provides an expenditure plan, includes specified branches, authors, or titles, or can be tailored for preferred genres.

Librarians creating an opening day collection may wish to collect statistics including grubby reports for well-used items in their library or branches with well-used collections, which may provide an opportunity to refresh these collections. Order lists for titles purchased in the last year or last few years can be repurposed as a starter collection in the case of a short timeline, with the added benefit of knowing that records for the titles will be in the catalog.

The opportunity to create a capsule or starter collection allows a collection development librarian to generate a list that may be retained for reorder purposes. This is an opportunity to plumb the YALSA Award and Selection lists for titles that are found on assigned reading lists, as well as award winners and authors, with whom library staff tend to be familiar.

Maintaining a Young Adult Collection

The flip side of the coin to making sure that popular and appealing titles are being added to a library's collection is ensuring that they can be found. In order for that to happen, it is vital that old, outdated, and grubby books are removed.

In a 2016 *American Libraries* magazine article entitled "Weeding Without Worry," Rebecca Vnuk points out that that the ongoing and regular weeding of a library's collection would negate many of the horror stories mentioned in the article, although it is always good to be prepared to communicate with library patrons when preparing for a large-scale weeding project. The benefits of removing damaged materials, keeping shelves tidy and easy to navigate, and removing outdated materials cannot be overstated. The best way to do this is at the shelves. Statistics seen through the Library's ILS or printed reports provide an initial starting point and a summary that may be adjusted to create reports to show titles that have circulated over a particular threshold, or that have not circulated for a particular period of time. Examining the books on the shelves not only provides the chance to examine each individual title to see if it is worn or broken, but also gives a bird's eye view of the section to see where or if newer titles are needed, allowing patrons a chance to ask questions at the same time.

References

Carstensen, Angela. *The Reader's Advisory Guide to Teen Literature.* Chicago: American Library Association, 2018.

Cart, Michael. "Just the Facts, Ma'am." *Booklist* 114, no. 14 (May 15, 2018): 35.

Horning, Kathleen T. *From Cover to Cover: Evaluating and Reviewing Children's Books.* New York: HarperCollins, 2010.

Hunt, Jonathan. "The Amorphous Genre." *The Horn Book Magazine* 89, no 3 (May/ June 2013): 31-34.

Milliot, Jim. "Print Unit Sales Increased 1.3% in 2018." *Publisher's Weekly* (Jan 4, 2019).

Summers, Kate. "Adult Reading Habits and Preferences in Relation to Gender Differences." *Reference & User Services Quarterly* 52, no. 3 (Spring 2019): 243.

Part 1

Nonfiction Genres

Chapter 1

True Adventure

Definition

More than any other genre, there is a strong parallel between the characteristics of nonfiction titles in this category and their fictional counterparts, although readers assuming that adventure titles will have some sort of swarthy character facing down an overt threat will miss out on a number of categories by relying on this cliché. The books included here feature stories of people facing challenges, overcoming great odds, and demonstrating remarkable courage and fortitude, and who are all the more remarkable for their veracity.

Appeal

Adventure is the genre in nonfiction most geared for escapist reading. While there are few studies of adult readers, consistent anecdotal beliefs persist that males are the primary readers of this genre. Books in this category's subgenres tend to be fast-paced, and feature people facing dire situations, competing with—or hiding from—their enemies, or overcoming odds to go farther, faster, or win in the end. These stories provide librarians with an opportunity to tempt readers who have seen *The Blind Side* into trying one of the remarkable underdog stories, for example, while fans of spy fiction will be captivated by Neal Bascomb's accounts of actual World War II missions.

Chapter Organization

This chapter starts off with "Survival and Disaster Stories," which provide readers with harrowing tales of disasters and people working to save others from them. This is followed by "Sports Adventures," true tales of athletes, teams, and sports figures overcoming stereotypes and odds. "War Stories" provide both historical and contemporary tales of bravery, valor, and resolve. The chapter concludes with tales of daring, danger, and determination, as men and women set off for parts unknown in the face of impossible odds and almost certain death in "Explorations, Travel, and Historical Adventures."

Survival and Disaster Stories

The popularity of these stories crosses both age and gender. As these titles frequently tell the stories of both genders, they have an intrinsic appeal to either, allowing them to experience life and death experiences that are more exciting than vicarious armchair travel, with the added benefit of knowing the stories are true. Readers interested in finding out what to do if they were to be caught in a situation where they needed their own survival kit can find some practical examples in the "Survival Skills" section of chapter 9.

Callery, Sean.

50 Things You Should Know About Titanic. 2016. 80p. **M**

There are some things widely assumed to be common knowledge about the *Titanic*'s sinking: it ran into an iceberg, there weren't enough lifeboats, and a large percentage of the passengers drowned. Those sparse details leave out a lot of interesting information for anyone interested in the doomed ship—details about its building, workforce, passengers, crossing, life on board, and the sinking itself, as well as the aftermath. This quick and informational book on a perennially popular topic is a boon for readers who enjoy books with facts, and will appeal to fans or readers interested in the ship itself.

Keywords: Shipwrecks • *Titanic*

Fighting to Survive

While the situations encountered by the people in the <u>Fighting to Survive</u> series are likely to be far outside the average reader's daily experience, they will appeal to anyone looking for thrilling stories to read from the comfort of their own home. Not even the introductions noting just how unusual it is to be attacked by a dangerous animal, or how much safer airplane travel is than driving, lessen the impact of reading about a survivor waiting for help. Photographs and maps add extra immediacy, while a list of resources and Web sites is also included.

Braun, Eric Mark.

Fighting to Survive in the Wilderness: Terrifying True Stories. 2020. 64p. **M J**

Dickmann, Nancy.

Fighting to Survive Animal Attacks: Terrifying True Stories. 2020. 64p. **M J**

Dickmann, Nancy.

Fighting to Survive World War II: Terrifying True Stories. 2020. 64p. **M J**

McCollum, Sean.

Fighting to Survive Airplane Crashes: Terrifying True Stories. 2020. 64p. **M** **J**

Raum, Elizabeth.

Fighting to Survive Being Lost at Sea: Terrifying True Stories. 2020. 64p. **M** **J**

Raum, Elizabeth.

Fighting to Survive Space Disasters: Terrifying True Stories. 2020. 64p. **M** **J**

Hale, Nathan.

Donner Dinner Party. <u>Nathan Hale's Hazardous Tales</u>. 2013. 128p. **M**

The penultimate actions of the Donner Party are so well-known as to have taken on tall-tale proportions among disaster stories. What is not as widely understood, and which is explained here in a format that makes the story both tragic and unbearably sad, is how such a large group could be brought to such a desperate end. The series of poor decisions made by the group, compounded by outside influences and weather, are made doubly ironic when rendered in comic format. **GGNT**

Keywords: Cannibalism • Donner Party • Westward expansion

Sherman, Casey, and Michael J. Tougias.

The Finest Hours (Young Readers Edition): The True Story of a Heroic Sea Rescue. <u>True Sea Rescues</u>. 2014. 176p. **M** **J**

The recounting of a storm so bad that it ripped two oil tankers in half off the Cape Cod coast on February 18, 1952, is dramatic enough to make hearts race. Coast Guard sailors determined to do their jobs set off to rescue the men stranded on the pieces of the *Fort Mercer*, completely unaware that the *Pendleton* had met the same fate. The authors make the readers care about the survivors and rescuers in recounting their stories from the ships' foundering through the aftermath of the rescue. It is notable that this amazing story, which was rarely mentioned in later life by the men involved and which is still the biggest open water small boat rescue in U.S. history, left the Coast Guard Motorboat 36-foot 36500 used by the four men who set out that night as the only boat on the U.S. National Register of Historic Places.

Keywords: Cape Cod • Coast Guard • *Pendleton* • Sea rescues

Strathdee, Steffanie, and Thomas Patterson, with Tessa Barker.

The Perfect Predator: A Scientist's Race to Save Her Husband from a Deadly Superbug; A Memoir. 2019. 352p. **A/YA**

> Steffanie Strathdee's terrifying mission to save her husband, psychologist Thomas Patterson, began in Luxor. Initially diagnosed with food poisoning, he was readmitted to the hospital and then airlifted out of Egypt when he was discovered first to have acute pancreatitis and then to have a football-sized cyst in his abdomen full of the deadly, multidrug-resistant superbug *A. baumannii.* Back in the United States, as every approved treatment failed, Strathdee looked for any alternative, finding a possibility in phage therapy, dismissed by clinicians a century ago. Almost as horrifying as this medical nightmare is a calmly detailed history of antibiotics and recounting of the difficulties faced by modern medicine, including the rise of drug-resistant bacteria. This story of two HIV researchers and a medical nightmare that could happen to anyone is an eye-opening thriller for readers interested in science and medicine.
>
> **Keywords:** Patterson, Thomas • Phage therapy • Strathdee, Stephanie

Sports Adventures

The men and women in these books have all of the best traits hoped for and expected from athletes, such as mental and physical endurance, an underdog's ability to overcome obstacles, and the determination necessary to make it to the finish line despite what life may throw in their way. The books in this category allow readers to go along for the ride. Well-written incorporations of the sport allow readers to appreciate the achievements of the books' subjects without having a background in the game being played, though fans of the sport will be drawn to them automatically. As the focus is on the achievement rather than a particular player, these books have a more lasting appeal and a longer life span in library collections.

Ballard, Chris.

 One Shot at Forever: A Small Town, an Unlikely Coach, and a Magical Baseball Season. 2012. 272p. **H A/YA**

> Lynn Sweet, already widely regarded with suspicion for his liberal teaching methods, had no intention of becoming the baseball coach in the small town of Macon. His unparalleled success with the team both on and off the field is a fascinating and thrilling story for both baseball fans and readers who enjoy rooting for any sort of underdog. Surprisingly, this story hasn't yet made it to a screen of any size.
>
> **Keywords:** Baseball • Sweet, Lynn

Brown, Daniel James.

The Boys in the Boat: The True Story of an American Team's Epic Journey to Win Gold at the 1936 Olympics. 2017. 357p. **M J**

Rowing is a sport that demands everything from the athlete taking part; for nine people in a shell to compete successfully they must ignore pain and move as one. Joe Rantz, who had been sent to live with his father at the age of four when his mother died, and turned out by his stepmother at the age of 10, was determined to make the University of Washington's team in order to stay at the school. The story of how nine working-class boys became national champions and then raced for the United States at the 1936 Berlin Olympics—defeating teams they were never supposed to defeat and surprising not only themselves, but their country and the world—is thrilling and inspiring.

Keywords: Olympics • Rowing

Now Try: One of the greatest classic underdog sports stories is that of a racehorse that defied all expectations in 1938, a media darling that garnered more attention than the leaders of the United States, Russia, and Germany. Laura Hillenbrand's classic *Seabiscuit: An American Legend* tells the story of the three men who believed in and trained the runty descendant of the great Man o'War when all indications were against them, creating one of the greatest legends of all time.

Hoose, Phillip.

Attucks! Oscar Robertson and the Basketball Team that Awakened a City. 2018. 224p. **M J**

The backdrop Hoose provides for the all-black high school basketball team that captured the attention of a segregated Indianapolis in the 1950s is the rise in that state of the Ku Klux Klan in the 1920s. One of the results was the creation of Crispus Attucks High School, a blacks-only high school created out of a desire to separate students by race and named after the first man to die in the Boston Massacre. It was denied entry into both the Indiana High School Athletic Association (IHSAA) and the Indiana Tournament, unable to compete in sporting events against other schools in the state until 1941, when the irony of denying playing opportunities to young men who would soon be fighting for their country was recognized. Hoose traces the development of the Attucks team during the years Oscar Robertson went from watching his older brother Flap play to ending up on the varsity team himself in his sophomore year. The years and teams after that tell a phenomenal story of leadership and basketball played out against a city that must decide whether to root for the team or their own deeply held prejudices. **ALA**

Keywords: Basketball • Crispus Attucks High School • Indianapolis • Robertson, Oscar

Neri, G., and Corbin Wilkin.

 Grand Theft Horse. 2018. 240p. **J** **H**

G. Neri presents the tale of his cousin, Gail Ruffu. Ruffu grew up devoted to horses, wishing above all other things for one of her own, and learning about the proper way to care for and train them in the various places she lived. She eventually became accredited as a trainer in Britain, where racing was free of habitual doping and overtraining; these root causes of the animal injuries and deaths so prevalent in American racing horrified her and made her determined to train the horse in which she owned a share a better way. When she found that the horse, Urgent Envoy, was in grave danger from these standard treatments, she decided to steal him and face the consequences. The true story of the following years is the story of two underdogs, as Urgent Envoy's other owners and the racing community remove Ruffu's credentials, ban her, and try to have her prosecuted while she fights for the safety of her beloved horse, putting up everything she owns while the system is set against her. This is a story for fans of horses, racing, and people determined to do the right thing at any cost, particularly when that cost will take time and effort rather than money and power. **GGNT**

Keywords: Graphic memoir • Horse racing • Ruffu, Gail

Sheinkin, Steve.

Undefeated: Jim Thorpe and the Carlisle Indian School Football Team. 2017. 288p. **J**

Sheinkin manages to do more than present a biography of one of the winningest football teams, and player, ever; he's written a gripping and involving account of a football player and team that will draw in even non–sports fans. While Jim Thorpe was a dominating force in athletics in the early 20th century, this book will also educate readers on the history of the Carlisle Indian Industrial School, created by Richard Henry Pratt as a direct result of his dislike of Indians, and the direct and formal measures that he integrated into the school to strip them of their language and background and assimilate them into white culture. **AENYA**

Keywords: Football • Thorpe, Jim

War Stories

This section presents adventure stories that take place during wartime and emphasize character traits such as endurance, bravery, and courage, which help ensure the survival of the people whose tales are being told. It is this that differentiates these stories from the "Human Cruelties" subsection in chapter 5.

Bascomb, Neal.

The Grand Escape: The Greatest Prison Breakout of the Twentieth Century. 2018. 288p. **M** **J**

To be held by the enemy in World War I was no guarantee of fair treatment; Germany neither signed nor adhered to the conventions agreed upon at The Hague around the turn of the century. As a result, of the 1.3 million prisoners of war in Europe, it should not be a surprise that among those held by the Germans were a large number who were determined to escape from the camps where they were being held. Bascomb provides a riveting tale of a number of those POWs detained at Holzminden, a camp designed to be escape-proof and in the charge of a particularly ruthless commandant. Readers are introduced to the men, combat pilots in the days when airplanes were only decades old, who faced certain death if shot down behind enemy lines. Bolstered by photographs, maps, and archival documents, this book tells the story of life in the camp, the men's daring escape, and the hope it brought to a war-torn populace.

Keywords: Prisoners of war • World War I

Bascomb, Neal.

The Nazi Hunters: How a Team of Spies and Survivors Captured the World's Most Notorious Nazi. 2013. 256p. **M** **J**

Adolf Eichmann, who by 1944 had been in charge of "Jewish affairs" for the Nazis for eight years, was by all accounts very successful in executing Hitler's plan for eradicating the Jews. An explanation of just how this was done, using the firsthand account of Holocaust survivor Zeev Sapir, from the day that Eichmann rounded up all 103 residents of Sapir's village of Dobradovo, Hungary, to take them to Auschwitz to the day he was found by the Russians in January 1945, is chilling. Eichmann, like many SS officers, managed to elude the Allies and the OSS after the war, escaping without a trace. Judged as one of the most wanted war criminals of World War II, he remained a person of interest for 15 years, until a person suspected to be Eichmann surfaced in Argentina. This fascinating and fast-paced narrative nonfiction follows the people determined to find him and return him to Israel for what would become one of the most important trials of the 20th century. **AENYA**

Keywords: Eichmann, Adolf • Nazis • World War II

Bascomb, Neal.

Sabotage: The Mission to Destroy Hitler's Atomic Bomb. 2016. 310p. **J**

While the Nazi invasion of Norway in 1940 was not met with indifference, the Norwegian military, as pointed out in Neal Bascomb's *Sabotage,* was severely outclassed. While the Nazis enacted martial law and some Norwegians went along with the occupying forces, readers are introduced to a professor and students at the Norwegian Institute of Technology (NTH), who were against this subjugation. Bascomb presents the frightening and exciting story of how close Hitler's Nazis came to finding an ideal location for the set-up and creation of an atomic bomb, as the British SOE (Special Operations Executive) worked, frantically and unsuccessfully, to derail the German's plans. It was up to a small contingent of determined men to not only save their country, but to change the outcome of the war itself.

Keywords: Atomic bomb • Hitler, Adolf • Military • Norway • World War II

Hale, Nathan.

Big Bad Ironclad! <u>Nathan Hale's Hazardous Tales</u>. 2012. 128p. **M**

This volume of the graphic series about a Civil War spy includes the story of a larger-than-life prankster along with the development of both sides' armored warships. Readers are introduced to the inventors of the *Merrimack* and the *Monitor*, two of the ironclad steam warships developed for use in the war, and shown their impact. One highlight of this series is its ability to integrate the quirks of historical characters, making them especially memorable; here, readers will certainly remember the ships' inventor, John Ericsson, who succeeded despite a timeline of 100 days, and be charmed and impressed by the antics of William Cushing, described in the source notes as a precursor to a modern-day SEAL.

Keywords: Civil War • Cushing, William • Ericsson, John • *Merrimack* • *Monitor*

Hopkinson, Deborah.

Dive! World War II Stories of Sailors and Submarines in the Pacific. 2016. 384p. **M J**

After the December 7, 1941, bombing of Pearl Harbor by the Japanese left much of the United States' fleet of battleships decimated, a small number of U.S. submarines became the Allies' ultimate hope for victory in the battle for the Pacific. Deborah Hopkinson brings readers along with the U.S. Submarine Force, as they face day-to-day life as well as the dangers from the battleships and planes above them. One such soldier takes readers aboard the *Seawolf*, where they are given the men's firsthand experiences of firing torpedoes and knowing survival could depend on the speed of the submarine's dive. Hopkinson includes a number of sidebars with different kinds of supplemental information to add to the text. These include further information about submarines or life on a submarine, background information about the war, or information from or about a particular person. Also included are statistics, facts and figures, and rosters from the U.S. Submarine Force, as well as a very thorough resource section. Readers interested in the subject may take advantage of virtual tours as well as the compiled bibliography.

Keywords: *Seawolf* • Submarines • U.S. Submarine Force • World War II

1

Webb, Brandon.

Navy SEALs: Mission at the Caves. <u>Special Operations Files</u>. 2018. 128p. **M**

As a teenager, Brandon Webb clashed with his father, and found both work and direction on the water. It was there he first heard about the SEALs and made a decision to join that elite arm of the U.S. military. This third person memoir presents Webb's route through the Navy, as he took several courses before qualifying for BUD/S and then endured the successively harder levels of training necessary to earn the coveted trident pin of a SEAL. Readers interested in the torturous phases endured by the candidates will be impressed by his descriptions, which do not stop once he joins his team. Webb began sniper training and was required to use it when, after the unfortunate events of September 11, 2001, his platoon, which had been deployed overseas in Kuwait, was assigned to Afghanistan as part of Operation Enduring Freedom. This soldier's account of how he used the skills he acquired during his training as a part of this mission will appeal to readers interested in military stories and the military.

Keywords: SEALs • U.S. Navy • Wars

2

3

4

5

Explorations, Travel, and Historical Adventures

The books in this subgenre provide readers with experiences that offer them a wealth of possibilities, as people set off for uncharted corners of the world, and hope to go higher, farther, and faster in order to find new places, species, or adventures. As they are taken along on these journeys, readers are given insights not only into the mindsets of the men and women who made them and the hardships they endured, but also the time and place in which they endured them. A series demonstrating incredible escapes allows readers to step into the shoes of the adventurers, allowing them to see firsthand if they have what it would take to survive, while *A World of Her Own* demonstrates that female explorers all too often were not given the credit they deserved.

6

7

8

Bertozzi, Nick.

Shackleton: Antarctic Odyssey. 2014. 128p. **M** **J**

Ernest Shackleton's determination to reach the South Pole led him to plan and lead one of the most ambitious expeditions of the early 20th century, the Imperial Trans-Antarctic Expedition, which was to culminate in an overland march by dogsled. How he and his crew survived after their ship, the *Endurance*, was locked into the ice 70 miles from the closest land, is both harrowing and inspiring.

Keywords: Antarctic expedition • *Endurance* • Graphic novel • Shackleton, Ernest

9

10

11

Now Try: Readers who enjoy this combination of danger, determination, and survival in an inhospitable climate will likely also enjoy Jennifer Armstrong's Orbis Pictus award–winning *Shipwreck at the Bottom of the World: The Extraordinary True Story of Shackleton and the Endurance*. Endurance takes on a dual meaning in this book as, after Shackleton's ship is trapped in the Antarctic ice 100 miles from land in 1914, he and part of his crew wait months on ice floes before attempting an incredibly perilous journey in an attempt to find a rescue ship. Pictures of his ship encased in ice will bring shivers, and this inspiring story remains a classic.

Lourie, Peter.

Locked in Ice: Nansen's Daring Quest for the North Pole. 2019. 336p. **M** **J**

The same people who thought Fridtjof Nansen's plan to ski across Greenland, an expedition that made his team the first to cross Greenland's polar ice cap, were guaranteed to be horrified by his idea to reach the North Pole. Nansen, an explorer whose innovations in boat design, science, and exploration are still being used, proposed to build and travel in a ship that could withstand the ice that had crushed previous vessels attempting to make the voyage. His strategy was to aim at the pole, locking the ship, the *Fram*, in the ice, with the idea that it would be taken by the currents to its goal. Along the way, he would gather previously unknown scientific information. After two years icebound, he came to the conclusion that he needed to abandon ship and, with one of his crew members and specially designed equipment, take to the ice to try and reach his final goal. The struggles experienced by the two men as they tried to survive over the next year are exciting and stressful. Lourie's presentation of Nansen's explorations and their lasting effects on science and exploration are supplemented by copious historical photographs and further information about the ship, its crew, their dogs, and the navigation and science of the time.

Keywords: Explorers • Nansen, Fridtjof • Polar exploration

Ross, Michael Elsohn.

A World of Her Own: 24 Amazing Women Explorers and Adventurers. <u>Women of Action</u>. 2014. 224p. **J**

The adventures to be found in this volume are exciting and noteworthy, as the women who made discoveries and traveled alongside men—and in many cases went higher, farther, and faster—were usually denied any credit. As pointed out by Lorie Karnath, the men who reached the North and South poles were members of the Explorers Club, which didn't admit its first female member for over 75 years, and did not have a female president until 2000. Here, readers will find out about women who have been drawn to explore and carry out their work in the most remote parts of the world, from the highest peaks to the most remote waterways. Painters, scientists, and researchers have devoted their lives to the study of their chosen subject, whether it be plants or herpetologist Kate Jackson's study of frogs. The presentation of the chapters is impressive, containing trivia that will entertain readers, such as Pamela Rasmussen's developed allergy to leeches when studying birds in South America.

Keywords: Explorers • Scientists

Sandler, Martin.

The Impossible Rescue: The True Story of an Amazing Arctic Adventure. 2012. 176p. **M** **J**

Winter in the arctic, where temperatures can drop to –60°F (fahrenheit and celsius meet at –40°), and there is no sunshine at any hour of the day, is not something to which the average person can easily relate. Even so, Martin Sandler is able, with the help of numerous period photographs and maps, to bring to life an incredibly dangerous and courageous journey undertaken in 1897 in this barren and desolate area. That year winter blew in early, causing ice to make things more treacherous for whalers, and encasing in ice eight American whalers and the men that manned them. President McKinley, upon hearing of the stranded ships, mustered a crew to undertake the 1500-mile journey to take food to the imperiled men, their only hope for rescue.

Keywords: Arctic • Rescue • Whalers

You Choose: Can You Escape?

The reader is presented with different scenarios and asked to choose which to take. Each scenario gives readers a slim chance for saving themselves from their current situation; no scenario is pleasant and any could end in death. All of the choices introduce factual information about the setting in briskly paced narratives, and numerous photographs help set the scene and add context to the stories. The variety of available locales allows readers to choose what kind of adventure they would like to have, as escaping from a locked cell offers different challenges than having no defense against the elements. The books themselves have a number of choices, allowing readers to follow different circumstances or skip to supplemental information about the topic, as well as some notable case studies.

Braun, Eric.

Could You Escape Alcatraz? An Interactive Survival Adventure. 2019. 112p. **M**

Doeden, Matt.

Could You Escape the Paris Catacombs? An Interactive Survival Adventure. 2019. 112p. **M**

Hoena, Blake.

Could You Escape a Deserted Island? An Interactive Survival Adventure. 2019. 112p. **M**

Hoena, Blake.

Could You Escape the Tower of London? An Interactive Survival Adventure. 2019. 112p. **M**

Consider Starting with . . .

Bascomb, Neal. *The Nazi Hunters: How a Team of Spies and Survivors Captured the World's Most Notorious Nazi.*

Lourie, Peter. *Locked in Ice: Nansen's Daring Quest for the North Pole.*

Neri, G., and Corbin Wilkin. *Grand Theft Horse.*

Ross, Michael Elsohn. *A World of Her Own: 24 Amazing Women Explorers and Adventurers.*

Strathdee, Steffanie and Thomas Patterson, with Tessa Barker. *The Perfect Predator: A Scientist's Race to Save Her Husband from a Deadly Superbug; A Memoir.*

Fiction Read-Alikes

- **Smith, Roland.** *Ascent.* Readers looking for a solid adventure can find one with any of the titles in Roland Smith's **Peak** series. Peak Marcello ends up with his father, the owner of a climbing company in Thailand, as the lesser of two evils when he is arrested climbing up a skyscraper in New York City. His home situation seems to put him in danger fairly consistently, but what is a guy going to do when he really loves to get to great places like Mount Everest and Hindu Kush? In his newest adventure, *Ascent*, climbing one of the most isolated mountains in the world may be the easiest thing he does.

- **Sands, Kevin.** *The Assassin's Curse.* Even before Christopher Rowe makes it to the court of Charles II, where he will save the king's life, he finds a member of his party has been poisoned and is almost garroted himself. Christopher is sent to save the true target of the assassin: the king's sister, Minette. He and his friends are off to the court of the Sun King, Louis XIV, in the third novel of the **Blackthorn Key** series.

- **James, Greg, and Chris Smith.** *Kid Normal.* Murph is definitely *not* excited about moving. Again. He has spent so much time moving that he figures he has spent at least a third of his life looking at yet another new and loathed house and wishing someone would blow it up. Little does he know he'll only have to wait a few months for it to happen, and that's just the start of his problems. His new junior high school finds him standing out in Capability Training, and he is the only student in school without a superpower. In Greg James and Chris Smith's illustrated and very funny novel, it turns out that it isn't necessarily the superpower that makes you super.

1

2

3

4

5

6

7

8

9

10

11

Chapter 2

True Crime

Definition

Books in this genre focus on a real event, usually a crime, whether solved or unsolved, and present a recounting of any related investigations and people. The enduring appeal of this genre is attested to by the continued popularity and proliferation of related film, reality, and television programming such as *Spotlight*, *Dateline*, and the *NCIS* franchise.

Appeal

True crime provides a vehicle for escapist reading. Humans have a desire to see criminals punished for their crimes, and tales of investigations into heinous and devious offenses offer readers a front-row seat to stories that also ponder the offenders' motives in order to determine how they committed the crimes. Titles in the "Intrigue and Espionage" subgenre take a larger-scale look at crimes that affect events on a much larger scale than one person generally sees, generally involving battles, wars, countries, and other historical events.

Chapter Organization

The chapter begins with "Cons and Crimes: Solved and Unsolved," which contains titles about recent and historical cons, crimes, and the men and women who tried (and occasionally failed) to solve them. A section with titles about the means used by investigators attempting to solve crimes follows in "Crime and Crime Science." The final section, "Intrigue and Espionage," provides titles in which spies and spying play a starring role.

Cons and Crimes: Solved and Unsolved

This section includes true accounts of crimes and cons, and a discussion of a culture that makes it permissible for a heinous type of crime to occur without appropriate punishment by society. Interestingly, almost all of the crimes discussed in these titles are historical, demonstrating that while our fascination with crimes and the people who commit them have not changed, forensics and laws have. Readers are shown how some criminals gained any notoriety they had only because of their crimes, while it took years for others to prove their innocence. In some cases, very graphic descriptions may merit thought prior to including titles in library collections.

Blumenthal, Karen.

Bonnie and Clyde: The Making of a Legend. 2018. 256p. **M J**

What is rightly pointed out in Karen Blumenthal's well-rounded and thorough biography of bank robbers and murderers Bonnie Parker Thornton and Clyde Chestnut Barrow is that they gained much of their notoriety after their deaths. The Oscar-winning 1967 film starring Warren Beatty is the best-known of the many books and movies of which they are the subject, although most titles give the same impression, by depicting them as legendary outlaws and omitting details of both the gang's crimes and the injuries they suffered committing them. This title both shows the crimes they committed, including information about the victims who were killed, and gives information about the couple's backgrounds and families, who stood by the wayward teenagers who ended up in a car riddled with bullets. The many photographs included allow readers to follow along the journey; presenting the faces shown in the narrative draws readers in at a human level. Information about how the legend of the twosome grew after their untimely deaths, the fate of the other parties involved, and a timeline that reinforces just how quickly the events unfolded are fascinating. With a subject that is so affected by legend and rumor, it is especially useful to have Blumenthal's reminders not only in the main narrative, indicating how difficult it was for information to be communicated at the time, but also in a comprehensive backmatter noting conflicting reports and family opinions.

Keywords: Bank robbers • Barrow, Clyde • Criminals • Parker, Bonnie

Bragg, Georgia.

Caught! Nabbing History's Most Wanted. 2019. 224p. **M J**

This book, as with Bragg's previous titles, contains short, narrative chapters that take the basic facts known about the volume's subjects and present them in a way designed to make them appealing to readers. In this case, they are presented in an active tone with a great deal of detail, humor, and language that readers will appreciate, whether describing Jesse James as a "momma's boy" or emphasizing just how poor a job the detectives searching for the missing Mona Lisa did.

Each piece is followed by a summary of facts and statistics about the case. Interested readers will also find a bibliography and list of online resources.

Keywords: Criminals • Gangsters • Pirates • Thieves

Faryon, Cynthia J.

Real Justice: Sentenced to Life at Seventeen; The Story of David Milgaard. <u>Real Justice</u>. 2012. 150p. **M** **J**

Gail Miller's rape and murder by Larry Fisher is told concurrently with the story of the road trip taken by 16-year-old David Milgaard and three of his friends in 1969. Milgaard, with a background that had given him a previous reputation with the Saskatoon police, was the one who was arrested, tried, and convicted of the crime, spending the next 23 years in prison before being exonerated because of DNA evidence. Trial transcripts, police reports, and other original documents are used to help give an immediacy to this true story of outright deceptions and failed justice.

Keywords: DNA • Judicial error • Milgaard, David • Murder • Rape

Geary, Rick.

Black Dahlia. <u>A Treasury of XXth Century Murder</u>. 2016. 80p. **H** **A/YA**

The unsolved murder of Elizabeth Short remains fascinating over 70 years after her body was discovered, cut in half and scrubbed clean, in a vacant lot in Hollywood, California. This volume in Geary's series uses his cinematic black and white illustrations to show just how perfectly "Beth" Short's life set her up to be a victim at the time: consistently short of money and determined to meet a man and be seen in Hollywood, she interacted with many men, several of whom were mobsters, in a city where they were very active and keeping police busy. Readers are given a picture of not only how the investigation into her very grisly death was complicated by all of these numerous relationships, but also how the grand jury questioned the police's own conduct.

Keywords: Murder • New York • Short, Elizabeth

Geary, Rick.

Madison-Square Tragedy: The Murder of Stanford White. <u>A Treasury of XXth Century Murder</u>. 2013. 80p. **H** **A/YA**

The details of this murder are particularly salacious, not only because the victim was a known hedonist with a fondness for younger women and living beyond his means but also because his murderer was a man who, while having even more loathsome and vicious habits himself, declared what he wanted was to destroy sinners. The discovery that White's wife,

Evelyn, had an abusive relationship with both men only adds a further layer of drama to this catastrophic tale.

Keywords: Murder • New York • White, Stanford

Geary, Rick.

The True Death of Billy the Kid. 2018. 56p. **M** **J**

Geary's dramatic tale of the notorious Billy the Kid starts off with a recounting of what little is known about Billy the Kid and his crimes and sentencing, then immediately builds up to the Kid's escape shortly before his scheduled hanging. The ensuing carnage, a carefully planned manhunt by Sheriff Pat Garrett culminating in the Kid's death at Fort Sumner, is depicted in suitably dark tones that postulate the true end of this legendary figure based on what is known and what might have happened. This is an exciting and fast-paced graphic novel that will entice readers to look for Geary's other books.

Keywords: Billy the Kid • Bonney, William H. • Garrett, Pat

Keyser, Amber J.

No More Excuses: Dismantling Rape Culture. 2019. 144p. **M** **J**

Studies have shown that sexual harassment is pervasive in American culture; while a 2011 study showed that 68 percent of high school girls had experienced it, both boys and girls in middle school were not immune, leaving them to face long-term negative effects. Keyser presents a book that hopes to move toward a future in which survivors of abuse will be believed, laws and criminal justice may be reformed, and rape culture as it is portrayed in the media will be eliminated. An introduction presents a relevant and painful example in which a very drunk girl at a party was raped by three boys who filmed the event and posted it on social media. The community rallied around the boys, including people who had been in attendance and did nothing to help or prevent the assault. Cases such as that against the producer Harvey Weinstein, which launched the #MeToo movement, demonstrate the power an attacker can use over a victim. Readers are asked to think about objectification and given examples such as schools that have been asked to question their dress codes, portrayals of desirability in the media, and slut shaming. More seriously, questions about reporting assaults, questions that are asked of victims, problems with believing victims, and myths about rapes are discussed. Keyser provides information about the criminal justice process, including where survivors can seek help and the tests they will need to undergo, as their body will be the crime scene being investigated. Faults in the system and legal loopholes make for frightening reading on a path that is a determined victim's only choice for justice. Chapters indicating paths forward to change the current culture, a bibliography, and further resources provide additional resources for all readers seeking to continue the conversation.

Keywords: Rape • Sexual assault • Sexual harassment

Miller, Sarah.

The Borden Murders: Lizzie Borden and the Trial of the Century. 2016. 288p. **M J**

Most people's familiarity with Lizzie Borden is limited to the few lines of doggerel about her, and with those they are left with the conviction that she was an axe murderer. The day that the bodies of Lizzie's father and stepmother were found in 1913 her remarkable composure was the first thing that made officials suspicious. During the investigation and subsequent trial Lizzie was hounded as the obvious, and later, only, suspect. This reconstruction, supplemented by historical documents including clippings and photographs, immerses readers into one of the fascinating mysteries of the early 20th century. **QP**

Keywords: Borden, Lizzie • Murder investigation • Stabbing • Trial

Mitchell, Don.

The Freedom Summer Murders. 2014. 256p. **H**

It is hard to overstate, as emphasized in the introduction and illustrated by several specific examples, the level of discord between white and black Americans in the summer of 1964, when a group of Klansmen and several police officers brutally and with forethought murdered three civil rights workers. By beginning with this action and then introducing each of the victims, Mitchell shows that the perpetrators were aware of the risks and believed in the importance of what they were doing, despite both their and their families' misgivings. The unfolding story of the long, increasingly significant investigation into the disappearance of James Chaney, Andrew Goodman, and Michael Schwerner, is fascinating and frustrating in equal measure, through the trial of the men who planned and carried out the brutal killing, and its aftermath. The volume is a page-turner, supplemented with copious photographs, a bibliography, and an author's note for any reader interested in pursuing more information about the case.

Keywords: Chaney, James • Civil rights • Goodman, Andrew • Ku Klux Klan • Mississippi • Murder • Schwerner, Michael

Slater, Dashka.

The 57 Bus: A True Story of Two Teenagers and the Crime That Changed Their Lives. 2017. 320p. **M J**

This book recounts the case of Richard, a teenager who set a lighter to the skirt of Sasha, an agender teen who was asleep on a bus in Oakland, California, in 2013. The author describes the charges and punishment that followed Richard and Sasha's parallel stories during a long and painful recovery. While Richard's actions are never in doubt, Slater is thorough in presenting the teens' varied backgrounds in this diverse city. What is also noted with startling clarity is documentation that many states habitually transfer juvenile cases to adult courts, and how much more frequently black and Hispanic offenders are to serve time once they are in an adult court. **AENYA BG-HB**

Keywords: Asexual people • Crime • Gender • Hate crimes • Oakland • Race

Swan, Bill.

Real Justice: Convicted for being Mi'kmaq; The Story of Donald Marshall, Jr. <u>Real Justice</u>. 2013. 179p. **M J**

This title in the <u>Real Justice</u> series looks at a fascinating and relevant case: a 1990 Royal Commission, in overturning the original verdict, found that race played a particular role in Donald Marshall's original arrest and conviction. The night Sandy Searle was knifed in Sydney, Nova Scotia, Marshall was at the scene. He was already known to police, who decided he must be the perpetrator and coached witnesses to help them prove it. The years Marshall spent in prison, the investigations into what went wrong, and Marshall's actions after having been released are an important case study of aboriginal rights and the Canadian justice system.

Keywords: Judicial error • Murder • Treaty rights

Swan, Bill.

Real Justice: Fourteen and Sentenced to Death; The Story of Steven Truscott. <u>Real Justice</u>. 2012. 150p. **M J**

Lorimer's <u>Real Justice</u> series presents cases in Canadian law where the justice system not only did not uphold the rights of the individuals it should have protected but, in cases such as Steven Truscott's, failed them utterly. In 1959, Steven Truscott was 14 years old when he was arrested for murder. Having been the last person to see Lynne Harper alive, he became the first, and then the only, suspect. At the time he was convicted of first-degree murder, the sentence was death by hanging. His case's journey to the Supreme Court, and the years until a documentary finally brought hope for a reversal in his verdict, make for a fast-paced, gripping story.

Keywords: Judicial error • Murder

Weinman, Sarah.

The Real Lolita: The Kidnapping of Sally Horner and the Novel that Scandalized the World. 2018. 320p. **AYA**

Readers familiar with Humbert Humbert, one of the best-known pederasts in literary fiction, are unlikely to know that Vladimir Nabokov found his inspiration for not only Humbert but the object of his infatuation in a real-life case. Here, Sarah Weinman explains not only Nabokov's difficulties in writing *Lolita*, but also presents the sad story of Sally Horner, taken from her home at the age of 11 and held for two years by a man with a predilection for young girls, before meeting a tragic end shortly after her release.

Keywords: Horner, Sally • Kidnapping • *Lolita* • Nabokov, Vladimir

Wood, H. P.

Fakers: An Insider's Guide to Cons, Hoaxes and Scams. 2018. 176p. **M** **J**

Con artists have been developing new and novel ways of scamming people as long as there have been opportunities to do so. In this intriguing and somewhat frightening book, readers are shown how to differentiate a short and a long con, along with a cogent description of different ways imposters have taken advantage of the unwary. The many examples given are as fascinating as they are illustrative. Wood then proceeds to show how fakery has been used in other areas, starting with carnivals and moving forward through psychics, science, medicine, war, and media. For readers who believe that they would never fall prey to such obvious or devious tricks, examples are included that makes this volume relevant today, including the hysteria over Orson Welles's *War of the Worlds* broadcast, as well as modern media scandals and current "fake" news. Also provided is as a definition of and warnings about catfishing, as well as examples of scams directed at college students. Interested readers will find lists of further reading and a thorough list of source notes.

Keywords: Con artists • Cons • Hoaxes • Imposters

Crime and Crime Science

These books discuss the changing nature of crime and the ways in which we view it.

Hanel, Rachael, and Erin L. McCoy.

Identity Theft: Private Battle or Public Crisis? <u>Today's Debates</u>. 2019. 144p. **J** **H**

This is a useful tool that contains information that is as horrifying as it is fascinating. Starting with a definition of identity theft, it moves quickly to the possible repercussions and likely targets, including children, seniors, or specific groups such as the recently deceased if the thieves are looking to take over an identity. The variety of these crimes is not only scary but staggering, with the thieves' likely financial gains ranging from financial to medical. Just how these thieves can accomplish this so easily is eye-opening. Chapters identifying famous thieves and cases of theft lead into a discussion of how to report theft and suspicious activity, and how identity theft is being dealt with around the world on a larger scale.

Keywords: Crime • Identity theft

Heos, Bridget.

Blood, Bullets, and Bones: The Story of Forensic Science from Sherlock Holmes to DNA. 2016. 264p. **H**

While many readers are drawn to reading about crimes, those that perpetrate them, and the investigators who work to solve them, there is an inherent fascination in looking at the techniques used in criminal justice. Heos looks at the early development of the need for coroners and medical examiners, a welcome change from the days when cases had been decided without looking at the evidence. This title looks at the many developments in forensics by examining prominent cases solved, from the development of poison tests in the 1700s through to the CODIS database available today.

Keywords: DNA • Fingerprints • Forensics • Poison • Profilers • Serial killers

Kyi, Tanya Lloyd.

Eyes and Spies: How You're Tracked and Why You Should Know. 2017. 135p. **M J**

Technology to monitor people has evolved exponentially over the years. Where surveillance used to consist of literally watching people, cameras are now so far advanced that they have been surpassed by other means of digital tracking, although they themselves are so ubiquitous that they have been used by police in solving crimes. This is a fascinating course in the various types of technologies used around the world to keep track of people and things, and many of the ways that they have been adapted that might make readers wary or angry, particularly in the chapter on data mining. Readers are given a final group of examples dealing with security and privacy to illustrate the difficulties in determining abusers and abuses of privacy, and the ways of monitoring them.

Keywords: Biometrics • Cyberbullying • Identity theft • Radio frequency identification • Surveillance

Mooney, Carla.

Forensics: Uncover the Science and Technology of Crime Scene Investigation. Inquire and Investigate. 2013. 119p. **M J**

This title brings readers into the crime scene, introducing each stage of a crime scene and how it is investigated by offering an explanation and then an activity that allows readers to understand and apply the science for themselves. It is one thing to see illustrations of the various whorls that differentiate the different types of fingerprints, and another entirely to have the opportunity to figure out which kind applies to you. Experiments progress involving fibers, tire tracks (which are translated to bikes for the purposes of nondriving readers), and trace analysis. There are a number of uses for this title, as it will appeal to the general reader and prove useful in the classroom.

Keywords: Crime scene investigation • Forensics

Intrigue and Espionage

These books provide a fascinating look at the business of spying. They provide readers with an understanding of how espionage works while giving them some notable examples that demonstrate how espionage and spies have affected the course of history.

Cornioley, Pearl Witherington.

Code Name Pauline: Memoirs of a World War II Special Agent. <u>Women of Action</u>. 2013. 208p. 🅼 🅹

Women made better Special Operations Executive (SOE) agents during World War II, because in Nazi-occupied countries they aroused less suspicion. The story of Pearl Cornioley, known at the time as Pearl Witherington—who grew up in Paris, possessed a photographic memory, spoke French like a native, was determined to return and work for the resistance, and was assigned to the Stationer network—is no different. The job of these operatives was to hinder the Germans in any way possible in preparation for the D-Day offensive, particularly by recruiting, organizing and training Maquis, resistance fighters, in France. Told from Cornioley's point of view and aided by her remarkable memory, readers parachute into France with her on September 22, 1943, and then follow along as she works as a courier and organizes the men of the Maquis under her code name, "Pauline." Supplementary material provides further information about the war, espionage, and Cornioley's work, and includes pictures showing her and others during the war. Cornioley's reflections on her actions and the war provide a unique insight into World War II and life afterward, in particular regarding the recognition—and lack of it—for the men and women who were involved in the resistance.

Keywords: Special Operations Executive (SOE) • Witherington, Pearl • World War II

Larson, Erik.

Dead Wake: The Last Crossing of the Lusitania. 2015. 448p. 🅷 🄰🄸🅈🄰

In May 1915 transatlantic crossings were still common, albeit more perilous, given a popularly held belief that the United States' neutrality in the war, which had begun eight months earlier, guaranteed a safer journey for its ships' passengers. That was the situation when the Cunard Line's flagship, the *Lusitania*, left New York for Liverpool, United Kingdom, with citizens from 18 countries, including 189 Americans. Larson presents the slow and inexorable collision between the unsuspecting ocean liner and the German submarine Unterseeboot-20 (U-20), the two vessels under the command of Captain William Turner and Kptlt. Walther Schwieger, respectively. These men, both capable and respected by their crews, were watched by their governments who, unbeknownst to them, each other, or much of the world for decades after, were monitoring German radio recordings. This early espionage, and its influence on the entrance of the United States into the war, adds a chilling layer to what is an already frightening and compelling maritime war story.

Keywords: *Lusitania* • Submarines • World War I

Mitchell, Don.

The Lady is a Spy: Virginia Hall, World War II Hero of the French Resistance. 2019. 299p. **J**

The story of how Baltimore native Virginia Hall became one of the first and foremost agents of the Special Operations Executive (SOE) operating in Vichy France during World War II is one of commitment, honor, and bravery. Hall was educated in Europe and worked for years for the U.S. State Department after an early and unfortunate accident resulted in the amputation of her foot. She returned to Europe after being denied permanent employment in the Foreign Service. Instead, working undercover as a reporter, she became the first SOE operative in France. Her importance to the resistance is demonstrated through examples of her interactions with other operatives. Hall left for London in 1942 after the pro-Nazi Vichy authorities became aware of her activities. She was awarded the MBE (Member of the British Empire) by the British government for her efforts, and only wanted to return to continue them. It would take more time, and further training with the OSS (Office of Strategic Services) branch of U.S. intelligence, before the "Limping Lady" could return behind enemy lines—this time as the radio operator for an operative code-named Aramis. Hall's actions over the next few years, as the French Resistance worked to overcome German occupiers, demonstrated her bravery. Hall's life after the war remains relevant today, as she continued to use her earned skills while being underpaid and overlooked for promotions. This volume will provide readers with a unique perspective on World War II.

Keywords: Hall, Virginia • Special Operations Executive (SOE) • World War II

McCormick, Patricia.

The Plot to Kill Hitler: Dietrich Bonhoeffer; Pastor, Spy, Unlikely Hero. 2016. 192p. **M J**

Dietrich Bonhoeffer grew up as part of a large family, intending to become a pastor. What he did not intend was for his ministry to evolve to include subterfuge, pleas to the church to join his cause against Hitler and, eventually, to become part of an assassination plot. That this is a true story is not only incredible but enticing to readers interested in World War II who might also wonder how a man of peace could be swayed into reconciling his beliefs with such an action.

Keywords: Anti-Nazi movement • Bonhoeffer, Dietrich • Hitler, Adolf • World War II

Now Try: Readers interested in more information about Dietrich Bonhoeffer's background and motivations will find it in John Hendrix's *The Faithful Spy: Dietrich Bonhoeffer and*

the Plot to Kill Hitler. Through a unique and compelling mix of illustrations and handwritten text, Hendrix helps readers understand Dietrich Bonhoeffer's actions during World War II by showing his deep religious background and his belief in the equality of all men; Hendrix documents Bonhoeffer's repugnance at the racism he witnessed in the Southern United States while traveling to experience church culture. The book provides a thorough timeline of the rise of Hitler and the Nazi party which, along with Bonhoeffer's beliefs, allow the reader not only to understand why he would become involved in the plot but also to care about what happened to him.

Twigge, Stephen.

The Spy Toolkit: Extraordinary Inventions from World War II. 2018. 160p. **H** **A/YA**

This book offers an introduction to the Special Operations Executive (SOE) formed in Britain to recruit agents to operate in occupied Europe during World War II. Potential agents would go through an interview before complicated preliminary training, involving testing to ensure they had the proper temperament and background. After that they would undergo additional training for sabotage, fieldcraft, and recruiting additional agents. Once sufficiently experienced, they would be able to appreciate the devices, disguises, and gadgets available to help them behind enemy lines.

Keywords: Espionage • Special Operations Executive (SOE)

Consider Starting with . . .

Heos, Bridget. *Blood, Bullets, and Bones: The Story of Forensic Science from Sherlock Holmes to DNA.*

McCormick, Patricia. *The Plot to Kill Hitler: Dietrich Bonhoeffer: Pastor, Spy, Unlikely Hero.*

Miller, Sarah. *The Borden Murders: Lizzie Borden and the Trial of the Century.*

Mitchell, Don. *The Lady is a Spy: Virginia Hall, World War II Hero of the French Resistance.*

Slater, Dashka. *The 57 Bus: A True Story of Two Teenagers and the Crime That Changed Their Lives.*

Fiction Read-Alikes

- **Carter, Ally.** *All Fall Down.* The first book in Carter's Embassy Row series introduces readers to Grace Blakely, now back to live with her grandfather on Embassy Row, three years after seeing her mother murdered. Grace, whose grandfather is the ambassador to a (fictional) European country, becomes certain she has found the man who killed her mother and that he is now part of a plot to assassinate someone else. If only everyone didn't think she made him up the first time.

- **Blas, Terry, and Molly Muldoon.** *Dead Weight: Murder at Camp Bloom.* The campers arriving at Camp Bloom in this amusing graphic novel have mixed reactions to spending their summer at a fat camp. Even returning campers who enjoy their time there are reluctant to give up their electronic devices and suffer pangs at the thought of giving up their sugary addictions. Newcomers are reassured that the camp's cook can be bribed to supply them with chocolate, and camp gossip is upstaged when two of the campers witness the murder of a counselor by a member of the senior staff. Blurred pictures, taken with a cell phone and shown to other campers, are used to convince the group of campers that it will be up to them to solve the crime.

- **Cook, Eileen.** *The Hanging Girl.* Skye Thorn knows that the tarot readings she gives are completely fake; she figures that is what makes her different from her mother, who actually believes that she is psychic. Convincing the police to use her so-called psychic abilities to help solve the kidnapping case of a classmate is convenient, as it lets her both take advantage of her inside knowledge of the crime and direct suspicion away from herself. When what was supposed to have been a prank and a way to raise funds turns dark and deadly, Skye will have to find a way to figure out what is going on. This is a thriller with many twists that will keep readers guessing.

- **Harvey, Sarah N., and Robin Stevenson.** *Blood on the Beach.* Alice and Caleb have very different reasons for winding up at INTRO, a week-long treatment program for troubled teenagers. Caleb, who assaulted the stepfather abusing his mother, is sentenced to attend, while Alice is sent for her own good by her mother, an overprotective police officer. They, along with six others, ranging from actual miscreants to misunderstood teenagers, find themselves forced to endure the circle talks of the three staff members. When one of the girls disappears and the adults seem unwilling and unable to deal with either finding her or arranging for help, it will be up to the teens to get themselves through the week and off the island.

- **Jackson, Tiffany D.** *Allegedly.* Mary B. Addison is in a group home, placed there six years after she was jailed for murder. At the time all that had mattered was that a white baby had died under the care of a nine-year-old girl and her churchgoing black mother; only she and her momma know the truth. Now all she cares about is Ted and their baby, but nobody wants to take the chance that she might kill again. She can't trust her momma, and the state doesn't trust her, but what will Mary do to protect her baby?

- **Riem, Elizabeth.** *Dancer, Daughter, Traitor, Spy.* Marina Dukovskaya has a privileged position in Moscow as the daughter of Sveta Dukovskaya, the

Bolshoi Ballet's prima ballerina. It isn't public knowledge that Sveta's second sight gives visions, or that she herself has begun to have them. When Sveta disappears, Marina and her father fear for their own safety and flee for the West. Marina is able to use her own Bolshoi training to find a place at Juilliard, which may be threatened when her visions show a future with a murder and intrigue in her own family, requiring her to question who she can trust.

- **Wynne-Jones, Tim.** *The Ruinous Sweep.* Bee finds herself at her boyfriend's hospital bed in the ICU, taking notes as he murmurs unintelligibly. She is completely unwilling to believe that he tried to commit suicide by throwing himself in front of a car after murdering his father; instead she is furious that she seems to be the only one who thinks so. It will be up to her to find out what really happened, as his vocalizations imply that even he doesn't remember the truth.

1

2

3

4

5

6

7

8

9

10

11

Part 2

Life Stories

Chapter 3

Memoirs and Autobiographies

Definition

Memoirs and autobiographies have remained consistently popular in recent years. They have several differences, although the principal and most significant is that a memoir describes a period or specific events in one's life, while an autobiography is a chronological story of a life. This helps to distinguish between the two.

Memoirs generally rely on the author's own recollection of the events being recounted and will not have the secondary sources and supplementary material that may be added to an autobiography. At the same time, they frequently have a greater sense of the author's viewpoint and emotions.

Appeal

As with biographies, the books in this chapter give readers a chance to explore other people's lives and learn from what they experienced. Titles are generally presented in the first person and range from tragic to uproarious. The subjects, which can range from celebrities to immigrants to other teenagers, put readers in situations that are completely foreign and yet still relatable.

Publishing in recent years has seen more titles that are either written by or about teenagers, making this a genre that will appeal to the young adult audience. Having titles with subjects dealing with issues that are relevant to readers both makes the books more appealing and increases the amount of time the titles will remain so. As they are rarely in need of updating, these are titles that may be weeded on condition and use.

Chapter Organization

While memoirs are plentiful, there are a smaller number of subgenres in which they are categorized. The chapter begins with "Coming-of-Age," in which the authors discuss the difficult and emotional times that helped them become the people they are today. These books are followed by "Overcoming Adversity," which deals with stories of adversity and triumph, such as Zeina Abirached's tale of growing up in war-torn Beirut. "Working Life Memoirs" presents tales of everyday life in the workforce at home and abroad, whether dealing with a chef or a congressman. The final section, "Humorous Memoirs," offers titles written with a lighthearted note, which may offer possibilities for reading aloud.

Coming-of-Age

Girls Write Now: Two Decades of True Stories from Young Female Voices. **2018. 250p.** 🅜 🅙

New York's Girls Write Now, a nonprofit writing and mentoring organization for girls, presents a compilation of 116 essays from young women written between 2007 and 2017. The essays are gathered in 10 groupings, each interspersed with thoughts and advice about books and writing from leaders such as Zadie Smith, Gloria Steinem, and Alice Walker. The girls write about their lives and the things that matter to them, including immigration, politics, race, and gender. The stories provide short and intimate glimpses of the girls' lives at the time of writing which, especially with many of the older essays, lets the reader see how the writer's life has changed, as biographical information is provided for each entry, including the author's place of birth and schooling.

Keywords: Girls Write Now • Personal essays

Georges, Nicole.

Fetch: How a Bad Dog Brought Me Home: A Graphic Memoir. **2017. 336p.** 🄰🅈🄰

Nicole Georges uses a traumatic moment at the quinceañera party she is hosting for her dog, Beija, to reminisce about their years together. Georges, whose unbelievably unstructured upbringing had neither dampened her enthusiasm for animals nor provided her with any ability to properly care for or train them, first acquired her dog at the age of 17 as a Christmas present for her boyfriend. While the years after didn't sweeten or change Beija's disposition, it also didn't bother Georges that her dog never warmed up to small children, men, or most other dogs, peed on her floors, and usually barked incessantly when kept apart from her. Beija remained her truest and most loyal friend throughout years of moving, changing relationships, exploring her sexuality, and extreme depression. Above all, Georges demonstrates the value of a relationship that lasts a lifetime.

Keywords: Dogs • Graphic memoir • Pet owners

Hartzler, Aaron.

Rapture Practice. 2013. 400p. **H**

Growing up in Aaron Hartzler's family meant an adherence to every rule in the Bible in order to be prepared and worthy for the coming Rapture. He, as a young boy, started wondering why he shouldn't go to an occasional movie or listen to songs played on rock music radio stations, and angered his parents with his acts of what they saw as rebellion. Hartzler's narrative demonstrates with startling clarity that parents and their children may have different worldviews, as it was his friendships, behaviors that went against his upbringing, and his desire to continue in singing and acting that stayed with him.

Keywords: Hartzler, Aaron • Rapture

Henigson, Jeff.

Warhead: The True Story of One Teen Who Almost Saved the World. 2019. 352p. **M J**

In 1986, Jeff Henigson was a normal 15-year-old, more concerned with girls and convincing his father to buy him a car than arguing with his dad about the current tense stalemate between the leaders of the United States and Russia. Everything changed the day a woman hit him with a car, and the ensuing tests revealed a tumor in his brain that turned out to be cancerous. When Jeff was offered a wish from the Starlight Children's Foundation, he asked to travel to Russia to speak to Mikhail Gorbachev about nuclear disarmament, hoping it would earn his father's respect. Even after his father made it clear he was against Jeff's trip, Jeff continued to plan. His relationships with his friends and family are shown to be both sympathetic and relatable, as are those with the people he met as he underwent treatment and worked to make his wish come true. Readers are taken on a bittersweet journey that is both meaningful and surprising.

Keywords: Cancer • Henigson, Jeff

Krosoczka, Jarrett J.

🏅 *Hey, Kiddo.* 2018. 320p. **M J**

Jarrett Krosoczka had an unconventional upbringing, raised by grandparents who believed that their childrearing days were behind them. Krosoczka presents an honest and forthright view of his household, surrounded by the outspoken Shirl and gruff Joe who took custody of him when their daughter, his drug-addicted mother, Les, disappeared. It was years later that he learned she was in prison. The bright light in Jarrett's days became an art class where a teacher introduced the students to comics, challenging them to stretch themselves and create new things. This love of art helped sustain Jarrett in spite of his personal life, dealing with his mother's rocky condition and the unknown that was his father. In a memoir that will appeal to a wide audience, Jarrett Krosoczka shares an important story of addiction and family. **AENYA ALA BG-HB GGNT QP**

Keywords: Graphic memoir • Krosoczka, Jarrett

Now Try: David Small's *Stitches* is a book about a young man in a dysfunctional family. As a chronically ill child, David was treated by his father, a radiologist, for a chronic sinus condition. David was the only person unaware that this had given him cancer, and that he was not expected to survive what he had been told was minor surgery to remove a cyst on his throat. He awoke with one vocal cord and without the ability to speak. Depicting the psychiatrist who helped him recover his voice as the white rabbit in his Wonderland, Small's Caldecott-winning book shows him learning to discover his voice and find a place with his art.

Lukasiak, Chloe.

Girl on Pointe: Chloe's Guide to Taking on the World. 2018. 208p.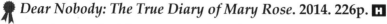

Chloe Lukasiak, best known as one of the cast members of the Lifetime show *Dance Moms* from 2011 to 2014, reflects on her time in front of the camera, giving readers a unique view of this type of life and the effects it can have. This is a unique perspective, as it is not the only area where she has obtained a measure of success. It was her ability in dance that brought her to the attention of the show's producers, but she has continued in acting and branched out into social media and clothing design. Where this book excels is in Lukasiak's ability to relate her experiences to readers, as when she shares her experience being cyberbullied for her appearance when appearing on television while undergoing medical treatments for a sinus condition. This, when coupled with advice for handling bullying as well as a list of resources, is offered as a recommendation from a peer who knows what she is talking about. By adding reminiscences, poetry, and short stories, Lukasiak has turned a book about her experiences into one that offers guidance, widening its appeal and use beyond readers that will be interested in reading about the celebrity.

Keywords: *Dance Moms* • Lukasiak, Chloe • Performing arts

McCain, Gillian, and Legs McNeil, eds.

🎗 *Dear Nobody: The True Diary of Mary Rose.* 2014. 226p. **H**

Reproduced with permission from her mother after her death from cystic fibrosis at the age of 18 in 1999, Mary Rose's diary recounts her life for the preceding three years. Mary Rose's early life was marked by resentment of her alcoholic mother's relationships with abusive boyfriends, especially as their behavior extended to Mary Rose; her mother frequently sided with the men. As she got older, particularly in the years documented in the diary, Mary Rose's own actions reflected her mother's, as she became more involved with the opposite sex, alcohol, and increasingly serious drugs. These had a negative effect on both her emotional and physical health, which became progressively erratic, as shown in a tragic document that is all the more affecting because it was only ever meant as a keepsake. **QP**

Keywords: Alcohol addiction • Drug addiction

Rodriguez, Gaby, with Jenna Glatzer.

The Pregnancy Project: A Memoir. 2012. 244p. **H**

Gaby Rodriguez grew up in a family where teen pregnancy was common: her mother got pregnant with the first of her eight children at the age of 14, and all seven of Gaby's older siblings became parents as teenagers. There is no doubt that this was a strong factor in her decision to fake a pregnancy for her senior project in high school. The reactions from her friends and family were harsh but unsurprising and served as a basis for a report on stereotypes, statistics, and rumors. After her project was revealed, reactions ranged from relief to feelings of betrayal, and then shock, after a local newspaper article was shared with the Associated Press, spurring a media frenzy and bringing Rodriguez to national attention. Gaby did what she intended to do with her project, as the book brings attention to teenage pregnancy and stereotypes. **QP PP**

Keywords: Pregnancy • Rodriguez, Gaby • Teenage pregnancy

Van Wagenen, Maya.

Popular: Vintage Wisdom for a Modern Geek. 2014. 272p. **M J**

If the popularity ranking for Maya Van Wagenen's middle school topped out with the "Volleyball Girls" ranking a 10, and the "Ignored" sixth graders being a zero, Maya, in beginning eighth grade, ranked with a negative number and only the teachers below her. In order to see if she could change this, she decided to follow exactly the advice proposed in a book published by a teenage fashion model in the 1950s, *Betty Cornell's Teen-Age Popularity Guide*. She did so without telling anyone but her parents and her best friend, while seeing if, throughout the school year, the implemented advice on diet, grooming, make-up, clothes, money, dating, and attitude would be noticed by her peers and raise her ranking. Taking part in this experiment gave Maya a new way to see not only how she felt about herself and others, but also to see how she felt about the way other people treated her and were treated, giving her a new view on what it meant to be popular, to be liked, and to be kind. **AENYA**

Keywords: Popularity • Van Wagenen, Maya

Walden, Tillie.

Spinning. 2017. 400p. **H**

Tillie Walden spent much of her life on the ice. She maintained a difficult routine, getting up hours before school for lessons with a figure skating coach, traveling to a different rink afterward to practice with her synchro team, and competing on weekends. Her memoir explores her evolving feelings about skating and the outside interests in her life, from her increased interest in art to dealing with—and letting her family and friends know about—her homosexuality, something she had been aware of since she was five.

Keywords: Figure skating • Graphic memoir • LGBTQ • Walden, Tillie

Overcoming Adversity

These books, which detail their subjects' stories of remembered pain, overcoming difficulties, and turbulent pasts, are perennially popular. They deal with a number of difficult and graphic subjects, including depictions of death, disease, disability, drugs, terrorism, and abuse, which makes them appropriate for older readers. Nevertheless, their frequent choice for readers' choice lists attests to their consistent and enduring popularity. Readers who enjoy fiction about people overcoming challenges may enjoy these nonfiction stories.

Abirached, Zeina.

 A Game for Swallows: To Die, To Leave, To Return. 2012. 188p. **H** **A/YA**

Zeina Abirached was born six years after Lebanon's civil war began. At that time East Beirut was for Christians, and West, for Muslims. Zeina's family lived in the middle of the war zone, an area rife with snipers. One day her parents went out to visit her grandparents a few blocks away and didn't return. This is a powerful book about what it is like to grow up in a place where normal is knowing that your loved ones may never really come back. **GGNT**

Keywords: Beirut • Civil War • Graphic novel • Lebanon • War zones

Burcaw, Shane.

 Laughing at My Nightmare. 2016. 208p. **M**

Being diagnosed with spinal muscular atrophy (SMA) at the age of three means that Shane Burcaw has been living with the shadow of his own mortality for all of his life. Despite that, he chronicles his experience and the physical obstacles he's faced without hesitation or protective coloration, putting down on paper stark and darkly humorous moments like learning how to drive a motorized wheelchair as a preschooler, trying to use a bedpan for the first time while hospitalized and bedridden with a full leg cast, and the planning and help that was required in order to get drunk for the first time. Burcaw communicates the realities of living with his disability and increasingly serious medical episodes while maintaining his positivity. The story of how he turned his experiences into his *Laughing at My Nightmare* blog and started a nonprofit organization is both enriching and rewarding. **AENYA**

Keywords: Burcaw, Shane • People with disabilities • Spinal muscular atrophy (SMA)

Now Try: Shane's second book, *Strangers Assume My Girlfriend Is My Nurse*, is a collection of essays that reflect on his life. It may be read as a stand-alone volume or a continuation of his first book, containing enough information about spinal muscular atrophy (SMA) on his daily life that readers will be able to understand the debilitating and devastating effects of the disease. Burcaw details the ups and downs he has experienced, using his disease and romantic relationships as examples, as well as humorous stories of difficulties encountered in everyday experiences, all of which help to illustrate that his is a life that deserves to be treated no differently than any able-bodied person, and all lives deserve respect and understanding.

Ebrahim, Zak.

The Terrorist's Son: A Story of Choice. TED Books. 2014. 112p. **H** **A/YA**

When Zak Ebrahim's mother woke him up on the morning of November 5, 1990, he believed her when she told him his father had been in an accident. It wasn't until later that he found out his father, El-Sayyid Nosair, was shot fleeing the scene after he had shot and killed Meir Kahane, the leader of the Jewish Defense League. Zak would go on believing in his father, even after his conviction and imprisonment, while his family was shunned and reviled, and he was consistently bullied in school as his family kept relocating. The situation for his family only worsened as his father kept up his activities from within Attica, helping to plan the 1993 bombing of the World Trade Center. Ebrahim paints a vivid portrait of what it was like to live as the Muslim son of one of America's most reviled terrorists, while at the same time demonstrating that it was growing up in that situation that allowed him to see what his father could not, and to value both peace and nonviolence. **Alex**

Keywords: Ebrahim, Zak • Muslim • 1993 World Trade Center bombing • Nosair, El-Sayyid

Etler, Cyndy.

The Dead Inside: A True Story. 2017. 304p. **H**

Cyndy Etler tried marijuana for the first and only time at the age of 13, believing it to be both a gateway to a social circle and an escape from her sexually abusive stepfather. At 14, she ran away and her mother sent her to Straight, Inc., ostensibly a recovery treatment facility. Cyndy and the other "Straightlings" were subject to unconventional treatments involving physical and mental abuse, sleep deprivation, and brainwashing as the staff attempted to cure her of her "druggie" ways. This frightening true story is validated by documents that provide a history of Straight. Readers will be taken on a harrowing journey as Cyndy tries to figure out how best to survive in more than one difficult environment, only to find herself unable to reintegrate into her life once she has been able to adapt to the facility.

Keywords: Drug addicts • Etler, Cyndy • Rehabilitation

Fleming, Melissa.

A Hope More Powerful Than the Sea: One Refugee's Incredible Story of Love, Loss, and Survival. 2017. 288p. **H** **A/YA**

As a child and a firsthand witness of the Arab Spring, Doaa Al Zamel's life experiences in Syria changed her from a shy child into a teenager willing to rebel against a repressive government. Doaa's story is both illuminating and heartbreaking, providing an account of the Syrian war that is both comprehensive and compelling, from the war's overall statistics to her personal narrative. Through her story, which includes both incredible bravery, loss, and the indignities of war, she remains a symbol of hope in a corner of the world where people are still suffering. **Alex**

Keywords: Syria • War • Zamel, Doaa Al

Hoge, Robert.

Ugly. 2016. 208p. **M**

This book's subtitle, generally left out of library catalogs, is "A Beautiful True Story about One Ugly Kid." Robert had a series of surgeries at a very early age to remove a congenital tennis-ball-sized tumor from the middle of his face, during which the stunted lower portions of his legs were also removed. His nose, replaced with one of his toes, would never look normal, and would lead to him being bullied throughout his childhood. This is a testament to the author's determination and grace, and an empowering, eye-opening look at learning to live with a disability.

Keywords: Bullying • Hoge, Robert • People with disabilities

Prout, Chessy.

I Have the Right To: A High School Survivor's Story of Sexual Assault, Justice, and Hope. 2018. 416p. **H**

In 2014, Chessy Prout was a 15-year-old freshman at the boarding school where her parents first met and at which her older sister was a senior when she was sexually assaulted by a senior as part of an annual competition among the boys. While she did speak to police and prosecutors, both she and her family were ostracized, bullied, and threatened, with the school trying to whitewash the situation and Chessy being either blamed or called a liar, demonstrating a common problem faced by victims of sexual assault. The presentation of Chessy Prout's story gives readers a firsthand look at how difficult it can be to navigate the court system, presenting statistics on just how few cases are reported. A lower percentage of cases are referred for investigation, and even smaller numbers are actually tried. The events of this book, which happened before the #MeToo movement, reflect cultural mores that have remained in place for decades, and which remain relevant in light of recent testimony in front of Congress. Prout's #IHavetheRightTo hashtag, list of resources, and author's note will provide support for any readers looking for it.

Keywords: Consent • Sexual assault

Rhodes-Courter, Ashley.

Three More Words. 2015. 320p. **H** **A/YA**

By the time Ashley Rhodes-Courter was ready to leave for college, she'd been with her adoptive family for a long enough time that leaving them was more nerve-wracking than the public speaking she did about her years in foster care. Rhodes-Courter met her boyfriend, later her husband, Erich, in college, and it was he, along with her adoptive parents, Gay and Phil Courter, who helped her navigate her troubled relationship with her biological mother and other family members. At the heart of this book, told as Rhodes-Courter earns her master of social work degree, are the stories of the foster children who stay with her and her husband as she works to better the lives of children and make sure that others avoid the pitfalls of a system that failed her for so many years.

Keywords: Foster children • Rhodes-Courter, Ashley

Now Try: Taken away from her mother at the age of three, Ashley Rhodes-Courter was placed into 19 foster homes over the next nine years, as detailed in her memoir *Three Little Words: A Memoir.* During those years she was lost by the system and was in a home so abusive that her foster parents were later jailed. This painful and poignant tale leaves out none of the horrifying situations that Ashley endured, even while she longed for the mother who was unwilling and unable to take care of her; in the telling she honestly depicts why she was unable to completely trust her life with her adoptive parents for years.

Uwiringiyimana, Sandra, with Abigail Pesta.

How Dare the Sun Rise: Memoirs of a War Child. 2017. 304p. **M** **J**

Sandra Uwiringiyimana was 10 years old when she witnessed the massacre in which she saw her mother and younger sister gunned down by rebels. Her journey afterwards, from the Democratic Republic of Congo to becoming an immigrant in the United States, shows a gulf that proves almost as insurmountable. This book is timely and relevant, not only in showing just how difficult it is to move to other places in the world but also how unwelcoming and alien new homes can be for those who attempt to assimilate. **QP**

Keywords: Acculturation • Emigration • Immigrants • Immigration • War

Yousafzai, Malala.

We Are Displaced: My Journey and Stories from Refugee Girls around the World. **2019. 256p.** 🄷

While Nobel-Prize winner Malala Yousafzai acknowledges that the story of her shooting is well-known, she points out that it was being deprived of her education and her country that led her on the path to understanding what it means to be displaced. The stories shared by the refugees in this book acknowledge the difficulties not only of leaving behind one's home, family, friends, and every belonging, but also how difficult it is to find a place in a country where one stands out as different and feels unwanted and unwelcome because of it. Each story begins with an introduction from Yousafzai, pointing out how she met the contributor and providing some context. Readers will discover that every entry, whether sharing a tale of a girl forcibly evicted from her country or one running from danger, shows that freedom is not a right but a privilege for which every person should be profoundly grateful.

Keywords: Displaced persons • Immigrants • Refugees

Working Life Memoirs

These authors use their work to offer an understanding of their world. Readers may gain insight into professions, other cultures, and places. Readers gain more than a chance to learn about the authors' work and lives, they can cross borders and formats, gaining a sense of Andrea Dorfman's film in her illustrated memoir, for example, or traveling to Jerusalem with Guy Delisle in his graphic novel.

Delisle, Guy.

Jerusalem: Chronicles from the Holy City. **2012. 320p.** **A/YA**

Cartoonist Guy Delisle's fourth graphic memoir is an account of his family's time spent in Jerusalem during his wife's tenure as a doctor for MSF (Médecin Sans Frontières/Doctors Without Borders). Given that Israel remains an even more volatile country politically than the countries shown in Delisle's earlier books, his day-to-day experiences, like attempting to buy groceries, travel across the border, and learn about the country, provide an illuminating look at a country that can be mysterious and misunderstood.

Keywords: Christian • Delisle, Guy • Gaza • Graphic memoir • Jerusalem • Jewish • Muslim • Palestine

Now Try: Delisle's best-known title provides readers insight into another little-known country. *Pyongang: A Journey in North Korea* chronicles the two months that Delisle spent working in Korea's capital city overseeing animators working for his French film company. As he was kept closely under watch during his entire visit, Delisle's book manages to convey what it is like to live under government oppression with a sense of humor.

Dorfman, Andrea.

Flawed. <u>National Film Board of Canada Collection</u>. 2018. 88p. **H** **A/YA**

Dorfman, a filmmaker and artist, recounts how she met her partner and eventually shared with him one of her deepest self-esteem issues, which had been exacerbated and brought to the surface by his profession. When Dorfman had a meet-cute with a wonderful guy, there was one immediate and inherent difficulty: finding out that Dave was a plastic surgeon, she found herself torn between liking him and her distaste for his profession—what she saw as a job aimed at finding flaws in people. Having grown up with a visible imperfection, she had worked hard to come to terms with her feelings of inadequacy. A series of communications, followed by a visit to her long-distance boyfriend where she was able to see him perform a reconstructive surgery, helped provide the basis for a relationship where the two were able to get to know each other well enough to share their stories and be willing to accept themselves and others as they are. Their tale, turned into an Emmy-nominated animated film for Canada's National Film Board and also shown on PBS, has now been recreated in this highly illustrated memoir.

Keywords: Dorfman, Andrea • Relationships • Self acceptance • Self esteem

Hodges, Henry, and Margaret Engel.

How to Act Like a Kid: Backstage Secrets of a Young Performer. 2013. 256p. **H**

Henry Hodges, who was already a Broadway veteran at the age of 13, saw his career launched at the age of four when his mother took him to his first audition. In this book, he shares his experience with all aspects of life on and off the Great White Way. In the process, budding thespians will be presented with everything they could possibly want to know about ways to become known in the business, along with a series of sidebars and Q&As from associated professionals, including a Broadway casting agent, a vocal audition coach, a dance teacher, and a producer. Hodges also describes what his life was like while touring, drawing readers into the book with pictures of himself with celebrities and mentions of his many accomplished performances. The author gives advice on how to become involved in acting, but more valuable is Hodges's candid information about his dyslexia, the chapters on his continued schooling, and dealing with ongoing challenges such as protecting finances and the transitions that come with moving into adulthood. A resource list for budding actors is included.

Keywords: Actors • Hodges, Henry

Knisley, Lucy.

 Relish: My Life in the Kitchen. 2013. 173p. **H** **A/YA**

Lucy Knisley, a cartoonist devoted to food, presents an ideal guide for the novice chef. As the daughter of a gourmet chef who never lost her own appreciation for the golden arches, her memoir is written around food, which she closely associates with the important moments in her life. Each chapter is accompanied by a recipe, all of which are illustrated in a style that shows clearly the steps for each recipe, with items that vary from carbonara to sushi. This is a lively and fun graphic memoir that can be enjoyed on its own but will tempt even the most kitchen-phobic reader into creating a shopping list and wandering into the cookbook section. **Alex GGNT**

Keywords: Chef • Cooking • Graphic memoir • Knisley, Lucy • Recipes

Lee, Stan, Peter David, and Colleen Doran.

 Amazing, Fantastic, Incredible: A Marvelous Memoir. 2015. 192p. **H**

Stan Lee would be the first person to acknowledge that he led a charmed life. Lee is the creator of many of the best-known characters and villains of the Marvel universe, making him one of the most renowned figures in the history of comics. His memoir, suitably presented in graphic format, introduces fans to many of his creations and his cocreators alike. It also allows fans to reminisce about his rise from publishing assistant to comics great while encountering difficulties with partners, Marvel's bankruptcy, and changes in the comics industry. **GGNT**

Keywords: Comic books • Comics • Graphic memoir • Lee, Stan

Lewis, John, Andrew Aydin, and Nate Powell.

 March: Book One. 2013. 121p. **H** **A/YA**

The first volume in the trilogy looking at civil rights icon John Lewis's life opens with the 1965 Bloody Sunday march, and then forwards to Lewis waiting for President Obama to be sworn into office. While he waits, he reminisces to two young visitors about key events that helped guide his path to nonviolence, specifically the Montgomery Bus boycott and a speech made by Martin Luther King Jr. The sharing of these seminal events from a first-person point of view with artwork that carries the reader into each scene makes for a compelling and absorbing journey. **CSK GGNT**

Keywords: Civil Rights • Graphic memoir • Lewis, John

Lewis, John, Andrew Aydin, and Nate Powell.

🎗 *March: Book Two*. 2015. 121p. 🅷 🄰/🆈🄰

The beginning of 1960 saw congressman John Lewis witness both John Fitzgerald Kennedy's victory in the presidential election and increasing violence in response to nonviolent protests for civil rights, leading up to his arrest and jailing on his 21st birthday in 1961. This look at the people wanting to change the status quo and what people were willing to do to maintain segregation is a harrowing and necessary look at America's past. **ALA GGNT**

Keywords: Civil Rights • Graphic memoir • Lewis, John

Lewis, John, Andrew Aydin, and Nate Powell.

🎗 *March: Book Three*. 2016. 121p. 🅷 🄰/🆈🄰

The final volume of the <u>March</u> trilogy starts with the bombing of the 16th Street Baptist Church in Birmingham, Alabama. This was followed by increasing tensions and threats of violence for activists, which eventually required them to ask themselves whether or not to continue to protest if it meant facing harm, or to leave their futures in the hands of leaders who weren't on the lines with them. Parallels to events citizens are facing today are chilling. **AENYA ALA CSK Printz Sibert**

Keywords: Civil rights • Graphic memoir • Lewis, John

Humorous Memoirs

Memoirs are occasionally simply stories to be enjoyed. Some authors are able to share their reminiscences in such a fashion that reading them makes one smile, whether or not there are lessons slipped in along the way. This may be easier for authors like Michael McCreary who, as a comedian, has likely had more practice in wordsmithing, or for Cece Bell, whose delightful *El Deafo* is a recommendation for a wide age range when looking for a memoir for readers unfamiliar with the genre.

Bell, Cece.

🎗 *El Deafo*. 2014. 121p. 🄼

This book offers a warm and positive account of Bell's childhood, starting from her losing her hearing at the age of four after contracting meningitis. Severely and profoundly deaf, she faced elementary school learning how to lip read while dealing with family, teachers, and classmates. She also learned to navigate a succession of hearing aids, including a "phonic ear" that allowed her to hear her teacher throughout her school, most notably in the washroom, and gave her a superpower that helped transform her into "El Deafo," modeled on a more powerful TV character of the day. The charming illustrations of people depicted as bunnies provide a wonderful vehicle for Bell's memoir while offering valuable insight into what it is like to live and learn as a deaf individual in a hearing world. **Newbery**

Keywords: Bell, Cece • Deafness • Graphic memoir

Chack, Erin.

This Is Really Happening. 2017. 272p. **J** **H** **A/YA**

Buzzfeed writer Erin Chack presents a series of autobiographical pieces that range from poignant to sharply funny. Chack largely centers her pieces around the people in her life, her work, and her battle with cancer, with which she was diagnosed at the age of 19. Much of the humor in the book is derived from her dealings with her boyfriend, whom she met at the age of 14. Their relationship is described at different stages, from an awkwardness that precludes speaking to an almost enjoined twin to his solid support for her during her chemotherapy in the years in between. Her cancer and her thoughts on the disease provide a theme for several essays that will also speak to readers, such as being able to witness the enthusiasm for John Green's *The Fault in Our Stars* while having different thoughts about death and dying. The experiences that Chack shares about her school, college, and her work at Buzzfeed are memorable, and will leave readers either laughing or wincing for her, recognizing that they have been on a memorable journey.

Keywords: Buzzfeed • Chack, Erin • Writers

Espinosa, Matthew.

Matthew Espinosa: More Than Me. 2017. 224p. **J** **H**

Espinosa, a prominent YouTube personality with more than 2 million followers, presents his story in a format that fans will recognize, and which new readers will be told is part of his style for "Vines and videos . . . telling a story in a blip," which has garnered the 19-year-old billions of views on Vine. In this highly illustrated volume, Espinosa alternates short sections that answer questions about himself with longer essays, which also include information about his work on his movie and his presence on Twitter and Instagram, speaking directly to readers in a chatty tone that offers advice along with biographical information.

Keywords: Espinosa, Matthew • Vine • YouTube

Inzer, Christine Mari.

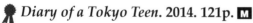 *Diary of a Tokyo Teen.* 2014. 121p. **M**

At the age of six, Christine Inzer relocated with her family to the United States from Japan, where she had been born in Tokyo to a Japanese mother and an

American father. At the age of 15 she took a two-month vacation to visit her mother's parents, diarizing her journey and reflecting on Japan, its culture and places, and her place in it. The pictures she produces, both literally in her illustrations and accompanying photographs and in the interesting, insightful, and funny commentary, allow readers to experience Japan's places, fashion, and food as Inzer does. This first-person perspective and Inzer's whimsical style will entice readers into learning about Inzer and Japan while accompanying her on an entertaining journey. **GGNT**

Keywords: Graphic memoir • Inzer, Christine • Japan

McCreary, Michael.

Funny, You Don't Look Autistic: A Comedian's Guide to Life on the Spectrum. 2019. 121p. **H**

Michael McCreary is able to dispel myths and provide realistic information about living and dealing with autism spectrum disorder (ASD) based upon his own knowledge, having been diagnosed at the age of five. McCreary's writing, which is intelligent and humorous, capitalizes on a love of performing, which he discovered early in elementary school and started honing when he began learning comedy as a method of therapy at the age of 13. Tales of his experiences as he progressed through school not only allow readers to get a better sense of what it is like to be on the autism spectrum, but also provide an opportunity to understand and relate to what someone with ASD is going through, by including many experiences that have commonalities with the neurotypical community, including feelings of awkwardness and inadequacy. Having these anecdotes told by a comedian ensures both life lessons and a punch line to smooth the delivery.

Keywords: Autism Spectrum Disorder (ASD) • Comedians • McCreary, Michael

Consider Starting with . . .

Bell, Cece. *El Deafo.*

Knisley, Lucy. *Relish: My Life in the Kitchen.*

Lewis, John, Andrew Aydin, and Nate Powell. *March: Book Three.*

McCreary, Michael. *Funny, You Don't Look Autistic.*

Uwiringiyimana, Sandra, with Abigail Pesta. *How Dare the Sun Rise: Memoirs of a War Child.*

Fiction Read-Alikes

- **Elliott, L. M.** *Hamilton and Peggy! A Revolutionary Friendship.* Elliott presents a fictionalized view of the lives of Alexander Hamilton and his sister-in-law Peggy Schuyler, the third daughter of Gen. Philip Schuyler. Peggy, brilliant at a time when being educated isn't considered as important as being pretty or serving one's husband, is fascinated by her father's work in the war and intimidated by her sisters' successes with the opposite sex. She is still able to perform a duty as an intermediary when her beautiful older sister, Eliza, captures the interest of one of George Washington's soldiers, Alexander Hamilton. As the war progresses, Peggy balances her interest in the events of the war with her own personal life.

- **Anderson, M. T., Candace Fleming, Stephanie Hemphill, Lisa Ann Sandell, and Jennifer Donnelly.** *Fatal Throne: The Wives of Henry VIII Tell All.* Of the six wives of Henry VIII, the best known is his second queen, Anne Boleyn, usually remembered either as the mother of Queen Elizabeth or for her death by beheading. Here seven well-known young adult authors have readers share the lives at court and the often-shorter marriages of Henry VIII with Katharine of Aragon, Anne Boleyn, Jane Seymour, Anne of Cleves, Catharine Howard, and Kateryn Parr. Fans of historical fiction, biographies, and memoirs will enjoy the ponderings of the characters as presented by each author. The authors consider the motivations behind their decisions, from Henry VIII's determination to have a male heir, which led him to create a new religion with himself at the head, to his wives' earnest intentions, which turned to despair, to the consistent political machinations of his advisors.

Chapter 4

Biography

Definition

A biography is the history of an individual's life. The term, coming from the combined Greek words *bios* (life) and *graph* (write) had its first English usage in Dryden's 1683 work *Lives of Plutarch*. Unlike memoirs, biographies generally share someone's whole life, rather than focusing on part of it.

Collection Development of the Biography Collection

As far back as 1991, librarians were recognizing that it was unacceptable to add outdated materials to the library collection.[1] At the time, biographies for young adults were seen as just compilations. It has been recognized in the interim that while the basic facts (birth, death, years in power) about a person of perennial interest would not change, it has become more important to present titles that are not only capable of presenting the point of view of the person rather than the author, but which can give the reader a better understanding of the times in which the subject lived and acknowledge the difficulties they faced. In the case of people who continue to remain in the public eye, such as Malala Yousafzai, it is not uncommon either for books to remain in print, new works to be published, or titles to be published for new audiences. In the case of Yousafzai, it should not be surprising that all three have happened; she has also become an author in her own right, having written a biography to share her story with younger children. Publication of new or revised titles presents an opportunity to discard older titles. Titles about celebrities may tend to be more ephemeral, as popularity may be fickle, or pass as a subject's fans age with them. Many teenagers' idols tend to also be younger, and thus lose their appeal or become outdated within a few years.

Biographies present a unique opportunity for librarians to share with readers stories of the wider world. People have an inherent curiosity about the lives of other people, and biographies remain the easiest window into the times, places, and perspectives of the books' subjects. Historians and biographers compiling events in both biographies and autobiographies should make sure that all events recorded are factual, complete, and verifiable, using both primary and secondary sources.

Chapter Organization

Not all libraries have a separate biography collection. For that reason, biographies have been grouped into the categories for which their subjects are best remembered. The first section, "American Presidents and Other Political Leaders," covers some of the most influential people in our lives. It is followed by "Outstanding in Their Fields: Professional Biographies," which contains the life stories of people lauded for their scientific achievements and career achievements. "Change-Makers and Activists" recognizes those devoted to making a difference socially and politically. The books in "Historical Biography" provide unique pictures of individuals and the times in which they lived. These differ from the titles in the "History" section of chapter 5 because the people, not the time period, are the focus of the books.

"Partner and Group Biographies" includes stories about more than one individual, such as the remarkable women in Margot Lee Shetterly's *Hidden Figures*. The public's ongoing fascination with fame is reflected in the next category, which contains titles about people in the public eye.

American Presidents and Other Political Leaders

The lives of arguably the most powerful people in the country are intrinsically fascinating to readers. Teachers are happy for their students to learn about the decision makers behind the laws and policies that shape our lives and our history. These interests make a good combination with authors that focus on national and world leaders. The titles in this subgenre provide the details of the time and the part the person played in it, and give the reader a sense of how people in a position of power got there and what effect they had on the country they led.

Blumenthal, Karen.

Hillary Rodham Clinton: A Woman Living History. 2016. 423p. **M J**

This is a solid introduction to the former first lady of Arkansas, first lady of the United States, Secretary of State, and presidential candidate. It presents a thorough overview of her background and the many details that make her such a fascinating individual, whether they involve notable firsts, such as serving as the first female senator from New York and the first female Secretary of State, or the notoriety of the scandal surrounding the Clinton White House. Thoroughly researched, this is a volume that does not spend time debating Clinton's ideas or looking at the opposition's positions in the 2016 election. This is a balanced title aimed at readers who are not of voting age.

Keywords: Clinton, Hillary • First ladies • Presidential candidates • Secretary of State

Brockenbrough, Martha.

Unpresidented: A Biography of Donald Trump. 2018. 432 p. **M J**

Approximately the first half of *Unpresidented* covers Donald Trump's life up to his decision to run for the presidency in 2016. Within that time frame readers are given a better sense of how Trump chose to conduct business, including his many bankruptcies, some of the 4,000 lawsuits in which he was involved on either side, and just what a driving force the Trump brand was to him. The lies and obfuscations seen in his daily life both personally and professionally make for fascinating reading as they become part of his political persona and message. Examples of this are the birther rumors he started and maintained about President Obama, years after the president produced his birth certificate. Trump's unconventional and outspoken tactics during his own presidential campaign are further evidence of how different a candidate, and a president, he is than the American public has seen before. This title will help readers learn about Trump's policies and rhetoric surrounding immigration, as well as the accusations of potential ties between Russia and the Trump camp. It also explains the events that followed the election, including the revelations of the Steele dossier and Trump's actions and reactions over the first months of his presidency. The book also includes a timeline of important events and biographies of important people in his campaign and legal team, and interested readers can use Brockenbrough's thorough documentation to lead them in further reading.

Keywords: Presidents • Trump, Donald

Hennessey, Jonathan.

🎗 *Alexander Hamilton: The Graphic History of an American Founding Father.* 2017. 176p. **M J**

This book offers a graphic telling of Alexander Hamilton's rise from living in poverty in the West Indies, with the stigma of being both illegitimate and orphaned, to becoming one of the most influential figures in United States history. This volume covers Hamilton's entire life and gives a thorough account of the timeline of the Revolutionary War and related key events that followed. The format will make it more appealing to readers who would not be interested in reading about economic policies, as there is a considerable amount of explanatory text included that would make this a very good introductory text about the period. **GGNT**

Keywords: Graphic nonfiction • Hamilton, Alexander

Now Try: Judith St. George looks at the events that brought Alexander Hamilton and Aaron Burr to Weehawken, New Jersey's, dueling grounds on July 11, 1804, in *The Duel: The Parallel Lives of Alexander Hamilton and Aaron Burr*. St. George looks at the many similarities between the two—they were both orphans and lawyers—and examines the effects of these similarities on the men in question, as well as the effects the men had on the nation, leading up to the duel that left one man dead and the other a fugitive.

Kanefield, Teri.

Abraham Lincoln. <u>The Making of America</u>. 2018. 240p. **M** **J**

The story of America's 16th president is presented in a well-researched narrative. More than a straight biography, this title explains not only the lasting importance of constitutional amendments but also demonstrates how the Democratic and Republican parties of today differ from their historical counterparts. It also provides examples of how Lincoln was able to win the White House by winning the popular vote, work in a bipartisan fashion to pass unpopular legislation, and bypass his government when he believed he knew best. This is a well-rounded portrait of an American icon, highlighted by a number of his writings and speeches, including the Gettysburg Address.

Keywords: Lincoln, Abraham • Presidents

Perritano, John.

John McCain: An American Hero. 2018. 192p. **M** **J**

While it is hard to say whether John McCain III will be best remembered for his service to his country during the Vietnam War or during his long political career, there is no doubt that he will be honored for his remarkable dedication to his country. As the son and grandson of U.S. admirals, it was expected that he, too, would enter the Navy, where he began a trajectory that eventually found him serving as a pilot and becoming a prisoner of war. The thorough recounting of the torture McCain suffered during his years in Vietnam is eye-opening and a testament to his character, which helps explain why he became one of the most steadfast voices in politics during the following decades. A timeline of McCain's life as a politician, from his election as a congressman through his decades in the senate to his bids for the presidency, demonstrates the influence he has had. The book is also complemented by numerous photographs that help introduce this vivid and larger-than-life figure.

Keywords: Aviators • Congressmen • McCain, John • Prisoners of war • Senators

Reef, Catherine.

Victoria: Portrait of a Queen. 2017. 423p. **J**

Victoria, Great Britain's second-longest reigning monarch after Queen Elizabeth II, became Queen at the age of 16 in 1837. The book covers changes to society during the Victorian era, including the introduction of the industrial age, several wars, and the increasing growth of the British empire, which saw Victoria becoming the empress of India in 1877. It also provides an intimate look at the politics and inside machinations of the royal family, and the people trying to benefit from their connections to it. Readers will be fascinated by an explanation of Victoria's family tree and her rise from fifth in line to the throne to its heir, along with the Kensington system devised by advisors determined to manage, if not outright control, the princess. This is followed by an equally engaging history of her reign and how she and her nine children were a part of the events of the day.

Keywords: Monarchs • Queen Victoria

Outstanding in Their Fields: Professional Biographies

This section includes people (other than politicians and social activists) who are thought of in conjunction with their field. Titles about them would be shelved under the Dewey number associated with their chosen profession. Covered in either single or group biographies, these people are exemplars, leaders, and innovators in their chosen fields. These titles provide insight into the subjects' work that can give interested readers a possibility for work in their own lives as well as information about heights to which they can aspire.

Aronson, Marc, and Marina Budhos.

Eyes of the World: Robert Capa, Gerda Taro, and the Invention of Modern Photojournalism. 2017. 304p. **M J**

Gerta Pohorylle and André Friedmann were a natural fit: he taught her photography, she supported his work. She also suggested they change their names to the less political Gerda Taro and Robert Capa in the increasingly anti-Semitic milieu that was 1930s Paris. Capa's work, photographing events for illustrated news magazines that had become increasingly popular across Europe, gave him a new purpose, and in 1936 he and Taro traveled to cover the Spanish Civil War. Side-by-side reproductions of their photographs give readers both a sense of their work and an empathetic sense of the events that magazine readers would never before have had. Capa and Taro were determined to bring the senselessness and news from the war to the public, and their work established a form of photojournalism that is still in use today. The book also demonstrates the costs they were willing to face in a search for truth. Appendices discussing controversial events and photographs are fascinating. **AENYA**

Keywords: Capa, Robert • Journalism • Photographers • Photography • Photojournalism • Taro, Gerda

Conkling, Winifred.

Radioactive! How Irène Curie and Lise Meitner Revolutionized Science and Changed the World. 2016. 240p. **M J**

The accomplishments of these two largely unheralded scientists, who between them won one Nobel Prize and were nominated another 15 times, deserve more publicity. This book provides insight into, and context to, their work, including its positive and negative effects. It begins with Curie and her husband's work in artificial radioactivity, which was initially used as a cure-all and led to inevitable poisoning. Meitner's accomplishments as a physicist and her experiments in nuclear fission were stopped when she fled Germany during World War II. The co-opting of the ladies' work for the war effort into the atomic bomb proved personally abhorrent to both women. The work of these scientists deserves to be lauded.

Keywords: Curie, Irène • Meitner, Lise • Nuclear fission • Radioactivity

Now Try: Another unlikely duo who overcame their initial doubts about each other and went on to have a long and productive relationship were Charles Darwin and Emma Wedgwood, the deeply religious woman he married. If he were to be proved right about his scientific beliefs, hers would be proven wrong. How she overcame her doubts and went on to become his partner, sounding board, and eventually the editor of his most important work, *The Origin of Species,* is the subject of a core title, Deborah Heiligman's Award of Excellence and Printz-honor winning title *Charles and Emma: The Darwins' Leap of Faith.*

Emmett, Dan.

I Am A Secret Service Agent: My Life Spent Protecting the President. 2017. 224p. **M** **J**

Dan Emmett made the decision to become a Secret Service agent at the age of eight, when President John F. Kennedy was assassinated. This book details the steps he took to achieve his goal, and then covers his life as an agent through training and as a member of several details including CAT (Counter Assault Team) and PPD (Presidential Protective Division) for presidents George H. W. Bush, Bill Clinton, and George W. Bush.

Keywords: Emmett, Dan • Secret Service

Now Try: Most people now recognize that SEALs are the crème de la crème of America's fighting forces. By that reckoning, Howard Wasdin was an unlikely candidate from the day he was taken home from the hospital as a three-pound, two-ounce preemie. The determination that took him through BUD/S training and served him well during his time in the service is detailed by Howard Wasdin and Stephen Templin in *I am a SEAL Team Six Warrior: Memoirs of An American Soldier.*

Hartland, Jessie.

Steve Jobs: Insanely Great. 2015. 240p. **M** **J**

Perhaps the perfect way to present the innovative and trailblazing Steve Jobs is through this graphic biography, which combines penciled illustrations with hand-drawn text. Readers following Jobs' remarkable career are given insight into the history of the personal technology industry. A double-page spread shows technology of the 1960s (big records, small records, and all games were played on boards!), long before he left college after a semester and went out on his own, beginning Apple Computer in his parent's garage. His personal story, along with his ability to develop items that became necessary and ubiquitous in the lives of the public, are inspiring and fascinating.

Keywords: Apple Computer • Computers • Graphic nonfiction • iPods • Jobs, Steve • Macs

Kapp, Diana.

Girls Who Run the World: 31 CEOs Who Mean Business. 2019. 320p. **M** **J**

The women included in this book demonstrate that creating a business from the ground up is not easy or for the faint of heart, and it can be done every bit as well, if not better, by a woman than by a man. The profiles of the business leaders are accessible, introducing both the women and the ideas that they developed into well-known and respected companies, from 23andMe to bareMinerals. They provide tips based on their experiences and discuss how they capitalized on early errors, faced near financial disaster, and made sure to keep having fun at work. After these inspiring stories, readers are provided with a toolkit to help them launch their own businesses, starting with a list of business concepts. From there, they are provided with the basics of business-plan writing, accounting, an examination of a business plan, and suggestions for idea-gathering.

Keywords: Business • Entrepreneurs • Entrepreneurship

Ortiz, Victoria.

Dissenter on the Bench: Ruth Bader Ginsburg's Life and Work. 2019. 208p. **M** **J**

This biography of well-known and respected jurist Ruth Bader Ginsburg presents a portrait of a lifelong student, a person whose upbringing instilled a respect for justice, education, and equality, and one who often disputed conventional opinions. Ortiz explains the background of Ginsburg's belief in the worth of dissent, particularly when she would have been expected to concur as a daughter, wife, and mother in her personal life. Supreme Court cases are described, providing readers with an understanding of several important constitutional challenges, alongside a description of Ginsburg's education and professional career path. Both show how she stood out among her peers, recognizing how unique it was for a woman to carve a path in the legal field to the top court in the nation, where she continues to recognize the rights of all individuals to be heard in matters of gender equality, civil rights, and human rights.

Keywords: Ginsburg, Ruth Bader • Supreme Court

Reef, Catherine.

Florence Nightingale: The Courageous Life of the Legendary Nurse. 2016. 192p. **M J**

This book's presentation of the well-known figure goes beyond the stereotypical image of a nurse wiping a fevered brow. Readers are shown that the mother of modern nursing was a girl raised in Victorian England, at a time when reputable girls were not supposed to work outside the home, much less in settings that were unrespectable, such as a hospital. That Florence gained fame nursing the British forces during the Crimean War was secondary to her study and beliefs about medicine, sanitation, and contagion, which led to her working to improve conditions for Britain's poor. Her dedication to furthering the nursing field is inspiring.

Keywords: Health care • Nightingale, Florence • Nursing

Samuelsson, Marcus, with Veronica Chambers.

Make It Messy: My Perfectly Imperfect Life. 2015. 212p. **M J**

Orphaned as a baby in Ethiopia, Marcus Samuelsson was adopted by a couple in Sweden, where he became part of a family that inspired his love of food. After an early hope of playing professional soccer didn't work out, he set out to learn the craft of cooking, across several countries and in the kitchens of renowned chefs, before opening his own highly recognized restaurant in New York City. His is an inspirational story of perseverance, determination, and achieving excellence in one's field.

Keywords: Chef • Cooking • Samuelsson, Marcus

Change-Makers and Activists

The people in this section are worthy of respect and admiration. They are memorable not only for what they have achieved, but for their struggles and the endurance they have shown. This makes for engrossing, enlightening reading, providing food for thought that lasts long after a reader has finished. These titles provide role models and demonstrate why people have taken up struggles and become involved in the movements for which they have been fighting, as well as the changes in those institutions.

Andraka, Jack, with Matthew Lysiak.

Breakthrough: How One Teen Innovator Is Changing the World. 2015. 256p. **J H**

Jack Andraka showed an affinity for math and science from an early age. He was both inspired and encouraged by a supportive family who allowed him to participate in science fairs and try to solve the mysteries that surrounded him. His projects found solutions to real-life problems, setting him on a path to compete nationally by middle school. These victories did not translate into his own life; he faced bullying and harassment. It was the devastating personal loss of his uncle to pancreatic cancer that inspired the research that became the Gordon E. Moore Award–winning four-cent paper strip capable of detecting pancreatic, ovarian, and lung cancers, a project he completed at the age of 15. His work shows that science is inspirational and demonstrates the importance of research.

Keywords: Cancer • Discoveries • Science • Scientists

Boyce, Jo Ann Allen, and Debbie Levy.

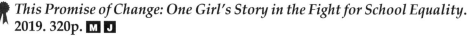 *This Promise of Change: One Girl's Story in the Fight for School Equality.* 2019. 320p. ⓜ ⓙ

The doctrine of "separate but equal," though guaranteed under the constitution, was ignored in Clinton, Tennessee, until a court decree declared that the town's high school would be integrated in 1956. Boyce's verse memoir gives readers an eye-opening view of the difficulties encountered by the students, particularly the difference between being allowed to attend the school and the limitations faced once inside, as well as the protests and increasing vitriol aimed against them in the community. The inclusion of headlines and historical material is both enlightening and frightening, and provides historical context that makes this incident all too relevant to current readers. **BG-HB**

Keywords: Clinton • Race integration • Social Activists • Tennessee

Jennings, Jazz.

Being Jazz: My Life as a (Transgender) Teen. 2016. 272p. ⓙ ⒣

Jazz Jennings notes in this memoir, penned at the age of 15, that she was born a boy but has always known she was a girl. It took several years for her parents, who came to accept this was a part of her when she was a few years old, to allow her to be female in public, knowing the difficulties she would face. As a sports-loving child, Jazz was denied the right to play on a girls' team. The struggle ended up with the United States Soccer Federation (USSF) creating a transgender inclusive policy. Through her first-person memoir, Jazz expresses the difficulties she experienced as a child and young teenager, knowing, in retrospect, that she and her parents have been able to make a difference for other children in similar situations. By the end of the book Jazz has met the president, and become the kind of role model she herself mentions meeting and admiring.

Keywords: Jennings, Jazz • LGBTQ • Transgender teens

Yousafzai, Malala.

I Am Malala: The Girl Who Stood Up for Education and Was Shot by the Taliban. 2013. 352p. **H** **A/YA**

> While there are very few people unfamiliar with the name Malala Yousafzai, her journey from being shot in the head at the age of 14 to becoming the youngest-ever winner of the Nobel Peace Prize at the age of 17 is well worth closer attention. This book will introduce readers to a country where human rights are severely limited, something that Malala continues to fight against, and which she is able to do because of her devoted family.
>
> **Keywords:** Pakistan • Taliban • Yousafzai, Malala

Historical Biography

While the authors in these titles use historical details to enrich their books, it is the person at the center of the of story, and not the time or place, that is the most impactful. By showing readers the effect that the atomic bomb had on one person, for example, Sachiko Yasui's biography offers a greater understanding of its effect. Titles where the historical events are featured more prominently than the subject of the biography may be found in chapter 5.

Conkling, Winifred.

Passenger on the Pearl: The True Story of Emily Edmondson's Flight from Slavery. 2015. 256p. **J**

> Emily Edmonson learned several important truths from her mother. One of the most important was not to marry a man before he had his freedom, as doing so would mean that your children could, and likely would, be sold. In 1848, to avoid this fate, she, four of her siblings, and another 65 slaves boarded a schooner in what was to be the largest attempted escape in American history. Conkling details what happened after the *Pearl* was caught in less than a day, with its captains jailed and the slaves sold south. It is because the 13-year-old Emily was in danger of being sold into the sex trade that she first came to the attention of the Rev. Henry Ward Beecher, whose sister, Harriet Beecher Stowe, would write *Uncle Tom's Cabin*. The author follows the lives of the Edmondson family and the ship's captains, and provides a timeline of developing antislavery sentiment at the time.
>
> **Keywords:** Edmondson, Emily • Slave trade • Slavery

Gill, Joel Christian.

 Bessie Stringfield: Tales of the Talented Tenth, no. 2. 2016. 158p. **M** **J**

> A frame tale has Bessie Stringfield recounting the story of her life to a young interviewer in this clever graphic portrait of a colorful woman. Brought to the

United States from Jamaica as a young child and abandoned by a father grieving over her mother's death, she was turned over to an orphanage, from which she found a happier adoptive home and a yearning for freedom. The rest of her life tells the story of a wanderer, played against the backdrop of the 20th century: she became the first woman to motorcycle across the country, constantly facing Jim Crow laws, escaped the Ku Klux Klan, served as a wartime courier, cycled across Europe after World War II, and married six times. Her chosen lifestyle earned her the moniker "The Motorcycle Queen of Miami" and a place as the first black woman to be inducted into both the Harley Davidson Hall of Fame and the American Motorcyclist Association (AMA) Hall of Fame. **GGNT**

Keywords: Graphic nonfiction • Jim Crow • Motorcycles • Motorcyclists • Stringfield, Bessie

Now Try: A classic account of a person at the center of a notable time in history is Phillip Hoose's multiple-award-winning biography, *Claudette Colvin: Twice Toward History*. It tells the story of how the 15-year-old girl, who failed to relinquish her seat on a Montgomery, Alabama, bus nine months before Rosa Parks was arrested, was removed from consideration for the bus boycott because of her age and the NAACP leaders' insecurity about winning an appeal of her case. Pregnant, unmarried, and disgraced by the time Parks was in the spotlight, Colvin stepped aside, but she still testified in the *Browder v. Gayle* case, which made bus segregation unconstitutional. Colvin stands as a true example of someone consistently doing the right thing.

Fleming, Candace.

The Family Romanov: Murder, Rebellion, and the Fall of Imperial Russia. 2014. 304p. **M** **J**

Candace Fleming introduces readers to Russia's last royal family, including a czar who never wished to be in power, his daughters who could not succeed him, and his hemophiliac son who would not likely live to do so. At a time of increasing discontent among the Russian populace, the last Romanovs sealed themselves away in a bubble, ignoring the unrest even as their people fought during World War I. A mysterious priest, Rasputin, was believed to be too close to the czarina, having a personal power so great that he could not be killed until he had been clubbed, poisoned, shot multiple times, and dumped into the river. While an autopsy determined that Rasputin was, in fact, killed by a bullet, the truth about the assassination of the Romanovs was not acknowledged for decades, leaving the government at odds about how to acknowledge their deaths. This is an intriguing and relevant look at the lives of people who were both revered and blamed for the ills of the country, at a time when a very small percentage of the population held all of the nation's power and most of its capital. **AENYA BG-HB OP Sibert**

Keywords: Rasputin, Grigori • Romanov

Hale, Nathan.

 The Underground Abductor: An Abolitionist Tale about Harriet Tubman. **Nathan Hale's Hazardous Tales.** 2015. 128p. **M J**

In this volume in Nathan Hale's graphic series, the eponymous narrator provides an illuminating and entertaining account of Harriet Tubman, a slave born Araminta Ross in the early 19th century in Delaware. Growing up, Ross saw several of her siblings sold and was threatened with the same fate; this was the deciding factor in her decision to make the dangerous trip north, where slavery was illegal. She then changed her name to Harriet Tubman and dedicated herself to helping others. **GGNT**

Keywords: Slavery • Slaves • Tubman, Harriet

Noyes, Deborah.

The Magician and the Spirits: Harry Houdini and the Curious Pastime of Communicating with the Dead. 2017. 160p. **M J**

Ehrich Weiss was born Erik Weisz in Budapest, Hungary, in 1897, to a loving mother and a rabbi who emigrated shortly thereafter to the United States and settled in Wisconsin. Having learned magic as a young boy, he turned to vaudeville at the beginning of his career for steady employment. It was at this point that he learned about psychic themes, such as mind reading, mediumship, and spirit conjuring, and incorporated them into his act. Later, after he developed the tricks that would make him one of the most renowned magicians in the world, he was also one of the most skeptical when spiritualism became a popular pastime and mediums were celebrities in the post–World War I world. His understanding of how magicians put their tricks together combined with his own desire to find verifiable proof of spiritual contact made him even more adamant in his determination to test and debunk each claimant. This is a fascinating look at Houdini's life and motivations and a history of spiritualism in all its forms.

Keywords: Houdini, Harry • Magicians • Spiritualists • Weiss, Ehrich

Now Try: The life of another showman, one who could legitimately be thought of as creating the precursor to reality television, is P. T. Barnum. While, as Deborah Noyes's book points out, Barnum had also testified against false mediums, he is better known for creating and then recreating Barnum's American Museum and becoming one of the earliest modern celebrities. Candace Fleming's *The Great and Only Barnum: The Tremendous, Stupendous Life of Showman P. T. Barnum* introduces a man who was born poor and made his life what he wanted it to be.

Ottaviani, Jim.

 The Imitation Game: Alan Turing Decoded. 2015. 240p. **H**

There is no dispute that Alan Turing had a gift for math; he not only preferred science and numbers, he saw them with perfect clarity and devoted himself to

them from a young age. He first garnered attention in attempting to solve what was thought to be an unsolvable problem in school, which was then used by machines for calculation. Later, Turing turned to ciphers and linguistics, doing important and unreported work leading a large group of cryptologists decoding German messages during World War II. He received the OBE (Officer of the Order of the British Empire award) for his service and tried after the war to continue with his work on computers, in a time when machines that are now ordinary were of little use. Ottaviani provides a painful and accurate recounting of homosexuality, which had been a crime since 1885. The story of a brilliant man in a world not yet ready for him, including exactly what his work at Bletchley Park entailed, is fascinating. Told from the perspective of people who knew him, his mother in particular, he is seen as the brilliant man he was, living in the looming shadow of what he missed, given the expectations of the time in which he lived and the possibilities of the discoveries he might have made. The author points out the ambiguity surrounding his death and provides a bibliography for readers interested in more information. **GGNT**

Keywords: Computers • Graphic biography • Science • Technology • Turing, Alan

Price, Planaria, and Helen Reichmann West.

Claiming My Place: Coming of Age in the Shadow of the Holocaust. 2018. 272p. **M J**

Gucia Gomolinska saw what happened to her native Poland when the Germans took over. As a young Jewish woman, she had both seen and faced discrimination, but when the Nazis took over she began to realize how bad it could really get, with the Jews being confined to a ghetto long before waves of people were sent off on train cars to a concentration camp, never to return. Eventually fear for her own safety led her to the realization that it was her almost-Aryan coloring and ash-blond hair, which allowed her to pass as Polish, that could provide her best chance of safety, if she dared use it. Taking on a new identity as Basia Tanska, she hid in plain sight in Germany, only to find out that escaping extermination was not the end of her ordeal. This is a remarkable story of courage and loss, written by Price with Basia's daughter.

Keywords: Holocaust • Poland • Tanska, Basia • World War II

Prins, Marcel, and Peter Henk Steenhuis. Translated by Laura Watkinson.

Hidden Like Anne Frank: 14 True Stories of Survival. 2014. 240p. **J H**

Of the 28,000 Jewish people who hid from the Germans in the Netherlands during World War II, approximately 14,000 survived. Marcel Prins gathered the stories of 14 children, including his own mother, in a volume that expresses the horror, fear, difficulties, and tragedies experienced by these children as they tried to escape the fate of the 12,000 who didn't. First-person accounts tell of deprivation, the need to move repeatedly to hide from soldiers, and children too young to know what it means to be Jewish wondering why they are being singled out. The book, which includes current pictures of the survivors, is notable for the stories that go beyond the Netherlands' liberation. Interested readers will be happy for the companion Web site.

Keywords: Holocaust • Netherlands • World War II

Now Try: No collection is complete without a copy of *Anne Frank: The Diary of a Young Girl*. Still considered to be one of the most evocative portraits of the Holocaust, the diary contains the reflections of Anne Frank, who spent two years hiding from the Nazis with her family in an Amsterdam attic before being sent to the Bergen-Belsen concentration camp. Her father, the sole surviving member of the family, found, edited, and published her diary after the war. The definitive 1995 edition translated by Susan Massotty added additional material to give readers a better understanding of Anne.

Schwartz, Simon.

The Other Side of the Wall. 2015. 112p. .

Simon Schwartz's parents met and married in the DDR, the Deutsche Demokratische Republik, more commonly known as East Germany. Two years after his birth in 1982, they emigrated to the other side of the Berlin Wall. This black and white graphic novel helps express the conditions at the time under the oppressive rule of the DDR's Socialist Unity Party, which kept his parents under watch. His parents' decision to leave the party caused a rift in his family and was considered a betrayal by both his father's family and the government. Readers are given a relatable picture that provides background for the greater historical events that precipitated the falling of the Berlin Wall while showing how difficult it can be to choose between one's beliefs and one's country.

Keywords: Berlin Wall • Germany • Graphic nonfiction • Schwartz, Simon

Stelson, Caren.

Sachiko: A Nagasaki Bomb Survivor's Story. 2016. 144p. M J

Sachiko Yasui was six years old when the atomic bomb was dropped on her hometown of Nagasaki on August 9, 1945. As a survivor, she spent the rest of her life dealing with the aftermath. This book presents a unique and personal perspective as well as a historical overview. Readers will find both components powerful and affecting, whether seeing a photograph of keloids covering scar tissue from radiation on a survivor's back, or one of Sachiko speaking to schoolchildren on the 50th anniversary of the bomb's release. **ALA**

Keywords: Atomic bomb • Nagasaki • World War II • Yasui, Sachiko

Turner, Pamela S.

🎗 *Samurai Rising: The Epic Life of Minamoto Yoshitsune.* 2016. 256p. **M J**

The life of Yoshitsune, one of the greatest warriors of the 12th century, is presented in a narrative that makes it accessible and interesting. Turner's careful reconstruction of source notes is necessary and laudatory, given the very complicated and violent time about which she is writing. She incorporates notes, timelines, maps and information about battles to enlighten readers about the soldier and his life. **AENYA ALA**

Keywords: Japan • Samurai • Yoshitsune

Wein, Elizabeth.

A Thousand Sisters: The Heroic Airwomen of the Soviet Union in World War II. 2019. 400p. **M J**

Wein takes care to point out that girls growing up in a communist Soviet Union in the period following World War I were presented with the same educational opportunities as boys. This also meant that young women believed they would, if needed, be fighting alongside their male counterparts if war was declared; however, by the time the Soviet Union joined World War II, even one of the country's greatest pilots, Marina Roskova, was initially denied a place at the front. She would eventually be put in charge of the 122nd Composite Air Group, which was comprised of three regiments of the Soviet air force. These pilots were not given uniforms, planes, or sufficient training before being sent to bomb the Germans. They also knew that Stalin had issued an order that retreating in the face of danger from the enemy was treasonous. Wein postulates that Stalin's order might explain Roskova continuing to fly into the bad weather that ended her life and offers readers the fascinating story of the night witches, as the Germans called the 46th Guards, who made up to 300 bombing runs nightly throughout the war. This is an impeccably researched volume that includes an update on the women after the war and a bibliography with a wide range of materials.

Keywords: Night witches • Roskova, Marina • Soviet Union • World War II

Partner and Group Biographies

It is occasionally impossible to look at one life without considering that person's relationship with other people. The interactions of these subjects make for involving reading. Challenges that authors can face when describing the accomplishments or challenges of multiple people can result in a book that gives a reader extra insight, such as with Margot Lee Shetterly's *Hidden Figures: The American Dream and the Untold Story of the Black Women Mathematicians Who*

Helped Win the Space Race, a title that has also been published in a young readers edition and was made into a motion picture.

Freeman, Sally Mott.

The Jersey Brothers: A Missing Naval Officer in the Pacific and His Family's Quest to Bring Him Home. 2017. 608p. **A/YA**

> In 2009, Sally Mott Freeman reopened the story of her uncle, held prisoner for three years during World War II by the Japanese. This is a remarkable narrative, all the more affecting because it is true. When the United States entered World War II, the three Mott siblings all contributed to the war effort in remarkable ways: Benny Mott was a gunnery officer on the *Enterprise*, one of the only ships to make it through the attack at Pearl Harbor; Bill Mott had been chosen by President Franklin D. Roosevelt himself to run the White House's Map Room; and Barton was a supply officer in the Navy Supply Corps. When General Douglas MacArthur evacuated army and not navy personnel from the Philippines, it was Barton, injured and left behind, who was listed as missing in action and then taken as a prisoner of war without any word to his family. It was left to his family to try and find him when he was lost to the horror of a long list of successive camps and Japanese atrocities.
>
> **Keywords:** Naval officers • Prisoners of war • World War II

Heiligman, Deborah.

 Vincent and Theo: The Van Gogh Brothers. 2017. 608p. **H**

> For most people, the name Van Gogh immediately brings to mind the mercurial artist, primarily known, if at all, for the murky incident of the loss of his ear. This beautifully presented biography presents a picture of the relationship that formed and maintained both his personal and professional lives, that of the artist and his younger brother, Theo. Vincent depended on Theo Van Gogh not only for financial support but also for emotional support, as the brothers both struggled with depression and maintained a correspondence that is incorporated in the entrancing narrative of this book. The years of the brothers' lives are divided into galleries, each featuring one of Vincent's pencil sketches. Supplemental materials include an insert with color reproductions, timelines, endnotes, source notes, and a bibliography. **BG-HB NBA Printz**
>
> **Keywords:** Art • Artists • Van Gogh, Vincent

Miller, Sarah.

The Miracle and Tragedy of the Dionne Quintuplets. 2019. 320p. **J H**

> By the time Dr. Dafoe came to help when Elzire Dionne went into labor two months early on May 28, 1934, she was already delivering her third of what would be five babies. Nobody present at their birth believed the babies would

live through the night. News of the miraculous occurrence, the multiple babies born with a combined weight of only thirteen pounds, seven ounces, captivated the public across North America in increasing numbers. At the same time, the babies required constant, specialized care, which caused an almost immediate rift in the family as medical staff took over the care of the infants. Oliva Dionne was left debating whether to use the public's enthusiasm for his children as a means to pay for their medical care, while Elzire Dionne resented being denied the right to mother them, although her own recovery kept her apart from her five older children. It was at this point the Ontario government stepped in with a proposal to take custody of the children for their own protection. The girls' move into their own private hospital across the street from the family home did little to quell public interest, and Quintland became a popular tourist destination. Miller explores how the enforced separation and publicity affected the Dionne family, playing a part in the painful family dynamics and secrets that affected the rest of their lives. Readers will look at this precursor to reality television with sympathy and understanding.

Keywords: Dionne family • Quintuplets

O'Brien, Keith.

Fly Girls: How Five Daring Women Defied All Odds and Made Aviation History. 2018. 352p. **H** **A/YA**

While airplane racing was seen as a glamorous sport between the world wars, it was also incredibly dangerous. Flying itself was viewed as something women should not do, and any woman who sought to become a pilot faced more than ridicule for trying to participate in a man's world; they also faced hostility and prejudice. This title recounts the stories of five women who dared to pursue their dreams of flight, facing the same dangers and disasters as their male counterparts, in order to fly, participate, and have a chance at the biggest race of the day. Readers who may only have heard the name Amelia Earhart will gain a great deal of respect for these women after reading about their continued bravery and determination.

Keywords: Pilots • Women pilots

Shetterly, Margot Lee.

Hidden Figures: The American Dream and the Untold Story of the Black Women Mathematicians Who Helped Win the Space Race. 2016. 368p. **H** **A/YA**

This is the gripping story of four human "computers"—four incredibly gifted African American mathematicians—and their unacknowledged participation in the aeronautics industry. During World War II, Dorothy Vaughan, Mary Jackson, Katherine Johnson, and Christine Darden worked in segregated conditions on any mathematical problem they were assigned.

In the years that followed they continued, working through increasingly more complex research and technological advancements, until they reached the point of working on supersonic planes and trajectory analysis for spacecraft. These are women worth celebrating.

Keywords: Mathematicians • NASA • Space race

Biography Collections

Biography collections serve several purposes. They provide a cursory introduction to readers who may not be familiar with a subject, introducing them to important people in an area or to biography as a genre, in the same way that a short story might introduce a reader to an author's writing. Readers, if intrigued by the subject area, may be open to offerings in that area. An attraction to the open-ended tales in Brenda Guiberson's *Missing! Mysterious Cases of People Gone Missing through the Centuries*, for example, could lead back to the "Cons and Crimes" section in chapter 2.

Bagieu, Pénélope.

 Brazen: Rebel Ladies Who Rocked the World. 2018. 304p. **M J**

This is an innovative, entertaining volume that presents short, informative portraits of 29 women from a variety of fields, cultures, geographic regions, and time periods; all of whom have overcome odds and made strides in their chosen professions by acting in ways that were not seen as appropriate or expected for women at the time. Their work and choices are both inspiring and interesting, from Temple Grandin's work in autism to Margaret Hamilton's decision to play the wicked witch in *The Wizard of Oz*. **GGNT QP**

Keywords: Graphic nonfiction • Hamilton, Margaret • Grandin, Temple

Gill, Joel Christian.

 Strange Fruit, Volume 1: Uncelebrated Narratives from Black History. 2014. 176p. **M J**

While the nine men and women whose stories are told here are likely to be unfamiliar to readers, that is just one of the things that they have in common. Readers will find stories of people who endured hardships, such as Henry "Box" Brown's arduous escape, introduced "firsts," including a surprise discovered after the death of America's first magician, Richard Potter, and had successes, like the career of Bass Reeves, the United States' most successful lawman. These unfamiliar chapters from early African American history provide enough information to intrigue readers. A bibliography is also available for more information. **GGNT**

Keywords: Brown, Henry • Graphic biography • Potter, Richard • Reeves, Bass

Guiberson, Brenda Z.

Missing! Mysterious Cases of People Gone Missing through the Centuries. 2019. 240p. **M J**

Guiberson presents the stories of six fascinating people, from a writing prodigy who penned and published her first book before the age of 10, to a man whose determination to fight for the rights of the working man led him to fall afoul of both the Mafia and the FBI, to two young princes who were both pawns and victims in a long-running fight for the crown. Their stories, along with three others, are presented in full. Readers are given a reasonable explanation why Jimmy Hoffa was most certainly killed after he disappeared on July 30, 1975, along with the most likely suspects, and why there has never been any satisfactory resolution to his case. While the commonality among these subjects is that none were ever found, not all were victims of violence, as with aviatrix Amelia Earhart, and hijacker D. B. Cooper, whose vanishings have remained a source of fascination, having spawned songs, movies, merchandise, and books.

Keywords: Cooper, D. B. • Earhart, Amelia • Hoffa, Jimmy • Missing persons

Prager, Sarah.

Queer, There, and Everywhere: 23 People Who Changed the World. 2017. 272p. **M J**

The 23 biographical portraits in this book demonstrate that throughout human history and around the globe there have always been queer genders and sexualities, and varying measures of accompanying acceptance. As the sexuality of historical figures is not often covered, this book is a refreshing and novel look at the private lives of well-known figures from Joan of Arc and Abraham Lincoln to Eleanor Roosevelt and Harvey Milk.

Keywords: LGBT • Queer

Schatz, Kate.

Rad Women Worldwide: Artists and Athletes, Pirates and Punks, and Other Revolutionaries Who Shaped History. 2016. 112p. **M J**

Especially relevant in the days of the #MeToo movement, this collection demonstrates that there have been competent and successful women around the world, throughout history and in all fields. Readers will find 45 portraits here that go well beyond the usual suspects, including humanitarians and activists who have left positive legacies around the world. A rad woman can be an Olympic athlete, a Nobel Prize–winning chemist, or a pirate. Their powerful stories can inspire in just a short biographical sketch.

Keywords: Biographies

Consider Starting with . . .

These are some recommended titles that are both accessible and captivating for readers new to the genre.

Bagieu, Pénélope. *Brazen: Rebel Ladies Who Rocked the World.*

Boyce, Jo Ann Allen and Debbie Levy. *This Promise of Change: One Girl's Story in the Fight for School Equality.*

Fleming, Candace. *The Family Romanov: Murder, Rebellion, and the Fall of Imperial Russia.*

Heiligman, Deborah. *Vincent and Theo: The Van Gogh Brothers.*

Miller, Sarah. *The Miracle and Tragedy of the Dionne Quintuplets.*

Fiction Read-Alikes

- **McCullough, Joy. *Blood, Water, Paint.*** A powerful and fascinating verse portrait of the 17th century painter Artemisia Gentileschi. The woman of the family from the time her mother died when she was 12, Artemisia followed in her father's footsteps as a painter, surpassing him in talent but lacking any recognition due to her gender. When, at the age of 17, she was unwilling to be silent after being the victim of unspeakable violence, she again found herself a casualty of her sex, in a story that remains sadly and profoundly relevant.

- **Palacio, R. J. *White Bird.*** The *Wonder* author presents an involving and touching introduction to the Holocaust, as Sara and Julian's backstories are given depth and meaning. As a young girl living with her family in unoccupied France in 1940, Sara Blum considers that her life doesn't change much. She remains a typical child, concerned more with pretty things and remaining aloof from the bullying of her classmates than the evolving anti-Jewish sentiments. Only when she is forced into hiding and is saved from both the Germans and the local gendarmes working with them does she truly begin to understand the danger in which she has found herself. The artwork in Palacio's graphic novel works seamlessly to support her theme, supporting the idea that it is through acts of kindness that it is possible to overcome acts of evil.

- **Ruillier, Jérôme. *The Strange.*** A powerful graphic novel follows an unnamed, undocumented immigrant after his arrival, as he tries to survive not speaking the language and interacting with those from whose perspective the story is told. Whether he is regarded as another potentially dangerous Strange who would poison and damage the country, or part of the Network determined to help the Strange, there is an inevitability when he is caught by the system just determined to follow the rules, in a powerful story that crosses borders and years.

- **Shabazz, Ilyasah.** *Betty Before X.* Malcolm X's daughter presents a fictionalized account of several years in her mother's life, starting in 1945, when Betty was 11 years old. Betty, feeling unappreciated by her mother, unhappy with her home life and her work with the Housewives League, which supports black-owned businesses, becomes drawn to the Civil Rights movement. An afterword helps place Betty Shabazz's importance in American history and provides additional discussion on the other people in the narrative.

Reference

Mueller, Mary E. "History and History Makers: Give YAs the Whole Picture." *School Library Journal* (November 1991) 37. Accessed September 3, 2018.

1

2

3

4

5

6

7

8

9

10

11

Part 3

Nonfiction Subject Interests

Chapter 5

History

Nonfiction history books provide information about events from the past relating to people, places, things, time, or countries. This continues to be a very prolific area for publishing; there is no way that every historical book or series published could be considered. The books contained in this chapter are meant to introduce the subgenres and all of them do meet the criteria for choosing nonfiction used in this guide, including accuracy, style, design, and documentation.

Appeal

While it is generally acknowledged to be a mainstay of libraries and a backbone of school curricula, nonfiction history has much more to offer. Recent years have shown the benefits of titles with credible sources demonstrating a verifiable accounting for important events, as well as the opportunity to provide additional points of view and, when possible, updating the historical record upon the uncovering of new evidence.

It is only by reading nonfiction in this area that readers are able to experience another time from the point of view of someone who experienced it firsthand and find out why they were there, as they would in Christopher Noxon's *Good Trouble: Lessons from the Civil Rights Playbook*.

Titles in this chapter offer many alternatives for readers who think history is boring, including titles that look at a subject from an unexpected angle or offer highly illustrated and graphic formats. Readers may read about the past through suspenseful books, narrative nonfiction, and fiction read-alikes.

Chapter Organization

Most readers think of history in terms of dates and will not be surprised to find "Defining Times" beginning the subgenres. This is followed by tales of disaster and dark days in "History's Darkest Hours," which is divided into two subcategories:

"Human Cruelties," covering man-made tragedies, and "Natural Disasters and Disease Epidemics," featuring naturally occurring disasters. Next are titles that narrow in scope to particular events and topics in "Micro-histories."

The books in the next section, "Historical Biography: Ordinary People in Extraordinary Times," differ from the titles in the similarly named section in chapter 4 in that it is the place and time, and not the people, that is the focus of the titles.

The subjects of the books in "Ideas of History" discuss subjects and issues that are wide-ranging and cannot be said to belong to one moment in history, such as the U.S. Constitution. "New Perspectives," the final subgenre in the chapter, contains titles that demonstrate how viewpoints change in response to new information, revisions in law, and changing attitudes.

Defining Times

A chronological organization is the most common way to explore history. It can be hard to understand history without dates. People wanting to find out about history frequently begin by looking for information about a particular time period, and then hope to answer questions about it. Students are taught to start with a particular era or period of time and then look at those dates and settings in order to determine how the events of the time affected the course of history.

Aronson, Marc, and Susan Campbell Bartoletti, eds.

1968: Today's Authors Explore a Year of Rebellion, Revolution, and Change. 2018. 208p. **M J**

Taking a detailed look at a time of cultural shifts provides insight into history in a way that an overview of a large period doesn't. When that time is still pertinent 50 years later, the first-person accounts provided by the authors of particularly relevant things from this watershed year make for engrossing reading. It is not just the body count of American and Vietnamese soldiers, along with the civilians caught in the crossfire, that draws the reader in. It is knowing that the draft and the thoughts of the presidential candidates (one of whom will be assassinated partway through the year) will ripple through the populace and into the succeeding years, in much the same way that today's government, youth, and all Americans are affected by the ongoing conflicts in the Middle East. Discussions of civil rights again mirror situations today, notably in the pieces by Laban Carrick Hill, who writes about being part of a racist family who preferred not to be called such, and Elizabeth Partridge's piece about two Olympic gold medal winners being ejected from the 1968 Olympics by raising gloved fists during the playing of the U.S. national anthem, foreshadowing today's kneeling football players. It does include lighter moments, with David Lubar's piece on the stand-up comics of the day and their material, which also resonates, given the lack of diversity and the plethora of political content. The importance of youth protestors then, as with youth voters now, and the effect of current events on their lives makes this a book that reinforces the weight of both.

Keywords: Activism • Cultural revolution • Kennedy, Robert F. • King, Martin Luther, Jr. • Vietnam War

Gates, Henry Louis, Jr., with Tonya Bolden.

Dark Sky Rising: Reconstruction and the Dawn of Jim Crow. 2019. 240p. **M**

Professor Henry Louis Gates and Tonya Bolden's title is a clear and lucid primer to America at the end of the Civil War, during Reconstruction, and up to the beginning of Jim Crow segregation. This slim volume includes many illustrations, documents, and sidebars, with quotations and information that supplements the text. Readers are introduced to important people and landmark events, including the *Dred Scott* case and *Plessy v. Ferguson*, which will provide them with a better understanding of the lives and tenuous rights of freedmen in the wake of the Civil War, as well as the long road that began with "separate but equal."

Keywords: Civil rights • Civil War • Jim Crow • Reconstruction

Now Try: One of the most interesting introductions to what life was like under Jim Crow laws in the South may be found in James Sturm and Rich Tommaso's Eisner Award–winning biography of the man who was arguably the United States' greatest baseball player. Reissued in 2019 with an introduction by Gerald Early, *Satchel Paige: Striking Out Jim Crow*, takes a look at the man who came to professional baseball at a time when the South was still segregated, and did it with such confidence and skill that he walked two men before striking out the next three in the 1942 Negro World Series. His career continued for another three decades before his induction into the Baseball Hall of Fame in 1971.

Partridge, Elizabeth.

Boots on the Ground: America's War in Vietnam. 2018. 224p. **M J**

The number of Americans who died in the Vietnam war, 57,939, is large enough to be both horrifying and ambiguous; it is almost impossible to relate personally to something on that scale. In order to do so, readers will experience the war by reading the stories of eight people who were actually there. These vignettes, which show firsthand the difficulties and misery of fighting, fear, and witnessing people suffer, alternate with short pieces that provide context about important events of the day and what was happening in the United States from the point of view of its political leaders as the war raged on. The format in this remarkable book gives an immediacy that is usually lacking in historical titles, its portrayal allowing readers to contemplate the merits of the presidents' decisions, and the increasing hostility against the war on the part of the American public, while sympathizing with and learning from the experiences of each profiled participant. **AENYA ALA**

Keywords: Minh, Ho Chi • Vietnam War

Now Try: Readers looking for information about the Vietnam War that provides an explanation of its political dynamics will find an interesting take in Russell Freedman's *Vietnam: A History of the War*. Freedman first gives a background in which the Vietnamese are involved in wars against other nations, including America, before Ho Chi Minh first joins with, then turns against, the allies in World War II. America is also seen doing a considerable amount of behind-the-scenes maneuvering prior to sending troops to Vietnam, even influencing the selection of the South Vietnamese leader, Ngo Dinh Diem. This is followed by a cogent history of the war itself that helps clarify why the withdrawal of American troops after 20 years was so difficult. An additional chapter discusses the period after the war and leaves the reader with a better understanding of the evolving world.

Wilson, John.

A Soldier's Sketchbook: The Illustrated First World War Diary of R. H. Rabjohn. 2017. 112p. 🄼 🄹

Russell Hughes Rabjohn was 18 years old when he joined the Canadian Overseas Expeditionary Force in 1916, identifying himself as an illustrator. Private Rabjohn's diary entries and drawings, kept during his three years serving on the front lines while he was assigned to draw dugouts and maps, accompany a timeline of the latter years of the war. Russell's own thoughts on the monotony of trench warfare and the horrors of war make this an accessible and compelling read.

Keywords: Rabjohn, Russell Hughes • World War I

History's Darkest Hours

Readers are often interested in a particular time or event. This subgenre captures the catastrophic, devastating events of our past, whether man-made or naturally occurring. Stories of man's past intentional inhumanities have important lessons for us in the present, as current governments across the globe continue to put lives at stake and it remains important to see that feelings and prejudices lobbied against a race, religion, or gender have led to tragedies on both a small and large scale. Readers will also find stories about the victims of war and desperate times. These are not only stories about suffering, but also about endurance, struggling, and overcoming oppression. Those drawn to these titles may also enjoy the books in the "Overcoming Adversity" section of chapter 3.

Human Cruelties

These are stories of dark times, tragedies, and unfortunate events visited upon mankind by other people. They include stories of battles as well as stories of individuals and groups dealing with oppression, attacks, and unimaginable horror. The books here run the gamut from individuals fleeing an oppressive regime to the victims of the Marjory Stoneman Douglas High School shooting.

Brown, Don.

🎗 *The Unwanted: Stories of the Syrian Refugees.* 2018. 112p. **J** **H**

Protests that began in 2011 to overthrow the tyrannical Syrian regime led by President Bashar al-Assad were met with increasingly brutal measures: imprisonment, torture, massacres. The unbearable and unlivable conditions, explained in detail in Brown's heartbreaking graphic novel, help to explain the plight of the Syrian people, making understandable why they would risk almost impossible conditions, leaving behind every possession for the hope of a future where they might find a home, a job, or an education for themselves or their children. At the same time, while the numbers of refugees fleeing to other countries burgeoned from thousands to millions, it is possible to see how they overwhelmed the ability of those countries to feed and house them. While the sympathies of the governments were and are with them, the unusual and overwhelming numbers were used in creating policy for subsequent immigration policies in several European governments and are relevant to current events. **ALA GGNT**

Keywords: Graphic nonfiction • Refugees • Syria

Freedman, Russell.

🎗 *We Will Not Be Silent: The White Rose Student Resistance Movement That Defied Adolf Hitler.* 2016. 112p. **M**

Today's youth can learn from a particularly scary point in history just what it is to defy the current government and belief system. Hans Scholl joined the Hitler Youth movement at the age of 14, followed by his three sisters. Only slowly did he and his sister Sophie become disillusioned with the group. They and a few friends formed their own student movement with the goal of speaking their minds and opposing Hitler's views. The daringness of their plans and actions right up to their executions is the personification of bravery. **ALA**

Keywords: Hitler, Adolf • Hitler Youth • Holocaust • Scholl, Hans • White Rose student movement

Goldstone, Lawrence.

Unpunished Murder: Massacre at Colfax and the Quest for Justice. 2018. 288p. **M** **J**

The killing of over 100 unarmed African American men in 1873 was known either as the Colfax Massacre or the Colfax Riot, depending on your political point of view and state of residency at the time. Goldstone presents a thoroughly researched account of the trials of the group of men accused of committing the cold-blooded mass murder, as they reached the highest court in the United States without any convictions for the accused. In this very timely book, it is Goldstone's explanation of the constitution's articles, the necessity of a Bill of Rights, and the development of a Supreme Court that had the power to declare any law unconstitutional, that will allow readers to understand the importance of any Supreme Court case decision in affecting the law for generations.

Keywords: Colfax County • Massacre • White supremacists

Hartfield, Claire.

A Few Red Drops: The Chicago Race Riot of 1919. 2018. 208p. **M J**

Hartfield provides a clear and detailed timeline of events to help readers understand that relations between the white and black communities in Chicago had been tense long before the death of Eugene Williams on July 27, 1919. The 17-year-old died after being hit with a rock for swimming in front of a beach perceived to be for whites only. The purposeful and systematic division between the black and white communities had taken place in Chicago over decades. It was demonstrated through labor, housing, and the activities of the Union Stock Yard and unions, as well as the Packingtown and Black Belt neighborhoods, in which whites and blacks lived, respectively. The exponential violence that followed from Williams' death may not be surprising, as the police chief repeatedly refused to call in extra help—though it is heartbreaking. One would hope that it is something from which a lesson can be learned, as Chicago tried to do in the aftermath.

Keywords: Chicago • Riot

Hoose, Phillip.

The Boys Who Challenged Hitler: Knud Pedersen and the Churchill Club. 2015. 208p. **M J**

This is the exciting and true account of seven Danish teenagers who defied their government and began the resistance movement when the Nazis took over in 1940. Denmark's military, completely outmatched by the occupying forces, did not put up a fight when the Germans invaded the country. While the nation was unhappy with this, there was no general uprising. This is the story of a group of teens calling themselves the Churchill Club, after the British Prime Minister, who spent five months in 1942 enacting acts of sabotage against the occupying forces. While they were caught, it was their acts that provided the impetus for the resistance in Denmark. **ALA**

Keywords: Churchill Club • Denmark • Resistance • War • World War II

Now Try: Deborah Hopkinson's *Courage and Defiance: Stories of Spies, Saboteurs, and Survivors in World War II Denmark* introduces readers to people determined to act against Hitler and the Nazis in any way possible, whether by protesting their actions, trying to find ways to hinder their progress, or subverting them by helping the allies. Their stories are woven together to provide a picture of Denmark's place in the war, along with the importance of fighting against a dictatorship. Examples of the ongoing resistance include the development of the Churchill Club and a concerted effort to rescue Danish Jews that saved the lives of more than 7,200 people.

Falkowski, Melissa, and Eric Garner, eds.

We Say #NeverAgain: Reporting by the Parkland Student Journalists. 2018. 272p. **H** **A/YA**

Edited by the journalism and broadcasting teacher at Marjory Stoneman Douglas High School, the teachers and students of MSD give visceral and moving first-person pieces that present their experiences, not only of February 14, 2018, but of how they came together afterward, creating a memorial edition of the school newspaper to write effective pieces in reaction to the tragedy, harnessing social media, effectively dealing with the press, meeting their representatives, and finding ways to remember and honor their fallen friends and teachers. They share their feelings about the day of the shooting and the days afterward, in a book that speaks not only to how they live within their community but to how they have worked on their media skills. The students have shared their journey with their newspaper in a spotlight that they neither sought nor shirked for the sake of the victims.

Keywords: Gun control • Marjory Stoneman Douglas High School • Parkland

Now Try: In *Glimmer of Hope: How Tragedy Sparked a Movement*, Marjory Stoneman Douglas students give a first-person accounting of the time between the immediate aftermath of the MDS shooting and the March for Our Lives six weeks later. The students communicate why they were determined not to have Parkland become a horrific media event, or synonymous with other, previous shootings, as something to be sad about and ignored by politicians. The students explain their rapid organization of a social media presence, a rally, an ever-increasing use of media, and a resolution to speak to legislators, knowing that it would take a combination of public awareness, activism, and actual legislation to make a permanent change. Reading about the contributors' personal experiences, including their memories of the MDS victims, thoughts about going back to school after the tragedy, and pride about the success of their movement and the marches around the world, should spur readers to look at the suggestions posed by the organizers of the movement for how to create change.

Kacer, Kathy, with Jordana Lebowitz.

To Look a Nazi in the Eye: A Teen's Account of a War Criminal Trial. 2017. 230p. **M** **J**

As a granddaughter of Holocaust survivors, Jordana Lebowitz felt an instant and personal connection when she visited Auschwitz. She was so affected that when she heard about the trial of Oskar Groening, a man known as the bookkeeper of Auschwitz, who was complicit in the deaths of more than 300,000 Jews, she made immediate arrangements to attend, traveling with a survivor and prepared to see a monster. Germany was no longer what she pictured, and neither was Groening. She recorded the events of the trial, as Oskar told the truth about what he did and said he believed that his actions should not be forgotten, as did the other survivors.

Keywords: Auschwitz • Germany • Hitler, Adolf • Nazis • World War II

Swanson, James L.

Chasing King's Killer: The Hunt for Martin Luther King, Jr.'s Assassin. **2018. 384p. M J**

It may be entirely reasonable to assume that Dr. Martin Luther King Jr., having been familiar with the killings of John F. Kennedy and Malcolm X, would be leery of his own fate. Swanson begins his page-turning and informative book with an earlier and bloody—but unsuccessful—attempt on Dr. King's life. The effect was not the one intended, leaving the recovered civil rights leader more determined to follow the path of nonresistance. A timeline of civil rights activities over the next several years includes events that many may not know, including the FBI leadership's dislike of Dr. King and their wiretapping of his activities. Most of the book follows the manhunt for King's assassin, James Earl Ray, who is properly described as a bland man who would not have been expected to commit the horrific crime that shocked an entire nation. The importance of the investigation cannot be overstated, nor can its difficulty, and reading about how it was accomplished is both exciting and fascinating. It is also relevant, given the current climate of distrust being stoked against law enforcement. The research and source notes that accompany this work are thorough and impressive.

Keywords: Assassination • Civil Rights • King, Martin Luther, Jr.

Now Try: Another murder committed against a black citizen that had long-lasting and wide-reaching effects happened in 1965, when 14-year-old Emmett Till was kidnapped and brutally murdered by half-brothers Roy Bryant and J. W. Milam. His murderers, insouciant during the trial, were acquitted after a white woman claimed Till had been whistling at her. Chris Crowe's award-winning *Getting Away with Murder: The True Story of the Emmett Till Case*, reissued in 2018, continues to provide readers with insight as to how this event angered citizens around the country and spurred on the civil rights movement.

Townley, Alvin.

Captured: An American Prisoner of War in North Vietnam. **2019. 256p. M J**

This book tells the story of Jeremiah D. Denton, a naval aviator shot down over Hanoi in 1966, and the subsequent years in which he was imprisoned and tortured. Denton managed not only to survive but to rally the American prisoners around him into resisting with him. Denton's determination not to give into the demands of his jailors manifested in various ways, including refusing to provide his captors with information or sign any statements, and in finding ways to communicate with his fellow POWs. This continued as he was transferred to several different prisons and endured increasingly harsh treatment over a period of years. Denton's story, that of a man held for 2,766 days in captivity, is both an example of the horrors and atrocities committed during war and the stamina and honor exhibited by the human spirit.

Keywords: Prisoners of War • Vietnam War

Warren, Andrea.

Enemy Child: The Story of Norman Mineta, a Boy Imprisoned in a Japanese American Internment Camp During World War II. 2019. 224p. 🅜 🅙

In 1941, Norman Mineta was a 10-year-old fourth grader in San Jose, California, when the Japanese bombed Pearl Harbor. He was a firsthand witness to the rights of Japanese Americans being stripped away until the people were forcibly taken away from everything they owned and moved into internment camps. An explanation of the perception and treatment of Japanese Americans in the years until the United States entered World War II helps prepare the reader for the author's description of his family's journey through the Santa Anita camp and their time at the Heart Mountain War Relocation Center. His life after the war includes a long and distinguished career in public service and ten terms in Congress; he is best known for the Civil Liberties Act of 1988. The meticulously researched and sourced biography also offers resources such as additional information about Japanese internment outside the scope of the book and a list of further print and multimedia resources suitable for both interested readers and the classroom.

Keywords: Evacuation and relocation • Heart Mountain • Japanese Americans • Mineta, Norman • World War II

Now Try: Jeanne Sakata's play about Gordon Hirabayashi, *Hold These Truths*, allows readers to learn about his courageous stand against what he believed to be the U.S. government's unconstitutional policies toward Japanese citizens during World War II. In 1942, when Hirabayashi was a college student at the University of Washington, he was arrested for staying out after the curfew and violating the exclusion order imposed on all citizens of Japanese descent. Hirabayashi's tale covers an incredible 40 years from his initial court appearance to the time his conviction was overturned and involves a trial in which his case was decided in 10 minutes, an appeal to the Supreme Court, and a long career in which he fought for human rights. A full cast audio production of the play, which has been performed across the United States, is available through L.A. Theatre Works.

Natural Disasters and Disease Epidemics

These are the records of naturally occurring incidents and traumas, due to plagues, weather, or some other unforeseen and uncontrollable event. Readers interested in disasters and the people who survived them may also be interested in the "Survival and Disaster" stories in chapter 1 and the "Survival Skills" section of chapter 9. Sandra Lawrence's tongue-in-cheek look at some of the ways in which people have died through the ages, whether naturally or with help, may be found under "Micro-histories."

Bartoletti, Susan Campbell.

Terrible Typhoid Mary: A True Story of the Deadliest Cook in America. 2015. 227p. **M J**

Mary Mallon, better known as "Typhoid Mary," largely remains a mystery. All that is known about her is that she was a healthy carrier of the typhoid bacteria that at the turn of the century was considered deadly. Because of the danger of the disease's rapid spread, the public health department was willing to take any and all measures it considered necessary to protect people, including quarantining and testing Mary against her wishes once she had been identified as a source of the disease. Mary's desire to keep working conflicted with that of the epidemiologist, George Sobol, determined to sequester her at all costs.

Keywords: Mallon, Mary • Typhoid fever

Bausum, Ann.

VIRAL: The Fight Against AIDS in America. 2019. 176p. **M J**

The first AIDS deaths, marked in 1982 in the United States, raised no immediate alarms in either the gay or the medical community, as there was no reason to suspect that they were related. By the time doctors began to realize that the rapidly rising numbers of mortalities were, in fact, exhibiting similarities, they were unable to obtain any attention from the government, as the affected communities, initially homosexual men or drug users, were not seen as top priority. Activism brought little change in America, where homosexual activities were highly stigmatized and could, in some areas, be prosecuted. Only slowly did the insidiousness and pervasiveness of the disease become apparent, through the visual presentation of the AIDS quilt and the shocking realization that even Hollywood stars like Rock Hudson could be afflicted. By the mid-1980s, when both the public and government were well aware of the reach and the progression of the disease, efforts to fight it were hampered by the lack of effective, affordable medications. Prevention, the best hope of all for saving lives, was still stymied by the Catholic Church, who saw both needle exchange programs and distributing condoms as affronts to morality. This is a well-researched history of the slow and inexorable battle to develop the effective medications that offered people with HIV/AIDS the chance to combat it; such treatment was not an option for previous administrations that did not see it as a priority, costing the lives of many.

Keywords: Acquired Immunodeficiency Syndrome (AIDS) • HIV

Davis, Kenneth C.

More Deadly Than War: The Hidden History of the Spanish Flu and the First World War. 2018. 304p. **M J**

The Spanish influenza, which is believed to have caused the deaths of five percent of the world's population in 1918, is overshadowed in history by the end of World War I and received little press at the time; there were few active media sources in Europe save Spain, from where it is believed coverage of the illness gave rise to its name. Davis gifts readers with a gripping presentation of both the devastating nature and spread of the flu, which started in the United States at Camp Funston with a private serving as camp cook and within two weeks had affected 24 of the army's camps. The pairing of the deadly story of the war with the rising toll of the disease sweeping across nations, and how it and the dead, dying, and infected were treated, makes for a riveting read.

Keywords: Bacteria • Disease • Influenza

Jarrow, Gail.

Bubonic Panic: When Plague Invaded America. 2016. 200p. **M J**

Gail Jarrow's history of this horrifying disease, which killed 40–60 percent of its victims, is pleasingly grisly, supplemented as it is with pictures of pits of skulls and bodies of transported victims. Statistics and stories of symptoms are detailed enough to satisfy the most avid researcher, as the narrative presents a thorough history of the pandemic's spread along with the fear, denial, and anger it engendered.

Keywords: Disease • Plague

Now Try: Falynn Koch's *Plagues: The Microscopic Battlefield* is a good choice for readers interested in either the medical or the historical aspects of plagues. As with the other volumes in the Science Comics series, this entry creates a frame story in order to introduce readers to a particular subject. In this case two plague germs find themselves being studied by a scientist who offers them the opportunity to become antibiotics. Hoping to persuade them, she instructs them about the various pathogens, including bacteria, germs, fungi, protozoa, and parasites, how they can infect and harm the body, and ways that they can be, if possible, prevented or fought off. Historically important plagues, such as Black Death in London and the malaria that affected the builders of the Panama Canal, are used to illustrate how these diseases were identified and controlled.

Jarrow, Gail.

Red Madness: How a Medical Mystery Changed What We Eat. 2014. 192p. **M J**

Approximately a century ago, an incredibly painful disease appeared for the first time in America, striking a victim in Georgia with the recurring symptoms of debilitating diarrhea, severe weight loss, and a red rash on his hands and feet that would turn into blisters and then scabs. The doctor he consulted learned that the illness, pellagra, was caused by eating spoiled corn. There was no cure, and cumulative effects could be fatal. More and more cases were reported until the spread was officially declared an epidemic. Highlighted by archival photographs and personal accounts, Jarrow details how public health officials worked to determine how the disease was caught and stop it from spreading, while doctors tried to find out how to treat the symptoms and scientists raced to find a cure.

Keywords: Diseases • Epidemics • Pellagra

Marrin, Albert.

Very, Very, Very Dreadful: The Influenza Pandemic of 1918. 2018. 208p. **M** **J**

The flu virus, largely held at bay today through the miracle of an annual vaccine, infected roughly one third of the world's population as World War I raged, claiming between 50 and 100 million lives. This fascinating book explains how the difficult conditions of war contributed to disease and provides an explanation of the flu (then called Spanish flu), how it was believed to have spread, its effects, and research that has been done in the years since. Readers will be convinced to keep their immunizations up to date.

Keywords: Flu • Influenza • Pandemics

Now Try: Epidemiologists categorize the severity of a disease by the size of its occurrence at a given point in time, from an outbreak, which affects relatively few people in a small area, to a pandemic, which strikes large numbers in many parts of the world. There have only been a few true pandemics, including the bubonic plague, which affected up to 44 percent of the world's population. Unlike the pandemics of the past, the next pandemic is likely to be caused by human activity. In Connie Goldsmith's *Pandemic: How Climate, the Environment, and Superbugs Increase the Risk*, case studies that look at SARS and monkeypox examine the methods used for identifying and containing the spread of infectious diseases. This is followed by chapters on climate change, the destruction of animal habitats, increasing world populations, and the rise of superbugs, all of which have wrought changes on existing viruses, making them stronger than ever. When the author poses several possibilities for the next pandemic, readers will be very interested in the offered suggestions for possible actions on their part.

Micro-histories

Composing a large subgenre for young adults, these books allow authors to narrow their focus to a single person, event, action, or object that fascinates them, starting when and where they like and adding as much detail as they choose. A study of one thing may then draw attention to its context and consequences.

Bausum, Ann.

Stonewall: Breaking Out in the Fight for Gay Rights. 2015. 128p. **M** **J**

In 1969 homosexuality was still seen as a sign of mental instability; however the Stonewall Inn did not come to the attention of the police because it was a gay bar. Rather, while it was definitely a hub for homosexuals, the attention paid to it was due to a blackmail operation. Ongoing raids on gay establishments had been stirring up dissatisfaction within the homosexual community, and two successive raids at the Stonewall led to chaos, with growing crowds, larger numbers of police, and the Stonewall itself facing most of the destruction. When violence broke out in the crowd, the officers were forced to retreat into the Stonewall. This further inflamed the rioters, who saw them as having taken possession of the Inn, and a tense night ensued. After Bausum's careful presentation of what happened up to and after the riot, readers are presented with a history of gay rights, including Harvey Milk, AIDS, and marriage equality.

Keywords: Homosexuality • LGBTQ • Stonewall Inn

Beccia, Carlyn.

They Lost Their Heads! What Happened to Washington's Teeth, Einstein's Brain, and Other Famous Body Parts. 2018. 192p. **M** **J**

The irreverence with which this title was written belies the research that went into it, although it is likely to appeal to its target audience. Presented with footnotes and black and white cartoons that add jokes for the reader, the main text alternates between information about historical forensic practices and grisly historical examples of missing and borrowed body parts. These would be enough of a combination of disgusting and fascinating to attract readers, even without the added lure of the stories being true. From Portugal's Pedro I trying to coronate the corpse of his great love to finding a forgotten leg, the stories are unforgettable. Sidebars entitled "Where Are They Now" ensure that the question is answered for any reader wondering what happened to the discussed parts.

Keywords: Forensics • Pathology

Brown, Box.

Tetris: The Games People Play. 2016. 256p. **H**

Tetris was a ubiquitous game in the 1980s, found on every and any kind of gaming platform. Its development, as discussed in this graphic history, both mirrored and reflected the time in which it was sold and demonstrates how games affect the people that play them. *Tetris* starts with a short history of games, noting that people have been gaming for millennia, engaging the prefrontal cortex while having fun. More complex games do

1

2

3

4

5

6

7

8

9

10

11

this more successfully, allowing the player to get lost in the game. When a bored Soviet computer programmer named Alexey Pajitnov turned a game he enjoyed called pentominoes into shareware, he had no idea of any possible ramifications. What ensued included several players fighting to assert themselves over rights, with Tetris being used as a hypnotically addictive pawn. Given that the political climate during the Cold War was reflective of today's, with the creator having no control, any businessman wanting rights for the game needed to deal with an agent of the Soviet government. Readers will find this an interesting look at how the world's most popular game became so.

Keywords: Graphic nonfiction • Tetris • Video Games

Now Try: Dustin Hansen's *Game On! Video Game History from Pong and Pac-Man to Mario, Minecraft and More* shows that the story of the development of the seminal games in the history of video games is as much, if not more, about their developers. Hansen, a game developer himself, introduces readers to the people who created the games that birthed and then revolutionized the video game industry, explaining their importance along the way. While young readers weren't yet born when Pong debuted in 1972 and will only ever see an original Atari game in a display of old technology, Hansen explains the attraction of the games in a way that makes clear their place in popular culture. This title shows why each designer made it more irresistible to keep playing as more complex games were developed, and ponders where games will be going in the future.

Jarrow, Gail.

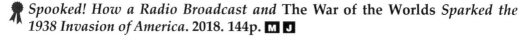 *Spooked! How a Radio Broadcast and* **The War of the Worlds** *Sparked the 1938 Invasion of America.* 2018. 144p. **M J**

For millions of Americans, one night in 1938 led to widespread panic and the belief that the country was being invaded—not by the Germans, but by aliens, the advance force from Mars, and they were attacking with overwhelming force. The broadcasted "alert" was actually a radio play, the brainchild of Orson Welles, but it led to immediate hysteria, several deaths and a backlash from local, national, and international media and governments. The story of this amazing spectacle is not only fascinating in and of itself, but relevant in the days of "fake news." Supplementary information about the people involved, additional resources, and information about other hoaxes round out a fascinating journey into what was an incredible moment in both radio and news. **ALA**

Keywords: Radio • *War of the Worlds* • Welles, Orson

Keyser, Amber J.

Underneath It All: A History of Women's Underwear. 2016. 96p. **M J**

Undergarments have changed considerably since the first bra appeared in the 15th century, but this fascinating history demonstrates that certain elements about them have remained relatively consistent, even while their purpose changed from a simple article of clothing to a fashion accessory. Both women's and men's underthings adapted regularly in response to fashion; for example, a woman's place in society in the 18th century was determined by her looks, which meant tight corsets and the larger the farthingale the better. Even so, readers will see that undergarments have moved from being viewed with shock to approbation, whether it was women wanting to wear bloomers and have pockets, Manet's 1877 painting, *Nana*, of a women wearing a blue corset, or Tyra Banks's empowering first appearance with the Victoria's Secret Angels. This is a fascinating look at what women have been wearing through the years.

Keywords: Fashion • Underwear

Lawrence, Sandra.

Hideous History: Death and Destruction. **2016. 63p.** **M**

Stories of brutality and atrocities abound in this short volume. From accounts of Boudica, leader of an Iron Age mob, to tales of the vengeful citizens in the French Revolution, to Al Capone and his henchmen in 1920s Chicago, readers will find an assortment of bloodthirsty tales, recounted in an economical fashion that will engage reluctant readers. This history shows that while their motives, weapons, and means vary, the results over time remain the same, whether there is one victim or thousands.

Keywords: Crime • Death • Violence

Newquist, HP.

The Book of Chocolate: The Amazing Story of the World's Favorite Candy. **2017. 160p.** **M**

This is a close look at the "food of the gods," an appropriate name for the foodstuff that has been used as currency and is loved around the globe. Chapters cover the growth of the cacao seed, its transformation into chocolate, the places where it is grown, the entrepreneurs who have formed and changed the industry, and the popular candy that is part of the multimillion-dollar business that exists today.

Keywords: Cacao • Chocolate • Chocolatiers

Sandler, Martin W.

🎗 *Apollo 8: The Mission that Changed Everything.* **2018. 178p.** **M** **J**

After the Soviet Union launched *Sputnik*, the first man-made satellite to orbit the earth, the space race began. This book describes some of the men and missions in the years between Sputnik in 1958 and the 1968 launch of *Apollo 8*. The story of Frank Borman, Bill Anders, and Jim Lovell traveling farther than man had ever gone, in the *Saturn V*, a rocket that had not yet been used in a manned launch, is both remarkable and fascinating. Readers may have seen the Earthrise photograph without realizing that it was taken by Bill Anders on the *Apollo 8* trip. This is a book that will appeal to both history and science lovers. **ALA**

Keywords: Anders, Bill • *Apollo 8* • Astronauts • Borman, Frank • Lovell, Jim

Sandler, Martin W.

Iron Rails, Iron Men, and the Race to Link the Nation: The Story of the Transcontinental Railroad. 2015. 224p. **M** **J**

Constructing a transcontinental railroad in the 1800s was a task comprised of an almost insurmountable list of impossible hurdles. The route, which would take over 1,800 miles, included deserts bereft of suitable materials and two mountain ranges through which it was doubted a suitable course could be found. If an agreeable route could be found, crews still needed to lay the track by hand. Lincoln's signing of the Pacific Railway Act set in motion one of the greatest and least-known contests, as two railway companies set out on an equally impossible task, the culmination of which would change the lives of citizens on both ends of the country. This is a fascinating look at the building of the railroad and the men behind it, as the Union Pacific moved west from Omaha and the Central Pacific laid tracks to meet them from San Francisco.

Keywords: Central Pacific • Transcontinental railroad • Union Pacific

Sandler, Martin W.

 The **Whydah:** *A Pirate Ship Feared, Wrecked, and Found.* 2017. 176p. **M** **J**

Piracy has been romanticized since Blackbeard and other pirates sailed the Caribbean in the late 1600s and early 1700s, pillaging ships and indulging in the slave trade. It has been because of discoveries like the *Whydah,* one of the largest and most recognizable pirate ships of its day, that a clearer picture has been formed about life on the Triangle trade route. Sandler provides a history of Sam Bellamy and his route to becoming the captain of the *Whydah,* trading up to stronger and faster ships as his crew took them over. This allows readers to understand just how vicious these men were, while being provided a history of the ship (one of the fastest pirate vessels) and all of its treasure. The ship was guided onto the Cape Cod reef and discovered by scientists hundreds of years later, rather than by the fortune hunters who searched for it in the immediate aftermath. **AENYA**

Keywords: Piracy • Pirates • *Whydah*

Walker, Sally.

Boundaries: How the Mason-Dixon Line Settled a Family Feud and Divided a Nation. 2014. 208p. **M** **J**

In this impeccably researched volume, Walker demonstrates that divides in religion and law existed between the Calverts and Penns over a century before the Mason-Dixon line was established. At the time Charles and George Calvert and William Penn were granted, respectively, royal charters to Maryland and Pennsylvania, the location of the 40th parallel had not been established. As the population grew and laws were determined by residency, determining borders became more important, especially as feuding became more prevalent. Walker's book explains in detail the work undertaken by Jeremiah Dixon and Charles Mason as they worked together to resolve the border dispute, with Dixon undertaking a ground survey and Mason, an astronomer, using celestial navigation to create an accurate boundary.

Keywords: Borders • Maryland • Mason-Dixon line • Pennsylvania

Historical Biography: Ordinary People in Extraordinary Times

This subgenre provides a place for books about people caught up in extraordinary times. Their names may be recognizable for their own works and lives, or they might have become known primarily because of their presence at a place or event. In either case, these books highlight a historical event, time period, or subject, rather than the life story of a particular person. This differentiates these books from those in the "Historical Biography" section in chapter 4.

Brimner, Larry Dane.

Blacklisted! Hollywood, The Cold War, and the First Amendment. 2018. 171p. **M J**

This is an exploration of post–World War II America, when U.S.-Soviet tensions were high and communist threats were so pervasive that the House of Representatives formed the House Un-American Activities Committee (HUAC) to investigate and eradicate them. What is not so easily understandable today is how and why Hollywood became the particular target of this committee. The story of the 19 men from the film industry chosen to testify in front of the committee and why they believed they should not have had to do so is a lesson in constitutional rights that will resonate with readers today.

Keywords: Cold War • First Amendment • House Un-American Activities Committee

Hale, Nathan.

🎖 *One Dead Spy*. <u>Nathan Hale's Hazardous Tales</u>. 2012. 128p. **M**

This volume is a witty launch to both this amusing graphic series and the author's historical namesake, the subject of its first entry. Introduced to the reader at the gallows, he is given a last-minute reprieve when swallowed and spit out by a history book and is allowed to give a full and funny recounting of his part in the Revolutionary War. This includes his interactions with and knowledge of important battles, actions, and people. **GGNT**

Keywords: Allen, Ethan • Graphic nonfiction • Hale, Nathan • Knox, Henry • Revolutionary War • Washington, George

Janeczko, Paul.

Secret Soldiers: How the U.S. Twenty-Third Special Troops Fooled the Nazis. 2019. 304p. **J** **H**

Fans of military history will find the third of Janeczko's examinations into wartime deception to be a detailed examination of a unique unit, its men, their work, and the influence it had on several key operations in World War II. In order to make the Nazis think they were facing forces that didn't exist, the men of the 23rd needed to come up with deceptions detailed enough to trick pilots flying overhead. They also needed to fool an enemy capable of seeing plausible facsimiles and close enough to notice a lack of noise, which would generally indicate large numbers of troops. Additionally, the Americans needed to blend in with the locals and move convincingly among several different units in different armies. How the set designers, actors, artists, camouflage experts, and other specialists learned how to use their expertise and parlay it into succeeding deceptions, influencing key operations from the Normandy Invasion to the crossing of the Rhine River, is a fascinating lesson in military and strategic operations.

Keywords: Camouflage • Ghost Army • Nazis • World War II

Kravitz, Danny.

The Untold Story of Henry Knox: The Man Who Saved Boston. 2015. 64p. **M**

While the Civil War actions of Henry Knox may not be untold, they are largely unknown. Henry Knox, who by the end of the war was second-in-command behind George Washington and served as Secretary of War from 1785 to 1794, earned his post through strategic acts that provided needed artillery to the Continental Army. This book provides a recounting of how, in June 1775, Knox came up with an idea to transport the weapons needed to overcome the British after the Battle of Bunker Hill. The only problem was that the cannons, mortars, and howitzers that could help defeat the Redcoats were a 700-mile round-trip away. This book provides a description of the journey taken, along with the weapons that allowed Knox to work with Washington to turn the tide of the war. In addition to illustrations and maps, supplementary and source materials include a timeline, glossary, further reading, source notes, and bibliography.

Keywords: Civil War • Fort Ticonderoga • Knox, Henry

Sheinkin, Steve.

🎗 *Port Chicago 50: Disaster, Mutiny, and the Fight for Civil Rights.* 2014. 208p. **J**

While the United States was embroiled in World War II, one of its busy navy bases, located in Port Chicago, California, maintained the navy's policy of segregation. The only possible job for black sailors was to load bombs. In 1944, a bomb destroyed most of the navy base, killing 320 men, including 202 black men who had been loading ammunition. This started a sea change, as 50 of the men refused to return to the same work. Their subsequent trial for mutiny shed light on the deeper issues around prejudice and segregation in the military. **ALA BG-HB**

Keywords: Civil rights • Mutiny • Port Chicago • U.S. Navy • World War II

Stone, Tanya Lee.

Courage Has No Color: The True Story of the Triple Nickles; America's First Black Paratroopers. 2013. 160p. **M** **J**

It is not hyperbole to say that discrimination ran rampant for the men serving in the military during World War II. In 1943 on the home front, while segregation was still being practiced among the enlisted men, the nine men who made up the 555th Parachute Infantry Battalion were determined to prove their abilities could not be measured by the color of their skin. Readers unfamiliar with the history of integration in the military will learn about the entrenched, unfortunate racism and stereotypes of the 1940s as they read the story of these brave and fascinating men.

Keywords: Military • Paratroopers • Triple Nickles • World War II

Winchell, Mike.

The Electric War: Edison, Tesla, Westinghouse, and the Race to Light the World. 2019. 272p. **M** **J**

It is hard to conceive of a time without power of any kind: no chargers, no outlets, no lights whatsoever. In the late 1800s, the men who could invent a way to light anything without an explosion were heralded as the geniuses they were. This is not only the story of how they fought to become first in that race, but also of how devious their tactics would become. While providing a clear and understandable explanation of the difference between alternating and direct currents, this book shows how Thomas Edison attempted to smear George Westinghouse by labeling his system, which used AC power, as the best possible choice for the electric chair. Winchell provides a tale of three men and their quest to light the world, undertaken in different ways and at vastly different personal costs.

Keywords: Edison, Thomas • Electricity • Tesla, Nikola • Westinghouse, George

Ideas of History

This section examines books in which the main subject is an idea important to history, but which cannot be defined as belonging to one specific point in history.

Blumenthal, Karen.

Tommy: The Gun That Changed America. 2015. 240p. **M** **J**

The Thompson submachine gun was created in order to save lives. Its developer, John Taliaferro Thompson, was an ordnance officer in the army whose primary goal was to provide the military with a weapon that would require fewer men up front in battle. Blumenthal provides readers with reasons for this, demonstrating proof of the success of the Gatling gun, and the devastation of World War I's trench warfare. The unfortunate truth—that Thompson's gun was mainly used by criminals—is fascinating, as the book provides a social history that is as illuminating as it is unfortunate. Readers are given a timeline of the National Rifle Association's involvement in legislation and the evolution of the Federal Bureau of Investigation, as Al Capone, Pretty Boy Floyd, and John Dillinger make use of the Tommy gun before it was finally adopted for use in World War II. A final chapter looking at the constitutional challenges that have kept guns in the hands of citizens is particularly relevant.

Keywords: Guns • Thomson submachine gun

Frankopan, Peter.

The Silk Roads: A New History of the World. 2018. 128p. **M** **J**

Peter Frankopan, Professor of Global History at Oxford University, examines history through the lens of the Silk Roads. This lushly illustrated volume includes maps that help to demonstrate the spread of ideas, religions, and commerce, which ensured the growth of nations and the exchange of faith and culture among peoples in the ancient world. Readers are shown the transmission of education and disease, as the Black Death spread along with the rise and fall of cultures in both the East and the West. The book also discusses the continuing migration around the world, from the Far East to Europe, and Europe to North America, as the centuries pass. Accompanying this discussion are explanations of the effects of world wars, civil rights, and other important world events on the human population. Originally published in 2014, the 2018 reissue of this title includes updated maps and an acknowledgement of the importance of the rising East.

Keywords: Silk Roads • World history

Khan, Khizr.

This Is Our Constitution: Discover America with a Gold Star Father. 2017. 224p. **M J**

Khizr Khan first gained national attention at the 2016 Democratic National Convention. As a lawyer and a Gold Star father, he gives a thoughtful and comprehensive introduction to America's most important legal document. An immigrant from Pakistan, a country where his rights were frequently limited, he brings to his analysis of each article and amendment of the Constitution an appreciation of the rights afforded to U.S. citizens. Also included is information about the government's structure, why the Constitution was needed, and the full text of both the Constitution and the Declaration of Independence. Landmark Supreme Court cases that hinged upon constitutional issues show just how relevant the Constitution, a living document, still is.

Keywords: Constitution • Government

Sarkeesian, Anita, and Ebony Adams.

History vs. Women: The Defiant Lives That They Don't Want You to Know. 2018. 144p. **M J**

Sarkeesian's volume was written to raise awareness of the little known, seldom mentioned, contributions made by women to history. They are divided into five sections, according to the area of influence for which the woman in question is known: rebels, scholars, villains, artists, and activists. Rebels, whether in the third or 20th century, fought for subjugated peoples against their own governments and existing cultural beliefs. While there is no doubt that there have always been brilliant women, there has also always been a patriarchy willing to doubt them, take credit for their work, or assume they must have had help. Examples of these brilliant women help to dispel such myths, along with the notion that women are the sweeter sex. Reading about a murderer, or a head of state who was every bit as capable as any man in the same position, is not only fun but demonstrates that a woman has just as many sides to her personality as any man. Offered in this volume are some fabulous firsts, including the woman credited with writing the world's first novel. The final section is made up of athletes, as women have historically been kept out of sports because of their physical limitations. The women who showed that they were stronger, faster, or more capable than men were derided as being unfeminine and therefore unattractive to men. This book raises awareness of the historical bias against women's participation and abilities. It also provides a short and fascinating introduction to several parts of history from different ages, races, and cultures in its 25 biographical sketches.

Keywords: Biographies • Women

Smith, Monique Gray.

Speaking Our Truth: A Journey of Reconciliation. 2017. 159p. **M** **J** **H**

Monique Gray Smith introduces the Seven Sacred Teachings and talks about what reconciliation means and why it is important alongside the painful history and legacy of residential schools. The book covers the lasting traumas exacted on the children in the schools, their separation from siblings and parents, and their being forbidden to speak their own language. Sidebars ask readers to reflect on what effect this would have on them, and a section is included with suggestions for specific actions they might take.

Keywords: Reconciliation • Residential Schools

New Perspectives

Over time, there is always the potential to discover new information that makes it necessary to revisit interpretations of the past. This can happen for any number of reasons, from cultural mores and changes in law, to technological and scientific advances, to the discovery of new evidence. For example, it may not occur to students that the founding fathers were also slaveholders, as pointed out by Kenneth Davis.

Davis, Kenneth C.

In the Shadow of Liberty: The Hidden History of Slavery, Four Presidents, and Five Black Lives. 2016. 285p. **M** **J**

Kenneth Davis introduces readers to five people, known to history only because they lived at a time in the United States when records were kept about enslaved people. These particular slaves were also owned by some of the greatest presidents of the United States, demonstrating the dichotomy of their ownership and actions. **ALA**

Keywords: Slavery • Slaves

Fleming, Candace.

Presenting Buffalo Bill: The Man Who Invented the Wild West. 2016. 288p. **M** **J**

Candace Fleming's entertaining presentation of the Wild West's greatest showman covers "Buffalo" Bill Cody's long and varied career—as well as his childhood, which he later plumbed for some of his most amazing stories. Fleming examines Cody's tendency to exaggerate, if not outright invent, his exploits in sidebars entitled "Panning for the Truth." The myths and legends of the Wild West and one of its most renowned figures make for an entertaining volume that is useful in demonstrating the value of quality sources and research, and particularly relevant in a time when the value of journalism is being questioned. **ALA**

Keywords: Cody, Buffalo Bill

Now Try: Andrea Warren gives considerable thought to the difficulties of Bill Cody's youth in her biography, *The Boy Who Became Buffalo Bill: Growing Up Billy Cody in Bleeding Kansas*. Warren explains the political situation that forced his father into hiding and terrorized his family, as well as the cumulative effect of the deaths in his family—all of which put pressure upon him to support his mother and sisters. This volume provides a different viewpoint from which to look at the young man who went to work for the Pony Express. Warren's biography includes notes on people and places associated with Cody, and links for readers to find further information.

Loewen, James W. Adapted by Rebecca Stefoff.

Lies My Teacher Told Me, Young Reader's Edition: Everything American History Textbooks Get Wrong. 2019. 256p. **J** **H**

Sociologist James Loewen first wrote his groundbreaking book after reviewing textbooks for their rosy views of important historical events and personages. The students he was teaching were often being presented with a picture that told only parts of the stories. Loewen felt that the textbooks generally portrayed their subjects in the most favorable light, with America shown as successful, operating solely with admirable intent, and viewed favorably on the world stage at all times. Stenoff's updated edition is a readable version for younger students, allowing them access to the more complete stories of famous figures and providing them with a rich discussion on the early peoples and populations of America. The portrayal of the arrival of various peoples to the Americas and how they were treated has changed significantly in recent years and may itself offer opportunities for classroom discussions. Loewen notes that recent textbooks are including more information on the recent past but have reverted to omitting controversial subjects. This volume is a good choice to fill that gap and help provide students with additional information that can show them there is more to know, leaving them with a sidebar that encourages them to question everything.

Keywords: Civil rights • Exploration • Government • History • Human Rights • Racism • U.S. History

Noxon, Christopher.

Good Trouble: Lessons from the Civil Rights Playbook. 2019. 192p. **H**

The "Good Trouble" of Noxon's title comes from a speech made by John Lewis, referring to the positive benefits of acting against injustices and the necessity for the troublemakers who do it. This is a unique and involving history of civil rights in America because it focuses not on what happened at events from boycotts to sit-ins, but because Noxon provides the takeaways of people who were there, as they speak about why they became involved and what it meant. The narrative, accompanied by drawings and presented in a format that mimics handwriting, speaks directly to readers. Readers will learn why people were present at the events and what happened to them afterward, and discover parallels between historical and current events. This book examines hard-earned truths and calls to action to affect change for the better.

Keywords: Activism • Civil rights

The Real Revolutionaries.

Each of the volumes in this series begins with a succinct recounting of the major accomplishments of the subject. This is followed by a chapter that corrects the myths and outright errors that have become accepted truths. In a time when it is increasingly important to learn how to question information presented with bias and without evidence, these topics offer valuable opportunities for discussion. The reader is provided with a fuller view of each revolutionary, as the author delves into his lesser-known achievements and examines darker truths, and looks at the subject's legacy. These interesting, easy-to-read titles are complemented by a number of supplementary materials, including illustrations, reproductions of historical documents, a timeline, internet sites, and suggestions for further reading. Students and readers interested in the subject area will find them a valuable and viable option.

Braun, Eric. *The Real Aaron Burr: The Truth behind the Legend.* 2019. 64p. **M**

Gunderson, Jessica. *The Real Benedict Arnold: The Truth behind the Legend.* 2019. 64p. **M**

Lassieur, Allison. *The Real John Adams: The Truth behind the Legend.* 2019. 64p. **M**

Smith-Llera, Danielle. *The Real James Madison: The Truth behind the Legend.* 2019. 64p. **M**

Sandler, Martin W.

1919: The Year That Changed America. 2019. 192p. **J** **H**

Sandler, an award-winning author, looks at what he explains is a pivotal year in American history. He presents readers with the events that made it so important and includes a timeline that demonstrates further developments and incidents in the area under discussion. This was a watershed year, with immigrants entering the country in droves along with soldiers returning from the European theater of war. Chapter discussions include the Red Summer, incited by the anger of hundreds of thousands of African American men who fought in World War I, along with the equal numbers who worked at home to support their efforts, only to be denied their civil rights after the war. Sandler segues into other parts of American life, including women's rights, the labor movement, and prohibition; these topics are not only fascinating but foreshadow societal issues of today. This

1

overview provides readers with a better understanding of how these events began, placing a summary of communism in the Soviet Union within an introduction to the Bolshevik revolution. The text is supplemented with pictures, colorful captions that draw the eye, and back matter that includes further reading and Web sites.

2

Keywords: Civil rights • Communism • Labor movement • Prohibition • Women's rights

Walker, Sally M.

3

Sinking the Sultana: A Civil War Story of Imprisonment, Greed, and a Doomed Journey Home. 2017. 208p. **M J**

4

5

Sally Walker's gripping narrative builds slowly, introducing the reader to a number of union soldiers who are to become prisoners of war, subjected to the inhumane treatment at Andersonville prison. This is balanced against an explanation of the importance of steamboats to the war effort and a description of how they were slowly built into bigger vessels, with more engines, boilers, and decks, until the *Sultana* was built, with its two engines, four boilers, and a legal capacity of 376 passengers and crew. The incorrect and speedy parole of all of the prisoners from Camp Fisk allowed 2,400 people to be on board when the boilers exploded on April 27, 1865. This was followed by the grisly task of identifying the dead. Walker describes the survivors' tribulations and frustrations as they found out that men who survived were listed as dead, and some of those who died were listed as alive in army records. At the time, people were determined that someone needed to be blamed, and the author discusses those possibilities, even though at the time the reason for the explosion was not understood. The story of the *Sultana*, the worst maritime disaster in U.S. history, remains timely as a reminder that important stories may be overshadowed by other events, as this news was eclipsed in its day by the assassination of John Wilkes Booth the day before.

6

7

Keywords: Civil War • Prisoners of war • *Sultana*

8

Now Try: Readers interested in taking a new look at events from the past will be fascinated by Pete Nelson's *Left for Dead: A Young Man's Search for Justice for the USS Indianapolis*. Eleven-year-old Hunter Scott first took an interest in the *Indianapolis* watching the movie *Jaws*, where Robert Shaw's grizzled Quint describes the horror of being in the water as the sharks picked off the men, one by one, after the ship was torpedoed by the Japanese in the final days of World War II. A history fair project on the ship's sinking led to Hunter working with the ship's survivors, who had been working for over 50 years to clear the name of Captain McVay, wrongly court-martialed by the Navy for the ship's sinking.

9

10

11

Consider Starting with . . .

Bausum, Ann. *VIRAL: The Fight Against AIDS in America.*

Brown, Don. *The Unwanted: Stories of the Syrian Refugees.*

Partridge, Elizabeth. *Boots on the Ground: America's War in Vietnam.*

Smith, Monique Gray. *Speaking Our Truth: A Journey of Reconciliation.*

Fiction Read-Alikes

- **Cart, Michael, ed. *Taking Aim: Power and Pain, Teens and Guns.*** While the stories contributed by Young Adult writers that make up Cart's collection look at guns from different points of view, take place during different time periods, and include different formats, the visceral impact that firearms can have, intentionally or not, is made clear. Guns are presented as something to be used with common sense. Teens accustomed to guns take them hunting, while teenage protagonists unused to guns find occasions to use them, either on a whim or because they think it will make a change in their own life. All too frequently, and unfortunately, they are correct in the latter scenario. In this, the stories mirror real life, as do the stories which recognize the all-too-realistic possibility of school shootings. Above all, the stories illustrate the lasting consequences of firing a gun, no matter the time period or reason.

- **Gratz, Alan. *Grenade.*** Hideki Kaneshiro is afraid of the approaching Americans in 1945 when battleships approach Okinawa. The Japanese give him, along with the other members of the student brigade at his middle school, the Blood and Iron Student Corps, two grenades, and tell them that they are to throw one to kill as many American soldiers as possible and to use the other to kill themselves. On an approaching battleship is a U.S. Marine a few years older named Ray Majors, who doesn't know much about Okinawans except that his fellow soldiers believe that they are as dangerous as the Japanese. He soon sees that their belief will lead them to kill any Okinawans trying to surrender, and that, given that the Japanese are using Okinawans as human shields, there is no way to separate out civilians on a battlefield. Both boys soon see the other side as monsters, and their meeting will change everything.

- **Hesse, Monica. *The War Outside.*** Margot and Toshiko meet in 1944 in Crystal City, an internment camp for families suspected of collusion. Toshiko's Japanese family and Margot's German family aren't groups that would socialize in the camp. Even so, the girls become friends and begin to share their feelings about being taken from the only homes they have ever known. When tensions grow in the camp, and Margot's father begins to rail against their confinement, the girls' relationship may reach a breaking point in this fictionalized tale inspired by the real camp of the same name.

- **Jane, Sarah.** *Maiden Voyage: A Titanic Story.* Three girls board the *Titanic* with wildly different expectations. Isabella doesn't want to be there and has no idea why her parents are sending her alone, carrying a letter that she is to open the night before the ship docks. Lucy is delighted to be traveling with her parents in such glamorous surroundings, and Abby, Lucy's maid, just hopes to keep her secret from her employers. As the ship travels across the sea the girls find out that things may not be as they seem. Their lives will never be the same, and not just because of the ship's inevitable fate.

- **Lawson, Julie.** *A Blinding Light.* While it isn't surprising that anti-German sentiment is rampant in Halifax during World War I, 15-year-old Will Schroeder and his 12-year-old sister are more preoccupied by mourning the loss of their father, who has died in a boating accident six months before, to pay any attention to gossip that he might have been a spy. Things change when Will, as a reporter for the school's newspaper, is on Citadel Hill the morning of December 6, 1917, and sees the collision of two boats cause the explosion that sets Halifax alight. The siblings are separated, starting more than one odyssey, as they try to discover whether blame for the event will be based on fact or prevailing assumptions.

- **Morrill, Stephanie.** *Within These Lines.* Even before the Japanese bombed Pearl Harbor, San Francisco teenagers Taichi Hamasaki and Evalina Cassano were hesitant to make their relationship public, given that interracial marriage was illegal in California. The internment of Taichi's family in Manzanar Relocation Center leads the two of them to deal with their feelings against a growing tide of anti-Japanese sentiment. Told from alternating viewpoints, Evalina's frustration against the unjust treatment of Japanese Americans continues to grow, while Taichi deals with both shame and anger, wondering how best to protect both Evalina and himself, as their future seems more fraught with difficulty.

- **Savit, Gavriel.** *Anna and the Swallow Man.* Anna Lania was only seven when the Germans took her father in the purge of intellectuals from Poland. The Swallow Man is not her father, but like her father he is very intellectual in that he can speak four languages—most unusually bird. Their travel through the war is seen from Anna's point of view. It is a difficult journey in a world gone mad, and there is no easy path.

- **Sepetys, Ruta.** *Salt to the Sea.* Freedom is the hope of thousands fleeing the Russians in East Prussia as Russian forces overtake the Germans in 1945. Among them are four people from different countries who end up working together, hoping to reach the *Wilhelm Gustlof,* a cruise ship they believe will be their salvation, but which may turn into just one more nightmare.

- **Wein, Elizabeth.** *Rose Under Fire.* American pilot Rose Justice loves to fly. She joins the Air Transport Auxiliary in World War II to help the Allied cause, and then finds herself captured by the Nazis and sent to the Ravensbrück concentration camp. Among the atrocities and horrors of war are moments of hope, friendship and strength in this companion novel to Wein's Printz Award honor title *Code Name Verity.*

Chapter 6

Science, Math, and the Environment

Definition

Science is generally defined as the systematic study of the nature and behavior of the material and physical universe, based on observation, experiment, and measurement, and the formulation of laws to describe these facts in general terms. Modern usage separates mathematics from the natural sciences, while maintaining and encompassing several larger subdivisions including physical sciences, earth sciences, medicine, engineering, biology, computer sciences, and social sciences. Science nonfiction, as such, is a widely inclusive genre that focuses on literature with scientific themes.

Appeal

Books in the sciences provide answers for people with an innate curiosity as well as those seeking answers. Readers wondering about how we got here may wish to start with either the adaptations of Darwin's *On the Origin of Species* or Neil deGrasse Tyson's *Astrophysics for Young People in a Hurry*, both of which introduce important concepts and discoveries that revolutionized science at the time of their publication and remain seminal works. Environmental works help inform us about changes in our planet and prepare us for the future, while books about research being done to further scientific knowledge are both interesting and inspiring.

Chapter Organization

The chapter starts off with a section on "General Sciences" before moving to titles that take a more rigorous look at scientists, discoveries, and research in "Adventures in Science." These two are followed by a section called "How Things Work," which looks at two areas, "General" and "Transportation," to further readers' knowledge about particular areas in science and math. "Micro-science" provides authors an opportunity to examine a subject in greater detail. Books in the "Environmental Writing" section examine the environment in terms of the earth, its inhabitants, and climate, and titles in the "Animals" subgenre deal with particular species.

General Sciences

The books in this section provide readers with explanations and introductions to topics in science, math, and physics. Rather than consisting of academic textbooks, this section includes both narrative nonfiction and highly illustrated titles with sidebars that have been condensed and formatted to be visually appealing and easily understood. Authors are experts in their field and able to make their subject matter not only comprehensible but enticing, appealing to readers who may not otherwise seek out titles in this area, and keeping the titles relevant for library collections for a longer time.

Darwin, Charles. Adapted by Rebecca Stefoff.

Charles Darwin's On the Origin of Species, Young Readers Edition. 2018. 176p. **M J**

The original edition of Charles Darwin's book, which first shared the scientist's groundbreaking theory, was published in 1859. Over a century and a half later it was chosen by the British public as the single most influential title ever published. The key elements of Darwin's book have been kept in this edition, with adaptations to make it accessible to a modern and younger audience. Stefoff notes that the original text is longer, containing many more examples. Where further developments in the study of evolution since the original publications have rendered Darwin's original hypotheses inaccurate, they have been removed. Language has been simplified for ease of understanding, and chapter titles, headings, notes, supplementary information in text boxes, and a glossary have been added for the same reason. This is particularly relevant in the chapter on heredity, as genetics was not a known science at the time of the original publication. This beautifully illustrated book will provide a fascinating introduction to readers interested in biology and the diversity of life on the planet.

Keywords: Adaptation • Natural selection • Species

deGrasse Tyson, Neil, with Gregory Mone.

Astrophysics for Young People in A Hurry. 2019. 128p. **M J**

While the basic fact that the universe originated with a big bang may be generally understood, an explanation that can help the reader understand what happened after that has been lacking. Here, readers will not only learn about matter, elements, space, and the cosmos, but also about many important discoveries in the field and the scientists who made them. This is not only a straightforward guide that would be appropriate as an introduction for readers new to the subject, it is also a book that could be used as a refresher for any older reader interested in the subject but not looking for the in-depth information of deGrasse Tyson's original book.

Keywords: Astrophysics • Elements • Galaxies • Particles • Universe

Gottlieb, Iris.

Seeing Science: An Illustrated Guide to the Wonders of the Universe. 2018. 152p. **H** **A/YA**

Readers are introduced to the complex and varied scientific wonders of the universe, presented in a way that is not only fascinating but also accessible and frequently funny. This volume offers a reading experience that combines enjoyment and learning. With the stated goal of making science less intimidating, Gottlieb offers a definition for what it means to be alive, and then divides her book into eight divisions of life science: anatomy, biology, botany, ecology, genetics, microbiology, neurology, and zoology. Rather than providing any textbook definitions, the categories are explained through examples accompanied by illustrations and pithy textual explanations, such as the comparison of glaciers to Snickers bars and the integration of examples from popular culture. Unusual and inventive on its own, these additions add a fun and inviting touch.

Keywords: Life sciences • Sciences

Green, Dan.

InstaGraphics: A Visual Guide to Your Universe. 2019. 128p. **M**

Green wanders the universe in this fun and attractive volume, presenting bite-sized pieces of facts artfully arranged over colorful, double-page spreads. This book is meant to impart information to readers who are captured more by visuals than text. It will be helpful to any student who prefers to have examples to help process scientific concepts, as with a section showing the fastest vehicles along with an explanation of the difference between speed and acceleration, and the use of the strongest animal bites to explain pounds of force.

Keywords: Life sciences • Sciences

Adventures in Science

The books in this section focus on the exciting and important stories of the people, discoveries, research, and technological achievements that further scientific knowledge, frequently impacting the world and its denizens. They are descriptive and frequently fast-paced, and in them readers will find knowledge about efforts undertaken by scientists around the world to gain knowledge to ensure the survival of the planet. Several examples of this are found in the <u>Scientists in the Field</u> series, which provides readers with a close-up look at a scientist's work on behalf of a specific species or ecosystem while giving them a greater understanding of the scientific method and what a scientist's job actually entails. More titles in the series, with a greater focus on the animals rather than the scientists, may be found in the "Animals" subgenre. Advances in photography, astronomy, and NASA's spacecraft mean that students interested in space will benefit from the wonderful photographs in books about Pluto. Given the time it will take for further information to be obtained about the Kuiper Belt, to give another example, these books will remain both current and appealing for quite some time.

Carson, Mary Kay.

Mission to Pluto: The First Visit to an Ice Dwarf and the Kuiper Belt. <u>Scientists in the Field</u>. 2017. 80p. **M J**

> Pluto was first discovered in 1930 by Clyde Tombaugh, who believed it to be a planet. At the time it was thought to be the ninth planet. Not until 1996 were scientists able to see with the Hubble Space Telescope what has since been identified as an ice dwarf. It was NASA that developed a spacecraft, *New Horizons*, to travel to and explore Pluto, on a journey of 3 billion miles over nine and a half years. This book introduces information about *New Horizons*, the team that developed it, its mission, and Pluto. For the first time, scientists were able to see Pluto's five moons and surface. This is a fascinating journey into the next frontier, and the story of the planning and research from the *New Horizons* journey to Pluto will leave readers eager to hear about the future information obtained from its next venture to the Kuiper Belt.
>
> **Keywords:** Kuiper Belt • Pluto • Space

Carson, Mary Kay.

Park Scientists: Gila Monsters, Geysers, and Grizzly Bears in America's Own Backyard. <u>Scientists in the Field</u>. 2014. 80p. **M**

> The 58 spaces that are America's national parks are some of the most unique and beautiful spaces in the world. Scientists and ecologists are assigned to study each of these ecosystems in order to better understand their unique features and protect the wildlife that lives within them. Here readers are taken to three parks, each with a singularly unique feature under study. The first to be visited is Yellowstone National Park, home not only to scientists studying a growing grizzly population, but also to geologists monitoring the unique thermal features of a location over a volcano, most notably geysers such as Old Faithful. Next, scientists in Arizona's Saguaro Park are shown using a variety of measures to keep an eye on the nocturnal denizens of their park; they track Gila monsters with radio transmitters, microchips, and citizen volunteer sightings. Citizens also help with another monitoring project: counting the fields of saguaro cacti to see

how numbers are keeping up. Lastly, a visit to Great Smoky Mountains National Park introduces the red-cheeked salamander, an amphibian unique to this part of the world, as well as some fireflies that demonstrate why they do so well in the Smokies. All of these animals and the scientists that work with them serve as examples of how and why spaces deserve to be protected.

Keywords: Animals • Conservation • Gila monsters • Grizzly Bears • Red-cheeked salamander • Saguaro cactus

Rusch, Elizabeth.

IMPACT! Asteroids and the Science of Saving the World. <u>Scientists in the Field</u>. 2017. 80p. **M** **J**

That a chunk of rock the size of a six-story building could fall from the sky and crush your classroom is unlikely, but not out of the realm of possibility. Just such an asteroid fell in Russia in 2013, injuring a large number of people from the shock wave alone. This fascinating if scary volume of the <u>Scientists in the Field</u> series looks at the everyday phenomenon of the fragments of asteroids floating in space, most of which burn up in our atmosphere before reaching Earth. Some of them pass through and very occasionally have had catastrophic effects, such as wiping out the dinosaurs. After an explanation of what asteroids are, the frequency with which they hit the earth, and the hunters who search for them, the author introduces scientists who are looking for ways to both predict and prevent possible asteroid impacts, including various ways of destroying them. This is an entertaining look at a scientific reality.

Keywords: Asteroids • Meteorite • Meteors

How Things Work

Books in this section provide readers with information that can help them add to their own knowledge of science, math, and physics. They also inform readers about the technology, innovation, and hard work required to advance scientific knowledge. They serve as a reminder that attaining that knowledge and deriving any benefit from it is time-consuming and part of a lengthy, rigorous process. This category is divided into two subsections, "General" and "Transportation."

General

These books provide readers with information about topics in science, math, and physics. They largely focus on the use of technology and math and use a narrower scope than the books in the "General Sciences" section to look at research, inventions, and how the scientific method is being put to use.

Andrysek, Jan, and Alex Mihailidis.

New Hands, New Life: Robots, Prostheses and Innovation. 2017. 64p. **M**

While today's students are used to being surrounded by machines, this book introduces the concept of looking at the human body as one, in order to introduce the concept of assistive technology to help support parts that aren't functioning correctly. This volume provides introductions to a number of topics, including why help would be needed in moving, and how robotics have been developed to fill this need. Information on how the field continues to advance, from 3-D printers that help make larger prostheses for growing children to the potential for mind-controlled body parts, ensure that there will be a revised edition down the road.

Keywords: Prostheses • Robotics

Drozd, Anne, and Jerzy Drozd.

Rockets: Defying Gravity. <u>Science Comics</u>. 2018. 128p. **M**

The introductory narrators of this volume in the <u>Science Comics</u> series, a couple of pigeons presented comically as having been related to the first rocket, begin by providing a thorough introduction to Newton's laws of motion before demonstrating how they all apply to a rocket launch. After this a succession of animals take over the narration to present a history of rockets and how they were used for entertainment and warfare before being sent into space. Important scientists and how their work was incorporated into rocketry are mentioned; the book includes innovators in design and delivery like Konstantin Tsiolkovsky, the founder of cosmonautics, and Mary Sherman Morgan, who discovered the propellant Hydyne. The future of rockets is considered through a look at current rocket capabilities and potential missions. A final timeline of the events discussed in the book is a useful tool for any reader looking for information for a report, as is the glossary and list of further reading.

Keywords: Laws of Motion • Rockets

McPherson, Stephanie Sammartino.

Artificial Intelligence: Building Smarter Machines. 2017. 104p. **J** **H**

Machines invested with intelligence suggest limitless possibilities in fields from medicine to the military, with computers, drones, and robots imbued with intellect and capabilities that could far surpass those of their human creators—but is this a realistic view of the future? McPherson looks at pioneers in the development of these fields to provide an overview of how, over time, computers have become sophisticated enough to handle complicated tasks that would previously have required humans. Examples include Charles Babbage's difference engine and the Roomba.

Keywords: Artificial intelligence • Computers • Drones • Robots

Redding, Anna Crowley.

Google It! A History of Google. 2018. 240p. **J** **H**

One of the world's most innovative companies began not with a bang but with two bickering graduate students at Stanford University. Google started in 1995 with Larry Page's idea to organize the information on the Internet for his PhD project. At the time, when the Internet had 10 million pages, the task of compiling the information seemed insurmountable. The explanations of how Larry and his partner, Sergey Brin, were able to reliably and consistently create their search methodology is told in a thorough, understandable, and humorous way. The technological aspects of their achievements and the ever-expanding use of their site are paralleled by the development and expansion of their business. It is fascinating to read about how the business was able to expand in order to keep up with demand while maintaining the company's positive culture and the entrepreneurial spirit that allowed for the development of Gmail, Google News, Google Maps, and Google Earth. The success of the company allowed Page and Brin to move from needing investors to being able to purchase other companies, including YouTube. The book also describes the company's support of computer science research, allowing for future developments in medicine, space exploration, and artificial intelligence.

Keywords: Computer science • Computers • Google

Scott, Mairghread.

Robots and Drones: Past, Present, and Future. <u>Science Comics</u>. 2018. 128p. **M**

As with the other volumes in the amusing and informative <u>Science Comics</u> series, a narrator accompanies readers through a history of the subject before providing information about it that would be suitable for anyone doing a research project. The guide introducing robots is Pouli, the "first machine capable of autonomous flight," built in 350 BCE. Pouli clearly explains how robots differ from machines before presenting a timeline of robots through history, demonstrating how they have adapted and developed as technology has improved. The book then discusses how robots differ from drones, their uses, and the kinds of work for which they are suited. The final part of the book looks at what goes into building robots and what their future may hold. A supplement includes 25 robots that represent steps forward in technology and a closer look at drones.

Keywords: Drones • Graphic nonfiction • Machines • Robots

1
2
3
4
5
6
7
8
9
10
11

Shibuya, Michio, Takashi Tonagi, and Office Sawa.

The Manga Guide to Microprocessors. 2017. 264p. **H**

Meet Ayumi, a champion at *shogi* (Japanese chess), who has an unbeatable record until she is challenged by a stranger, Yuu, to play a match against his computer, the Shooting Star. When she loses, she wants to learn all about the thing that has managed to beat her, and Yuu teaches her all about the history and inner workings of the computer. Using a format that combines comics and text, information about CPUs and microprocessors is explained by an expert. This book includes information about how computers work, process mathematical operations, and use integrated circuits; it also covers various languages including assembly language.

Keywords: Computers • Microprocessors

Transportation

A child's interest in toy cars evolves into a teenager's deeper fascination with modes of travel as they get closer to the age at which they will be taking control of their own vehicle. These titles explain the different types of transportation, how they work, and why they keep us enthralled. Is there a reason for anyone other than James Bond to have an amphibious vehicle? What are a car's different systems, and should one really be touching them before calling roadside assistance? How does a plane actually achieve lift? Books in this category can provide a basic history and answer enough basic information to help prepare readers to own, operate, and maintain their own cars or bicycles.

Tech on Wheels

While it isn't difficult to believe that there are a wide variety of sporting, amphibious, electric, high-tech, and utility vehicles in use by individuals and the military, it is surprising that their history goes back almost 100 years. The volumes in the Tech on Wheels series each provide a look at the history, design, and purpose of a specific type of vehicle. Numerous photographs help illustrate the vehicles' features, while sidebars introduce some of the novel concepts and technologies that make the machines unique, from the development and introduction of software and artificial intelligence to environmentally friendly technologies and alternative power sources. The books also look at some of the next steps in development for future vehicles, while acknowledging hurdles that still need to be overcome. Readers will also find a glossary and resources for more information.

Chandler, Matt. *The Tech behind Amphibious Vehicles.* 2019. 32p. **M J**

Keywords: Amphibious motor vehicles

Chandler, Matt. *The Tech behind Concept Cars.* 2019. 32p. **M J**

Keywords: Cars • Experimental automobiles • Technological innovations

Chandler, Matt. *The Tech behind Electric Cars.* 2019. 32p. **M J**

Keywords: Cars • Electric cars • Technological innovations

Chandler, Matt. *The Tech Behind Off-Road Vehicles.* 2019. 32p. **M J**

Keywords: All-terrain vehicles • Technology

Chandler, Matt. *The Tech Behind Self-Driving Cars.* 2019. 32p. **M J**

Keywords: Artificial intelligence • Autonomous vehicles • Technology

Goldsworthy, Steve. *The Tech Behind Race Cars.* 2019. 32p. **M J**

Keywords: Cars • Sporting vehicles • Technology

Schweizer, Chris.

Maker Comics: Fix a Car! <u>Maker Comics.</u> 2019. 128p. **M J**

The frame story in this volume of the <u>Maker Comics</u> series has four teenagers, two old enough to drive and two not yet driving, brought together at Car Club by their interest in learning about how to take care of their cars. The teens are given a thorough introduction to preventive maintenance as their teacher walks them through her car's systems, showing them how to check a car's various fluids. Further meetings of the club discuss changing a tire and detailing the car to ensure the inside looks like new, adding both practical and lifelong skills. While not every reader would need to know how to undertake some of the repairs explained in the book, having the information will help to ensure vehicles are maintained and repaired correctly and entice interested readers. Systems and major parts not included in the club's lessons are summarized at the end of the book.

Keywords: Car repair • Motor vehicles

Walker, Dave.

The Cycling Cartoonist: An Illustrated Guide to Life on Two Wheels. 2017. 144p. **H A/YA**

Cyclists of all ability levels will appreciate this unique take on bikes and biking. Dave Walker, an experienced if indifferent bicyclist, illuminates not only the sport itself, but many of the quirks and challenges that go along with it. These range from intellectual problems—such as what to do when dealing with a race or trying to deal with commuting to work—or the more practical, like keeping the parts of the bike in working condition. The book is delivered in a humorous style that will amuse riders and nonriders alike.

Keywords: Bicycles • Graphic nonfiction • Recreation • Sports

Now Try: An earlier introduction to the bicycle's history is Sue Macy's award-winning *Wheels of Change: How Women Rode the Bicycle to Freedom (With a Few Flat Tires Along the Way)*. Macy's book shows how the bicycle was a means for gaining greater freedom for women, particularly as fashion adapted to make it easier for them to ride—much to the chagrin of men around them. Period photographs showing that cycling has been a liberating exercise for well over a century are quite enjoyable.

Wilgus, Alison.

Flying Machines: How the Wright Brothers Soared. <u>Science Comics</u>. 2017. 128p. **M**

The story of the Wright brothers and how they sought to develop a machine that would actually fly is told in this volume of the <u>Science Comics</u> series by their sister, Katherine, as she explains their story to a classroom. Included in the discussion are a timeline of the development of the airplane and the mechanisms of flight. Katherine, a college graduate that managed her brothers' household and answered questions from aviators, is a figure that both fits into the story and can be set apart from it, appearing in grayscale in both the historical information and scientific explanations. This entry will provide information for readers interested in the aviators, their creations, and how they harnessed and overcame the elements.

Keywords: Airplanes • Aviation • Aviators • Wright, Orville • Wright, Wilbur

Micro-science

The term "micro-science[1]," was first developed for use by Sarah Statz Cords (2006). This topic remains an appropriate and popular subgenre that complements the "Micro-history" category and allows authors to narrow their focus to a single object or subject, starting when and where they like and adding as much detail as they choose. The study of their chosen subject, whether the climate or the weather, may then draw attention to its context and consequences.

Eamer, Claire.

Out of the Ice: How Climate Change is Revealing the Past. 2018. 32p. **M**

Claire Eamer explains how the melting of the earth's cryosphere has caused a whole new field in research known as glacial archaeology. As permafrost, glaciers, and mountaintop patches have slowly been decreasing around the world, they have been revealing artifacts and remains both natural and grisly that provide information about the earth and the people that existed eons before us. The importance of this work is in both the speed at which it requires the scientists to work, as any remains disintegrate quickly upon exposure, and in the new information it can provide about our history. Also included are sources for further information and a timeline noting that Antarctica's oldest ice dates to 2,700,000 BCE, over two million years before the emergence of *Homo sapiens*.

Keywords: Climate change • Glacial archaeology

Mihaly, Christy, and Sue Heavenrich.

Diet for a Changing Climate: Food for Thought. 2019. 128p. **J**

In this novel take on climate change and its impact on sustainability, the authors take a look at the food habits and diets of a number of alternative food movements, such as locavores, invasivorism, and entomophagy. The discussions of these movements are accompanied by a number of photographs that can help, for example, to identify a snake that is not edible and the parts of a dandelion that are. Whether or not readers are convinced that foraging is better for the environment, or that some of the suggested ingredients have just as high a nutritional value as ones with which they are familiar, they may remain dubious about the recipes, which include nettles and crickets. More adventurous gastronomes will find a list of bug-serving restaurants, including several in North America, and a conversion table for the recipes.

Keywords: Cooking • Entomophagy • Invasivores • Locavores

Mosco, Rosemary.

Solar System: Our Place in Space. <u>Science Comics</u>. 2018. 128p. **M**

In this volume's frame story, a girl entertains a very bored friend stuck at home with a cold with information from the book she has been reading about the solar system. What follows is a trip through the planets in the ship the girls have invented, narrated by a crew that presents information about each planet in a humorous and inventive way. As the ship passes each planet readers are presented with a concise and useful "report" summarizing key information about it. Neither the origin of the universe nor its expansiveness is overlooked, and a glossary is included, making this a fun and informal trip through the eight planets composing our solar system in the Milky Way.

Keywords: Graphic nonfiction • Planets • Solar system • Universe

Roach, Mary.

Gulp: Adventures on the Alimentary Canal. 2013. 96p. **H** **A/YA**

Mary Roach takes a detailed look at what humans will and won't eat, and what happens to food as it passes through the body's systems. In taking a look at the various parts of the body that are involved in eating and digesting nutrients, Roach takes readers on a remarkable journey, looking at cultural influences that guide what we eat and what can affect taste, and providing segues into various theories on how best to eat, digest, and effectively pass food. Squeamish readers may wish to avoid the stories of constipation and megacolons, culminating with the medical history of Elvis Presley, who died at the age of 42 in his bathroom. A look at bacteria, generally believed to be universally harmful, will leave readers with a better understanding of its function in the body; the book also discusses bacteria as a promising potential treatment for ailments caused by the products of bodily functions.

Keywords: Alimentary canal • Digestion • Physiology

Roach, Mary.

 Stiff: The Curious Lives of Human Cadavers. **2003. 320p.** **H** **A/YA**

Mary Roach's award-winning first book is a fascinating look at what happens to people's bodies after they die. Some of the possible uses for human cadavers throughout history may leave readers feeling nauseous while still admiring the scientific research that went into both this book and the use of the cadavers themselves. The book moves beyond gore by including stories that are funny, amazing, and surprising. This title will appeal to high school readers who enjoy narrative nonfiction and science. While death is universal and inexorable, the beliefs and practices surrounding it around the world vary widely, both now and throughout history. **Alex**

Keywords: Death • Human anatomy • Physiology

Now Try: In *After Life: Ways We Think about Death*, Merrie-Ellen Wilcox looks at what happens to the body after one's death, the ways in which humans have dealt with the loss of a loved one, and the many diverse traditions and religious understandings that go along with that passing. The author does not overlook potentially difficult topics like hospice care, suicide, and dealing with grief, in a title short-listed for the Norma Fleck book award. This is a title suitable for readers either looking for more information about the process of death or dealing with it in their own lives. Mortician Caitlin Doughty's *Will the Cat Eat My Eyeballs? Big Questions from Tiny Mortals About Death* provides an informative look at what happens to the body after death, but with a twist—she answers questions she has received from kids. The fluid prose and macabre humor she uses to answer these frank and funny questions—which are largely about corpses and their treatment post-mortem—will appeal to a much wider and older demographic.

Wagstaffe, Johanna.

Fault Lines: Understanding the Power of Earthquakes. **2017. 96p.** **M**

A meteorologist and seismologist, Wagstaffe presents a competent and understandable explanation of the science behind earthquakes, showing their causes and effects and what happens to the planet during an earthquake. Additional information includes facts about earthquakes, ways to prepare for one, and eyewitness accounts from around the world.

Keywords: Earthquakes • Fault lines • Plate tectonics • Seismology

Winchester, Simon.

When the Sky Breaks: Hurricanes, Tornadoes, and the Worst Weather in the World. 2017. 96p. **M J**

In addition to the clear, cogent descriptions of what makes hurricanes so destructive, the feature that makes this such a fascinating and appealing book is the photographs. Journalist and self-described avid weather-watcher Simon Winchester has added a plethora of pictures of both the storms themselves and the damage they have wrought. Satellite imagery looks at hurricanes and typhoons and their intensity and paths, while readers are shown before and after pictures of storm damage, visceral indications of the power these storms have. Winchester uses specific storms to explain how storms work, how they can be predicted, and the damage they can do. Key examples include Hurricane Sandy, Hurricane Katrina, Typhoon Haiyan, and the Joplin, Missouri, tornado of 2011. This book offers an incredible discussion of the causes of storms, including seasonal changes, climate changes, and global warming.

Keywords: Climate change • Hurricanes • Tornadoes • Typhoons • Weather

Environmental Writing

The last several years have seen a decrease in books being published as introductions to climate change. Rather, given that there has been a general acceptance of climate change, the titles on this topic have evolved to discuss what needs to be done in response to this disaster. Titles such as *Overview: A New Way of Seeing Earth* give tangible proof of the effects man has had on the planet, while Nancy Castaldo offers several cases of animals whose endangered status has significantly improved.

Castaldo, Nancy.

Back from the Brink: Saving Animals from Extinction. 2018. 176p. **M**

Nancy Castaldo's introduction points out that if, as scientists believe, this is the sixth era of mass extinction, the fault lies directly with humans. That being said, countries around the world have "recovery plans" to rescue endangered species, and this book discusses six cases where species formerly on the red list have been able to make a substantial recovery due to direct intervention from scientists. Animal lovers will find it heartening to read about the recovery of whooping cranes, which had formerly dwindled to a flock of 15 birds, to the point where scientists are working on breeding programs. The bald eagle population, dramatically affected by the pesticide DDT, had been reduced to one nesting pair in New York state at the time of the country's bicentennial, when work began to reintroduce the species. The birds were not only able to survive but to breed. These stories, and other examples involving wolves, condors, Galápagos tortoises, and alligators, all validate the efforts done by environmentalists and the need to maintain and keep working on behalf of the many species at risk.

Keywords: Bald eagles • Conservation • Whooping cranes • Wolves

Grant, Benjamin, with Sandra Markle.

Overview: A New Way of Seeing Earth, Young Explorer's Edition. 2019. 160p. **M** **J**

The author of *Overview* explains that its title comes from the wonder experienced by astronauts as they gaze down upon the earth from space, an experience that gives them the drive to protect it. The photographs contained in this volume give readers a chance to see the earth from a completely different vantage point. The journey goes beyond the earth's most famous points, including magnificent vistas that demonstrate the world's immensity. The book provides tangible evidence of man's interaction with the natural world, including powerful before and after pictures of forest fires and deforestation. Information is provided on the technology used to take the pictures; as the book also includes further reading and suggested Web sites for readers interested in conservation and environmental protection.

Keywords: Conservation • Environment • Satellite photographs

Montgomery, Sy.

Amazon Adventure: How Tiny Fish Are Saving the World's Largest Rainforest. **Scientists in the Field.** 2017. 80p. **M** **J**

The Amazon Basin, the area that provides one-fifth of the world's oxygen, is also home to the richest variety of the world's wildlife, including the most widely regarded and best-known aquarium fish. The annual farming of these fish is a practice that not only helps the *piaba*, the "small fry," but was the main support for the local economy until the 1990s. This title looks at the conservation efforts for the *piaba* and the *piabeiros* that harvest them, as well as the other wildlife in the area that would be affected by their disappearance.

Keywords: Amazon • Conservation • *Piabas* • Tetras

Walker, Sally M.

Champion: The Comeback Tale of the American Chestnut Tree. 2018. 144p. **M** **J**

Sally Walker presents a history of the possible restoration of a tree that was part of eastern forests in the United States for over 12,000 years, until a blight started wiping out the population in the early 20th century. The discovery of the blight's origin and path, and the virus that caused it, makes for a fascinating tale of both science and nature.

Keywords: Blight • Chestnut tree • Virus

Animals

Books that take a detailed look at animals tend to be great titles for reluctant readers, as they frequently are highly illustrated, focus on high-interest topics, or use design and format in ways that highlight captivating and pertinent information. This subgenre also contains titles about research on endangered animals.

Hirsch, Andy

Dogs: From Predator to Protector. <u>Science Comics</u>. 2017. 128p. **M J**

The average person might be surprised at how much there is to learn about dogs. This introduction to the species is narrated by one in particular, Rudy, an unassuming and friendly animal easily distracted by balls but still able to convey information to the reader about the classification of the species and how it is that dogs, the world's most diverse species, have evolved over time. Readers will find a wide variety of information, from the impact of dominant and recessive genes to the characteristics of different breeds and the work that they do, in a colorful and fun presentation.

Keywords: Canines • Dogs

Koch, Falynn.

Bats: Learning to Fly. <u>Science Comics</u>. 2017. 128p. **M**

When a small brown bat flies too close to some campers and is swatted out of the sky, he is taken to a bat rehabilitation clinic for treatment. Readers are provided information along with Little Brown Bat, as he learns all about bats, various species, and why humans do not get along with them and what can be done about it. For what seems like a very sweet and unassuming story, there is a surprising amount of information, from scientific classification to methods of handling wild animals and a plan for building bat boxes in a suitable area. Supplements include further reading and information about related careers and volunteering.

Keywords: Bats • Graphic nonfiction

Montgomery, Sy.

Chasing Cheetahs: The Race to Save Africa's Fastest Cats. <u>Scientists in the Field</u>. 2014. 80p. **M**

The cheetah, a species that had diminished in the wild from 100,000 to fewer than 10,000, becoming Africa's most endangered wildcat, became the focus of a group called the Cheetah Conservation Fund (CCF), headquartered in Namibia. CCF, under the leadership of *Time* magazine "Hero of the Year" Laurie Marker, has managed to rescue and return to the wild over 900 of these amazing animals. This book in the award-winning series gives readers an introduction to Marker, the cheetahs she loves, and the ongoing conservation work to help save them.

Keywords: Cheetahs • Conservation • Marker, Laurie

Montgomery, Sy.

 The Hyena Scientist. <u>Scientists in the Field</u>. 2018. 80p. **M** **J**

Readers are immediately drawn into this volume in the <u>Scientists in the Field</u> series by one key point: hyenas are weird. Their eccentricities make them an entrancing subject for the general observer. They are also important for research, as their anomalies can be studied for other purposes; the strength of the enamel on their teeth, for example, the strongest in the animal kingdom, may be adapted for commercial use. After an introduction to these unique animals, readers will learn about their Kenyan habitat, as well as the scientists and students who devote their days to studying them and helping to dispel some of the misunderstandings around them. Nic Bishop's wonderful photographs bring the animals and their surroundings to life. **ALA**

Keywords: Holekamp, Kay • Kenya • Spotted hyenas

Turner, Pamela S.

Crow Smarts: Inside the Brain of the World's Brightest Bird. <u>Scientists in the Field</u>. 2016. 80p. **M**

Readers travel to New Caledonia with crow researcher Gavin Hunt, where they will be shown ample evidence that crows are one of the most intelligent species on the planet, humans included. Separating themselves from other animals by their use of tools and ability to reason, New Caledonian crows, small cranial size notwithstanding, beat groups of children in controlled tests back in the United States. This is a fascinating look not only at these birds but also the development of intelligence and what we know about it. The copious and beautiful photographs enrich the text and capture the imagination.

Keywords: Birds • Crows • Intelligence

Viola, Jason.

Polar Bears: Survival on the Ice. <u>Science Comics</u>. 2019. 128p. **M**

Jason Viola's volume in this graphic novel series starts by having a mother polar bear educate her two cubs about the characteristics of their species. The two frolicsome bears, while willing to believe that they are indeed much better than any other bear, are more interested in learning about hunting. Their mother then informs them they have much to learn before they become subadults at the age of two-and-a-half, and runs through other polar bear habits like mating, finding a den, and reproducing. She also discusses the physical demands reproduction, nursing, and hibernation place on the polar bear physiology. This segues neatly into climate change, as decreasing ice will irreparably affect the polar bear food web. A list of suggestions for how to help concludes the volume.

Keywords: Arctic • Climate change • Polar bears

Wicks, Maris.

Coral Reefs: Cities of the Ocean. <u>Science Comics</u>. 2018. 128p. **Ⓜ**

The narrator of this volume in the <u>Science Comics</u> series starts off by reminding readers of the difference between plants and animals, as corals are animals. This is a thorough guide to corals, covering their biological classification and how it differs from Homo sapiens. It also discusses life cycle, several major types of coral, and where each type is found. As reefs are one of the most biodiverse ecosystems on the planet, the author also includes information about the many other animals that can be found living there and why the health of the world's reefs is important to the planet. This leads into a discussion of the effects of climate change, the water cycle, and how reefs are being affected by global warming. Easy suggestions are offered for helping to keep these amazing places healthy.

Keywords: Biodiversity • Coral • Reefs

Consider Starting with . . .

These are some recommended titles for readers new to the genre.

deGrasse Tyson, Neil, with Gregory Mone. *Astrophysics for Young People in a Hurry.*

Montgomery, Sy. *The Hyena Scientist.* <u>Scientists in the Field</u>.

Fiction Read-Alikes

- **Baguchinsky, Jill.** *Mammoth.* Plus-sized blogger Natalie Page knows that a large part of what makes her awesome and keeps her fashionista followers is her knowledge of and dedication to paleontology. Unabashed fossil fan that she is, she can't wait to spend her summer as an intern at an Ice Age dig, earning her way there on merit. When she gets there, she finds out that one of the other students, Quinn, is actually the daughter of one of her icons, Dr. Ronald Carver, a paleontologist she frequently

1

2

3

4

5

6

7

8

9

10

11

quotes or links to on her blog. The summer turns her expectations upside down when it seems the great Dr. Carver may not be so great after all. Natalie, while digging her way out of some potential pitfalls of her own, will learn what it really means to be awesome.

Reference

Cords, Sarah Statz. *The Real Story: A Guide to Nonfiction Reading Interests*. Genreflecting Advisory Series. Westport, CT: Libraries Unlimited, 2006.

Chapter 7

Sports

Definition

This topic offers the opportunity to develop a section of the collection that will teach new things. Publication and popularity often reflect current events and familiarity. There are more books published about winter sports around the time of the Winter Olympics, and it is more likely that students will seek out books about figures with whom they are familiar. Baseball, a ubiquitous sport in the United States, is not as common in Canada, which has only one major and one minor league team, so there are likely to be more titles found on school and public library shelves in the United States. Titles about sports figures may become dated depending on the sport and the subject. A biography about a recognizable figure, especially one with information about the sport or from the athlete, has more staying power than a book about an athlete who is not as well known or unfamiliar to teenagers. Elena Donne, Steph Curry or Carey Price are much more likely to be known to today's teenagers than players from the PGA.

Appeal

Sports remain a popular source of entertainment, with both individual competitors and teams having dedicated fans that follow their wins and keep up with their statistics. Titles in the "General Information and Statistics" and "The Greatest Games" sections of this chapter frequently contain numerous photographs showing athletes in peak condition or demonstrating how to perform signature moves, making them highly appealing to reluctant readers. Readers do not need to play a sport to find a book appealing. A book about a sport or one of its legends has an intrinsic fascination, while the grand spectacle of a major event such as the Olympics or a championship may drive publication of books about the event. These books might also appeal to readers interested in the "Sports Adventures" titles from chapter 1.

Chapter Organization

The first section, "Sports Biographies," contains engaging and inspiring titles of sports heroes and people who have worked hard to achieve their goals and become the best at their chosen activity, frequently breaking barriers for the athletes who followed them. This is followed by "General Information and Statistics," in which readers will find titles that explain particular sports and how to participate in them, along with information about some of their greatest moments. A final section, "The Greatest Games," contains books with sports histories and titles where sports legends reflect on what the game means to them.

Sports Biographies

Athletes are heroic icons to many people. The qualities necessary to become a top competitor in any sport are admirable—strength, determination, self-discipline, and courage. The story behind the struggle to get to the finish line, the podium, or the end of a season has many elements that draw readers, including exciting competitions and teamwork. Titles that show athletes overcoming greater obstacles to participate in sports, whether internal or imposed by society, can validate readers' own struggles. Titles also include biographies about athletes who have overcome racial or religious bias to compete in their sports, as well as inspirational Paralympians like Jessica Long, providing readers with many options for champions to admire.

Biles, Simone, with Michelle Burford.

Courage to Soar: A Body in Motion, a Life in Balance. 2016. 256p. **M** **J**

Simone Biles was drawn to gymnastics at a very early age, having been a particularly energetic child. While this alone may not have made her unusual, the talent she displayed in beginner classes, performing moves usually made by gymnasts several years older, did. Biles does not flinch from mentioning the difficult beginning she and her siblings experienced, or the loving grandparents who became like parents to her, supporting her efforts right through the Rio Olympic Games. Family, faith, and friends are central to Biles's work ethic, and while she freely admits her imperfections, her many successes serve as an example of just how far an athlete can go when determination and drive are married to her kind of ability.

Keywords: Biles, Simone • Gymnastics • Gymnasts • Olympians

Donne, Elena Delle, with Sarah Durand.

My Shot: Balancing It All and Standing Tall. 2018. 272p. **M** **J**

While basketball fans know Elena Donne as the 2015 WNBA MVP and a 2016 Olympic gold medalist, what they may not know is that she has always been outstanding at the sport—so much so that she was offered her first college scholarship at the age of 13. That talent, along with the accompanying pressure that she felt to live up to it and be the best member of any team on which she was playing, caused her to start to hate the game. Eventually she walked away from a scholarship at UConn and the chance to play for its incredibly well-regarded program, instead choosing to move closer to home and the family she believed needed her. Readers will learn how she slowly came back to basketball, playing with the University of Delaware's much lower-ranked Blue Hens. Under her leadership the team made it to the Sweet 16 semifinal round of the NCAA tournament before she was chosen second overall during the WNBA draft.

Keywords: Basketball • Donne, Elena Delle • WNBA

Ignotofsky, Rachel.

Women in Sports: 50 Fearless Athletes Who Played to Win. Women in Science. 2017. 152p. 🅼 🅹

This book presents biographies of 50 legendary women athletes who led the way in their chosen sports. Ignotofsky points out that women have traditionally been stereotyped as the weaker sex and denied the right to compete at the same level as men, if at all. It is because of women with outstanding abilities that generations that followed have earned the right to contend, participate, and play in their chosen sports. Readers will enjoy learning about athletes such as Olympic medalist and world champion Gertrude Ederle, who not only became the first woman to swim the English Channel but set a 34-year record in doing so. The book covers pioneering women from around the world who have played a wide variety of sports like golf, track, and sky diving, from the beginning of the 20th century to the present day, with a look at several notable sports teams. Resources include books, statistics, and a list of Web sites where further information may be found.

Keywords: Athletes • Sports

Long, Jessica, with Hannah Long.

Unsinkable: From Russian Orphan to Paralympic Swimming World Champion. 2018. 112p. 🅼

Long, winner of 13 gold medals at the Paralympics, makes a particularly prescient observation of her younger self, noting that she felt particularly at home in the water because it was the one place where her normal situation was reversed; she found herself in a situation where other people were chasing her. She presents her story in a clear, compelling, and forthright voice, summarizing the fascinating tale of a girl born in Russia with a birth defect that affected the development of the bones in her lower leg. After

Jessica and her brother, Joshua, were adopted by the Longs and brought from an orphanage in Irkutsk, Russia, to the United States, it was discovered that her lower legs needed to be amputated. This didn't stop the toddler from learning how to use her prosthetics or developing an early love of gymnastics that would translate to other sports and then to the water. Jessica's success in and out of the water make for an inspiring and motivating read.

Keywords: Long, Jessica • Paralympics • Swimming

Muhammad, Ibtihaj.

Proud: Living My American Dream, Young Readers Edition. 2018. 304p. **M J**

Ibtihaj Muhammad has always been competitive and athletic, which isn't unique in her family. What does make her stand out, however, is her ability with a saber. Growing up, it made her uncomfortable to feel different or to be denied a chance to participate because of her hijab. This outward symbol of Muhammad's misunderstood and misrepresented faith is what allowed her to find the sport where she would finally excel; it was fencing, where all the athletes are fully covered, that made her feel that she did not stand out. She started to progress through the ranks, gaining national and international standings. Muhammad's accomplishments have made her more than a model for Muslims, athletes, and girls. Her drive and determination have helped her become the first U.S. Muslim competitor at the Olympics, an Olympic medalist, a businesswoman, and one of *Time* magazine's 100 most influential people.

Keywords: Athletes • Fencer • Muhammad, Ibtihaj • Olympian

Rondina, Catherine.

Carey Price: How a First Nations Kid Became a Superstar Goaltender. Recordbooks. 2018. 152p. **M J**

Montreal Canadiens goalie Carey Price has a list of accomplishments long enough to amaze any sports fan. What is truly inspiring is the support he received from his family. Price grew up in Anahim Lake, British Columbia, a small town where kids played pond hockey. His dad was so determined to help his son get better at the game that he drove, and later flew, him 300 kilometers (approx. 186 miles) biweekly to Williams Lake, the closest community with a house league. Readers will enjoy Price's journey through the WHL, international competitions, the NHL, and the Olympics. Catherine Rondina gives readers a sense of his family life, including his mother's determination to share her indigenous family heritage as part of the Ulkatcho First Nation. Sidebars are divided between information about hockey, hockey players, and biographical information. A glossary and list of career highlights is included.

Keywords: Hockey • NHL • Price, Carey • WHL

General Information and Statistics

Readers interested in becoming competent participants in, or well-informed observers of, a sport need look no further than these titles. They include information about the sport's rules, equipment, and setup, and are generally written by people with a close association to the sport. Titles are usually highly illustrated, which will appeal to reluctant readers. There is a potential crossover with the "Sports Biographies" section for readers with an interest in a particular sport.

Bertolazzi, Alberto.

Soccer for Kids: An Illustrated Guide. 2018. 100p. **J**

This quick and informative guide provides historical information about the world's most popular sport, showing readers how play has been modified over the years to its current form. Colorful illustrations accompany information about the game's rules, moves, techniques, tactics, formations, and exercises to improve play. Information is provided about international competitions, soccer-playing countries, and the most-recognized players. The book also includes statistics about the best-known international soccer clubs. Readers will enjoy this crash course in a sport that has over a billion players.

Keywords: Soccer • Sports

Dornemann, Volker, and Wolfgang Rumpf.

Taekwondo Kids: from White Belt to Yellow/Green Belt. 2013p. 144p. **M**

This is an introductory guide to taekwondo intended for beginners; it offers instructions in the exercises associated with the white belt to the yellow/green belts. Before beginning the exercises, readers are presented with a short history of the martial art, an explanation of the various belts, and a discussion of appropriate behavior for the training hall. Each exercise is presented with a narrative explaining the body movements. Illustrations show characters with related backstories getting older and gaining more experience for each successive belt. Terminology is explained at the end of each section. This book will allow prospective students to see if they are interested in taekwondo and offers help with newly acquired skills.

Keywords: Graphic nonfiction • Martial arts • Taekwondo

Frederick, Shane.

Hockey is a Numbers Game: A Fan's Guide to Stats. <u>Know the Stats</u>. 2018p. 32p. **M**

Frederick offers a novel way to better understand the game of hockey by explaining some of its aspects, providing statistics about those aspects, and then using the statistics to help explain the game. For example, the section on penalties lists the types of penalties and describes how statistics for penalties are counted, then includes a list of the players with the highest number of accrued penalty minutes. By explaining how statistics are tallied, fans can keep track of the players and teams that are playing well and see how the game has changed over time. Scoring statistics have changed significantly, for example, partly due to the increase in size of a goalie's equipment. This highly illustrated book is a fun way to find out about the game and how it is currently measured; readers will learn about some of its greatest players as well.

Keywords: Hockey • Hockey players

Full STEAM Sports

Titles in this series break down sports through the lenses of science, technology, engineering, arts and mathematics (STEAM). The books explore topics like the force behind all motions to get balls where they need to go, the technology that creates better helmets to prevent concussions, the engineering of better equipment and stadiums, and the numbers behind statistics that calculate a player's worth for salary and draft number. These narratives are presented smoothly and will help explain each game to readers unfamiliar with it, while allowing fans to appreciate the explanations and additions of the full-color photographs, glossary, and suggestions for additional resources.

> Helget, N. *Full Steam Baseball: Science, Technology, Engineering, Arts, and Mathematics of the Game.* 2018. 32p. **M** **J**

> Helget, N. *Full Steam Basketball: Science, Technology, Engineering, Arts, and Mathematics of the Game.* 2018. 32p. **M** **J**

> McCollum, Sean. *Full Steam Football: Science, Technology, Engineering, Arts, and Mathematics of the Game.* 2018. 32p. **M** **J**

> McCollum, Sean. *Full Steam Soccer: Science, Technology, Engineering, Arts, and Mathematics of the Game.* 2018. 32p. **M** **J**

Gifford, Clive, and John Malam.

The Complete Book of Soccer. 2016. 300p. **H** **A/YA**

This book provides readers with everything they need to know about the world's most popular sport. The authors provide a history of the game, describing similar games that date back 2,000 years; while examples can be found all over the globe, the original version likely dates from a game played in Asia roughly 2,200 years ago (the current version was adapted in English schools). This is a guide that will appeal to both interested novices and fans, as the book not only explains the subject matter, providing history, rules, and statistics, but does so with full-color photographs and reproductions of historical documents where appropriate. Readers are given information about the World Cup, other important championships, profiles of important FIFA and national teams, notable players and managers, and noteworthy statistics.

Keywords: Soccer • Sports

Now Try: Younger readers or readers looking for a more basic introduction to the sport will find it in Andrea Mills's slim and involving volume, *The Soccer Book: Facts and Terrific Trivia*. The book offers a wide variety of facts about the game, including its history, its greatest players, and the top tournaments and stadiums. Find out who would make up the all-time dream team—and who you would never want on that team. A combination of fun statistics and trivia alongside information about the game makes this a fun and informational read for fans and newcomers alike.

Keywords: Soccer • Sports • Trivia

The Greatest Games

The books in this subgenre include histories of particular sports and legendary players. These titles will appeal both to fans of a particular sport and readers looking to learn more about why some people find them so compelling.

Freedman, Lew.

Football Stadiums: A Guide to Professional and Top College Stadiums. 2018. 320p. **H** **A/YA**

Fans of America's most popular sport will enjoy the glossy photographs of, and statistics about, the homes of their favorite teams. The story of each location starts with a sidebar that provides basic information including the stadium's architect, opening date, and capacity, followed by memorable moments in its history. An entertaining narrative expands on the team histories, usually commenting on the ownership or coach. After learning about NFL stadiums, readers are taken on a cross-country tour of college stadiums. Each is accompanied by photographs and a short history of the stadium, team, and any notable events. The photographs in particular communicate the immense size of the vast NFL stadium bowls. Sports fans will enjoy these stories, but even readers who are not football fans will find this book worthy of their time.

Keywords: Football • NFL • Stadiums

Milton, Steve, ed.

The Baseball Game I'll Never Forget: 50 Major Leaguers Recall Their Finest Moments. 2018. 192p. **H** **A/YA**

Compiled from a segment in *Baseball Digest*, America's longest running publication devoted to the sport, insiders describe the game that meant the most to them. For the pitchers, catchers, and outfielders sharing their stories, it isn't only their winningest games that became their most memorable or defining moments. In more than 50 years plumbed for memories, the players describe what they learned from wins, losses and trying situations, determining whether they were worthy of playing in baseball's greatest forum. Reading about what made particular games noteworthy in careers marked by lifetime achievements makes this a title that sports fans will savor.

Keywords: Baseball

Sitterson, Aubrey, and Chris Moreno.

The Comic Book Story of Professional Wrestling: A Hard-Core, High-Flying, No-Holds-Barred History of the One True Sport. 2018. 184p. ⏹

Wrestling as a sport has been around for millennia. The professional version, as described by Sitterson and Moreno, takes this sport and makes it entertainment. The sport got its start in carnivals, where the point of the fighting was to gain the public's attention and money. Arranging a splashy finish to a fight ensured both; by the 1880s it was understood that wrestling in America was fixed. In order to draw crowds it was necessary to create a spectacle, establishing match rules, creating desirable matchups, and hiring legitimate fighters. The book describes the progression of the sport, the rise of villains such as Gorgeous George, the legacy of the Hart family, and the advent of television, which brought wrestling to a whole new audience. *Lucha libre* (a form of Mexican wrestling) and the World Wrestling Federation (WWF) also raised its profile. By the time Hulk Hogan brought Hulkamania to a wider audience, wrestling was a familiar television phenomenon. Readers may not know about Dwayne "The Rock" Johnson's wrestling background, but his familiar eyebrow raise is portrayed here to good effect as one of wrestling's superheroes. Even Donald Trump's connection to the sport is not overlooked in a history covering two centuries of wrestlers and wrestling.

Keywords: Graphic nonfiction • Professional wrestling • Wrestling

Wahl, Grant.

Masters of Modern Soccer: How the World's Best Play the 21st-Century Game. 2018. 272p. ⏹

Hall takes a close look at the game of soccer by examining each of its positions and how it is played by one of the stars of the sport. By showing how the best players think, act, and strategize, readers will discover a new appreciation for the game. From midfielder American phenom Christian Pulisic's early lessons on the first touch to center back Vincent Kompany's ability to deliver the right pass, Wahl presents conversational pieces that will entertain and enlighten soccer fans learning about important players and their skills.

Keywords: Soccer • Techniques

Zweig, Eric.

Everything Sports: All the Photos, Facts, and Fun to Make You Jump! **National Geographic Kids Everything.** 2016. 64p. ▣

> This photo-filled overview of sports introduces the wide world of team and individual sports beyond the ones generally covered on television, played in stadiums, and taught in schools. While there is information about basketball, football, and hockey, the information here is about leagues, the equipment used in uncommon sports, and the most common sports played around the globe. Statistics about the greatest players and most victories are provided. Readers will also become more familiar with many of the competitions played at the Olympic games.
>
> **Keywords:** Sports • Trivia

Consider Starting with . . .

These are suggested titles for readers new to the genre.

> Muhammad, Ibtihaj. *Proud: Living My American Dream, Young Readers Edition.*

> Sitterson, Aubrey, and Chris Moreno. *The Comic Book Story of Professional Wrestling: A Hard-Core, High-Flying, No-Holds-Barred History of the One True Sport.*

> Zweig, Eric. *Everything Sports: All the Photos, Facts, and Fun to Make You Jump!*

Fiction Read-Alikes

- **Aronson, Marc, and Charles R. Smith Jr., eds.** *Pick-Up Game: A Full Day of Full Court.* Nine young adult authors present stories of games that take place over one day at the "Cage," the West 4th Street courts in New York City. Seamlessly interwoven with pieces by Charles R. Smith, readers meet a lanky, irretrievably gawky Korean player coerced into playing because of his height, scouts who are watching over a prospect named ESPN, and a player whose main goal is to get into NYU film school, in pieces that can be read singly or as one connected narrative.

- **Reynolds, Jason.** *Ghost.* **Track.** Castle Cranshaw, better known as "Ghost," doesn't know anything about running when he is recruited by a former Olympian to join one of the city's youth track teams. What he does know is stealing, lying, and guns, courtesy of the night his dad tried to shoot him and his mom in their apartment. The team gives him a chance to join in and meet new people. When it turns out he has real talent, sprinting gives him the chance to move beyond the events that are holding him back.

- **Sandor, Steven.** *Stick Pick.* <u>Lorimer Sports Stories</u>. On the way home from a provincial hockey championship, Janine Burnett and her parents are in a car accident that leaves her paralyzed from a spinal cord injury. Told she will be in a wheelchair for the rest of her life, she turns away from everyone and everything. Janine's BFF, Rowena, takes her to a sledge hockey practice and tells her that she will learn how to play too if she will stick with it. In job-shadowing her father, a sportswriter, she comes to understand the inaccessibility of the world for people in wheelchairs while managing to find a sport where she can still excel.

- **Ukazu, Ngozi.** *Check Please! Book 1: #Hockey.* Former figure skater Eric Bittle leaves his small town in Georgia to start college on a hockey scholarship at Samwell University in Samwell, MA. The first volume of this graphic novel duology introduces readers to Eric, a devoted baker who chose Samwell because he thought it would be more open to the LGBT community than Georgia had been. When Eric, whose skating background gives him speed and dexterity, finds himself frozen when confronted with physical threats on the ice, he receives help from the team's captain, a star player, which leaves him both grateful and more than a little awed.

Chapter **8**

All about You

Definition

Adolescence is defined by Britannica.com[1] as the "transitional period of development between childhood and adulthood." The World Health Organization stipulates adolescents to be any youth between the ages of 10 and 19. Adolescents undergo significant changes during these years, primarily in two areas. The first has to do with physical changes and the second, broader area deals with psychological, social, and emotional issues. Titles in this chapter deal with both the physical changes as well as the issues of well-being teens deal with in their daily lives.

Appeal

Adolescence is a time when independence becomes increasingly important and increasingly valued. Titles in this chapter speak directly to the reader about issues that matter to them, frequently in areas about which they would rather not ask friends, family, or other adults. Books that can provide an opportunity to take charge of their own situations and gain a measure of control are frequently in demand. It can be very comforting to learn that something potentially embarrassing is normal and has happened to others as well. The increase in published titles offering suggestions for dealing with stress is both an acknowledgment of the pressures of daily life and a positive step toward teaching teenagers about work-life balance. This is reflected in the career section, where recently published titles encourage teens to think about alternative careers, lifelong learning, and transferrable skills.

Chapter Organization

The chapter begins with a section on "Personal Growth" before moving on to "Health and Wellness," which looks at overcoming stress and dealing with life's changes. This is followed by "Relationships and Sex," which offers titles with straightforward answers to questions teens might have. "Tough Stuff" follows, including titles about difficult issues from abuse to mental health. Lastly, a number of titles give suggestions for jobs, training, and education in "Career Directions."

Personal Growth

Self-esteem involves a person's feelings of worth. While an adult's self-esteem might incorporate feelings about abilities, intelligence, behaviors, and characteristics, there is an overwhelming tendency among teenagers, particularly teenage girls, to measure their self-esteem by how they feel about their looks. As they get older and gain greater life experience teens develop coping skills that help them deal with these doubts. Books in this section offer assistance in a range of areas for ways to feel more comfortable with oneself, in social situations among others. Readers looking for more traditional titles to help them present themselves in a different light will find options in the "Beauty and Style" section of chapter 9.

de Heer, Margaret.

Philosophy: A Discovery in Comics. 2012. 120p. **M J**

Margaret de Heer begins her inviting, illustrated introduction to philosophy by asking what makes humans different from other animals. The answers to this question lead to explanations, humorously supplemented by cartoon accompaniments, of different philosophies, beginning with ancient Greek philosophers like Socrates, Plato, and Aristotle, and moving on to writings from the Middle Ages, including Augustine, Thomas Aquinas, and a particularly clear explanation of free will. Other important philosophers are also mentioned. This book will appeal to readers who would like to find out how humans have thought of themselves over the centuries or who might like to take their own inward look.

Keywords: Aristotle • Philosophy • Plato • Socrates

Heinrichs, Jay.

Thank You for Arguing, Third Edition: What Aristotle, Lincoln, and Homer Simpson Can Teach Us About the Art of Persuasion. 2017. 480p. **H AYA**

At the heart of Heinrich's dense, thorough, and entertaining text is instruction in the formulation and delivery of a winning argument. Heinrich points out the ubiquity of arguments in many aspects of daily life, including advertising, mediating, interacting with family and friends, and making arbitrary decisions. By using readily relatable references, the author makes it easy to understand the difference between a fight and an argument and gives a series of examples for every step in constructing an argument, demonstrating the value of logic and rhetoric. This book can be used to polish language, speech, and debate skills, as many if not most of the examples show how the argument may be turned back on the speaker. It is not surprising that the book is divided into sections on offense, defense, and advanced defense, including a chapter on giving a persuasive talk, a look at the styles of Barack Obama and Donald Trump, the parts of a persuasive essay, and a guide to creating an effective college essay.

Keywords: Persuasive arguments • Rhetoric

Hemmen, Lucie.

The Teen Girl's Survival Guide: 10 Tips for Making Friends, Avoiding Drama, and Coping with Social Stress. Instant Help Solutions. 2015. 208p. 🇯 🇲

Hemmen, a psychologist who works primarily with teenagers, notes a gender difference in approaches to high school, with boys looking at it as something to be endured, and girls rating their days as good or bad by the quality of their social interactions. In order to encourage success, she offers suggestions in 10 areas for the improvement of the quantity and quality of social connections. Each covers an area with a broad reach, starting with encouraging positive thinking and working up to making contact and communicating. Difficult topics are also covered, such as how to weed out inappropriate social habits. Information is presented in a conversational style, with numerous examples provided from actual teenagers. Each section includes exercises and quizzes, presented in a format that encourages the reader to grab a pen and paper and tally their answers, meaning that the book should not be marked on its first circulation, but will be available for many teens looking to widen their social circle.

Keywords: Confidence • Self-esteem

Kay, Katty, and Claire Shipman.

The Confidence Code for Girls: Taking Risks, Messing Up, and Becoming Your Amazingly Imperfect, Totally Powerful Self. 2018. 320p. 🇲

The tween version of Kay and Shipman's *New York Times* bestselling guide to confidence is a practical and easy-to-read look at the factors in developing, having, and maintaining confidence. The authors note that any included exercises which involve writing may be done in a journal if using a library book. Knowing the benefits of being confident, the authors provide plenty of real-life examples to demonstrate what they deem the keys to confidence, including: the value in trying new things, the upside in failing, determining real friends, dealing with negative and difficult thoughts, navigating social media, and being true to oneself. By doing these things, readers will step outside their comfort zone, doing something new without taking time to overthink it, and at the same time knowing they are doing something by choice that they will enjoy.

Keywords: Confidence • Self-esteem

Pham, Tiffany.

Girl Mogul: Dream it. Do it. Change the World. 2019. 224p. **J** **H**

The author, Tiffany Pham, is the developer of Mogul, the company that is Google's most consistently returned search result. Here Pham presents a guide for teens on navigating and thriving in the teen years. Divided into three main sections, Pham gives advice on how to develop and maintain confidence, keep a strong support system, and look to the future. Discussions about relationships consider how to deal with both positive and negative interactions, as well as providing guidance about how to approach mentors, which is demonstrated in the text by the inclusion of suggestions from key figures. This component illustrates Pham's theory on seeking out and taking advantage of ties from the available and knowledgeable community. Readers will recognize that Pham maintains a level of respect for their choices, encouraging them to consider their interests, what they think is fun, and the things they do well. Above all, she promotes positivity and the idea that any girl can apply herself to become a mogul in her own right in the way that she did.

Keywords: Confidence • Entrepreneurism • Self-esteem

Health and Wellness

A number of factors are singled out on the Canadian Pediatricians' Web site Caring for Kids as being important to a teenager's emotional and physical health, including nutrition, physical activity, and coping with stress.[2] Titles in this section provide readable guides with practical suggestions. Rather than concentrating on improving one's health through dieting, these titles look at overcoming stress and attaining a more peaceful, balanced lifestyle. This does offer them a potential for a longer lifespan, as particular diets are more likely to be weeded as another diet, implement, or food gains popularity.

Andrus, Aubre.

Project You: More Than 50 Ways to Calm Down, De-Stress, and Feel Great. 2017. 160p. **M** **J**

This is a practical, fun list of realistic methods for coping with the many stressors of daily life. With only a short, to-the-point reminder of what stress can do to the body and some information about where to go for help should it be needed, the choices here are fun and suit a wide variety of situations and personalities, including advice on how to exercise, relax, or clean out physical or mental clutter.

Keywords: Mindfulness • Relaxation • Stress

Now Try: Teens are by no means immune to stress in their everyday lives. In order to find relief from these stressors, Gina Biegel's *Be Mindful and Stress Less: 50 Ways to Deal with Your (Crazy) Life* introduces the basic practices of mindfulness. This is followed by suggestions on how to apply them to self-care, providing tips on how to keep a healthy body, mind, and self-esteem. Each section includes explanations, practical ideas, and takeaways. Any reader interested in mindfulness will find this a practical and useful volume.

Bialik, Mayim.

Girling Up: How to be Strong, Smart, and Spectacular. 2017. 177p. **M J**

The actress, mother, and neuroscientist has penned a practical, thorough, and surprisingly readable text that covers the nuts and bolts of what young women might want to know about what their bodies are made of, how they will change, and how to take care of them during the teenage years. While the author, a PhD, offers a thorough chapter with concise, practical information about the physical changes that the body will go through during puberty, the book goes beyond this to discuss nutrition, mindfulness, relationships, and stress. Bialik, who will be familiar to readers from her years on television, writes in a straightforward manner and equates information to practical experience without condescension, making this an offering that would be suitable for research as well as advice.

Keywords: Health • Puberty • Relationships

Daldry, Jeremy.

The Teenage Guy's Survival Guide: The Real Deal on Going Out, Growing Up, and Other Guy Stuff. 2018. 192p. **M J**

This is a guide appropriate for middle schoolers on up about what to expect with the onset of puberty and how to deal with it, presented in a lighthearted and entertaining way. Readers will find practical advice about how to deal with dating, relationships, sex, breakups, and the inevitable changes they will experience in their bodies. Daldry does not overlook more serious issues such as drugs and pornography, or Internet hazards like catfishing. Older readers and girls may also find this a potential choice for its refreshing and straightforward advice and the included list of resources.

Keywords: Adolescence • Puberty • Relationships

Okamoto, Nadya.

Period Power: A Manifesto for the Menstrual Movement. 2018. 368p. **M J**

When Nadya Okamoto was in high school, firsthand knowledge about homelessness made her determined to increase knowledge and awareness about menstrual hygiene. She founded a nonprofit organization called PERIOD at the age of 16, dedicated to advocating that menstrual care is a basic right. This book goes beyond serving as an educational tool, although it begins by providing information about exactly what to expect with a period, a menstrual cycle, and complications that can ensue. Okamoto then moves beyond this to discuss and dispel taboos around periods, which she ties into the purpose, goal, and work of her nonprofit. As part of her work includes delivering menstrual products, an explanation of the different types and benefits of each, and instructions where suitable, are included. Girls will appreciate Okamato's chapter on the stigmatization of the period in the United States and will be won over to her fight against what she calls period poverty, as well as her commitment to making products affordable for all. The author is well versed in policy and can speak to the need for legislation at different levels of government, as well as instances where menstruation has been mentioned either positively or negatively in the media. This book is a winning read not only for those interested in health care but also in the social sciences.

Keywords: Health • Menstruation • Puberty

Rissman, Rebecca.

Yoga for Your Mind and Body: A Teenage Practice for a Healthy, Balanced Life. 2015. 208p. **M** **J**

A simple introduction offers the ancient and low-tech practice of yoga to readers as an all-purpose way to improve health, as it is believed to de-stress, strengthen, boost brainpower, and make the body more limber while stretching. Readers can decide whether their goal is to be more relaxed, stronger, or smarter, and start learning the poses with that aim. Rissman, a certified yoga instructor, provides an explanation of basic yoga equipment and how and why to warm up before working out. Each pose starts out with a picture of the final, desired position, which may be off-putting to beginners or people who do not read the text. The book also includes many reminders to not overstretch and to stop if anything hurts. Each pose includes numbered steps to achieving the position along with notes as to where equipment may best be incorporated to help make the pose easier. After the first few poses paragraphs are added to indicate the intended benefit of the pose. The author also includes suggestions for further information and motivators.

Keywords: Exercises • Health • Yoga

Shy Guides

The four volumes in the <u>Shy Guides</u> series are intended to provide quick and practical suggestions for readers who find themselves uncomfortable in social situations, whether uncertain about dealing with a personal relationship, dealing with anxiety and suffering related effects, or looking for advice on overcoming worries. Each provides a list of further resources and has sidebars with "life tips" that speak to the reader directly. Explanations for the ways the various systems of the body respond to anxiety lead naturally into suggestions for how to deal with it and prevent it in the future. These highly illustrated titles emphasize that several things can contribute to making a person more or less shy, introverted, or extroverted. They also provide suggestions for things readers can do if they would prefer to overcome a natural shyness.

Bjorklund, Ruth. *The Science of Quiet People: The Shy Guide to the Biology of Being Bashful.* 2019. 48p. **M** **J**

Kenney, Karen Latchana. *Getting Out and Getting Along: The Shy Guide to Friends and Relationships.* 2019. 48p. **M** **J**

Kenney, Karen Latchana. *Quiet Confidence: The Shy Guide to Using Your Strengths.* 2019. 48p. **M** **J**

Peterson, Megan Cooley. *That's Awkward! The Shy Guide to Embarrassing Situations.* 2019. 48p. **M** **J**

Relationships and Sex

During adolescence children develop secondary sexual characteristics, such as a deeper voice in boys and breasts in females, as their hormonal balance shifts toward the adult state. Adolescence is a time when there are significant changes not only in a person's body but also in their identity and independence. It is not surprising that their relationships would change and shift at the same time, along with the potential for the formation of romantic relationships. Books in this section provide frank, forthright information about these changes, letting teens and tweens know that they are not the only ones with questions in this area and that all of their questions deserve a valid answer. More books are being published that deal with sexuality and gender, making this an area that will likely need to be updated and watched in order to have outdated material removed.

Green, Laci.

Sex Plus: Learning, Loving, and Enjoying Your Body. 2018. 528p. **H**

This book is a thorough, frank, and above all completely positive guide to sex and sexuality. Laci Green, a well-known advocate in the field of sex education, answers questions that teenagers likely didn't know they had, in a volume with information vetted by physicians. Her inclusion of actual examples from both personal experience and her readers makes this a much more relatable text than many alternatives, starting with male and female anatomy and moving through the parts of the body, gender identity, masturbation, and sex. Further, because it is better to have information up front, she provides information about sex toys, knowing when to have sex, how to prepare for it, variations of it, and dealing with possible consequences. Readers will also find information on relationships and a list of resources.

Keywords: Anatomy • Intercourse • Pregnancy • Puberty • Sex

Hemmen, Lucie.

The Teen Girl's Survival Guide: 10 Tips for Making Friends, Avoiding Drama, and Coping with Social Stress. <u>Instant Help Solutions.</u> 2015. 208p. **J** **H**

The tips in this book, accompanied by simple quizzes, are intended for teens who could use some help communicating, which is quite likely to say any of them willing to pick up the book. The first, a personality quiz, points out that no matter where they fall on the introvert-extrovert scale, there are things they can do to improve their interactions. The following chapters cover making friends, improving communication, decreasing conflict, writing on social media, and practicing balance.

Keywords: Communicating • E-mail • Friendships • Social media

Madrone, Kelly Huegel.

LGBTQ: The Survival Guide for Lesbian, Gay, Bisexual, Transgender, and Questioning Teens, Third Edition. 2018. 270p. **M** **J**

In the third edition of *LGBTQ*, the author points out advances in LGBTQ rights since previous editions, noting the added category of married same-sex couples on the 2010 census, as well as studies that note the increasing acknowledgement and acceptance of LGBTQ individuals. This title provides a wide range of useful material, both for queer teens and anyone hoping to help create a more positive community for them. In a culture where understanding of gender and sexuality is expanding rapidly, the very useful vocabulary provided helps to inform any reader while providing information for teens about questioning and gender identity. Information is included about binary and nonbinary identities, with pullouts that add stories from teens and resources for teens seeking more information. Chapters are included on a wide variety of topics, including homophobia and transphobia, coming out, school life, friendship, dating and relationships, sex and sexuality, staying healthy, religion and culture, and life after high school. This last chapter is useful in that it contains practical suggestions for finding colleges and employers with LGBTQ-friendly communities and nondiscrimination policies. Running through the book are reminders to know your rights and keep a strong support system, which is still necessary given societal pressures, cultural beliefs, and long-held misconceptions.

Keywords: Gender identity • LGBTQ rights • Sexual identity

Witton, Hannah.

Doing It! Let's Talk About Sex. 2018. 352p. **H**

Blogger Hannah Witton provides a frank and up-front discussion of all things having to do with sex, from relating to the other person to the various aspects of the act and any possible repercussions. Chapters also cover related topics like porn and body issues. What makes this book so relatable is Witton's conversational tone, which includes numerous personal anecdotes that draw the reader into the narrative. Witton also adds stories from friends and other people to further illustrate and explain the topic under discussion.

Keywords: Gender Identity • Relationships • Sex • Sexual identity

Tough Stuff

Books in this category cover some of the darker issues that teens deal with during adolescence, including abuse, depression, and mental illness. The books present first-person accounts of impactful stories that will resonate with readers, as the authors write about how their lives were affected and what they did to try and endure, take charge, or recover from the situations in which they found themselves.

Bluel, Amy.

Project Semicolon: Your Story Isn't Over. 2017. 331p. 🄷

These powerful, frequently painful, and always impactful stories will resonate with those who have grappled with or are familiar with depression, anxiety, or mental illness. The semicolon tattoo is intended to represent a pause rather than an end; rebirth, hope, and the possibility of a new future after enduring pain and hardship are all recurring themes in this gritty and honest collection. A resource list of hotlines is provided.

Keywords: Anxiety • Depression • Mental illness • Sexual assault • Short stories • Suicide

Burkhart, Jessica, ed.

Life Inside My Mind: 31 Authors Share Their Personal Struggles. 2018. 320p. 🄷

While having a mental illness in any form is not uncommon, it can be painful, awkward, and incredibly difficult, especially when a person is ignorant of their condition, unaware of treatment options, or loathe to seek help. Thirty-one authors share the histories of their struggles dealing with a panoply of mental health illnesses: anxiety, ADHD, OCD, alcoholism, suicidal thoughts, Alzheimer's, depression, bipolar disorder, and body dysmorphic disorder. The stories recount the effects of these conditions on the authors' lives and what they have done in order to take back control of their lives, including noting that stigma around mental health is wrong and dangerous. The mechanisms that they use to regain and maintain balance in their lives will speak to all readers, reassuring any that would like to know that there are ways to seek help and that having a mental illness is not a choice one makes.

Keywords: ADHD • Alcoholism • Anxiety • Depression • Mental illness • OCD

Demetrios, Heather, ed.

Dear Heartbreak: YA Authors and Teens on the Dark Side of Love. 2015. 187p. **M** **J**

Nineteen young adult authors answer one letter each from thousands submitted by teenagers across the United States, Mexico, and Europe. The letters are, appropriately, sent to "Heartbreak" and contain the senders' real and tough feelings; the writers feel inadequate, are suicidal, abused, betrayed, or cheated upon, or are choosing to stay single. The emotions in the letters acknowledge that heartbreak is painful, devastating, and above all, universal. Each author, having chosen a letter that spoke to them, shares their experience, writing their answers in a way that lets readers know there are others who understand, have felt the same things, and have been able to move on. A list of hotlines is included.

Keywords: Abuse • Relationships • Suicide

Jensen, Kelly, ed.

🎖 *(Don't) Call Me Crazy: 33 Voices Start the Conversation about Mental Health.* 2018. 331p. **H**

Acknowledging that discussing mental illness is the best possible way to help remove any stigma about it, the authors of these essays address the ways in which mental illness, in varying shapes and forms, has had an effect on their lives. The contributors are an eclectic group that includes a wide variety of recognizable names, including well-known young adult authors and artists from a number of fields. They discuss the possible definitions of "crazy" and how mental illness is viewed and portrayed in society. The essays also take readers on a journey with depression, anxiety, and specific forms of identifiable disorders and behaviors, showing them that these are not shameful and definitely not something to be hidden. A list of resources is provided for more information about mental health issues. This title was chosen as the Young Adult winner of the Schneider Family Book Award.

Keywords: Anxiety • Depression • Mental illness

Career Directions

Career planning continues to become more complex, as it is more likely for people to work more than one job during their professional lifetime; in many states a first job can legally be obtained by the age of 14. This section contains titles about many different types of careers and the education levels they require. Unlike some previous guides, many of these books speak about transferrable skills and encourage teens to think about nontraditional careers. These books introduce the jobs in very practical ways, with information about the educational requirements, potential salary, and prospects; the jobs that are considered and the subject matter make them an appealing option for readers.

Bondy, Halley.

Don't Sit on the Baby! The Ultimate Guide to Sane, Skilled, and Safe Babysitting. 2012. 128p. **M** **J**

This slim volume is an exceptionally practical and thorough guide. It can help prepare anyone considering taking a babysitting job and serve as a step-by-step guide for situations that can arise before, during, and after sitting. The author starts by providing a very handy quiz to determine the kind of sitter the reader is before offering some useful tips before the first job—notably to take advantage of one's siblings for practice. Advice and explanations are offered for feeding, changing, bathing, playing, supervising, and, if need be, disciplining the children. All of these examples offer variations for differing ages, including babies, toddlers, preschoolers, and kids ages five and up. Difficult situations and communicating with parents are also fully covered, including sections on medical emergencies and expectations for the job. The book also offers advice on how to discuss ending a working relationship. This is a useful guide to a profitable and practical life experience for any teenager.

Keywords: Babysitting • Careers

Cool Careers without College.

This series was developed to acknowledge that the increasing costs of a college education leave many students thinking about alternatives to dealing with hefty student loans. Each book focuses on a different industry, starting with a short introduction that lists the reasons for considering jobs in that industry without postsecondary education. Each career choice is presented with a breakdown of what the job entails, what a prospective employee would need to know, and pay and prospects for the field. Further information for each industry includes a list of organizations that offer training and books and blogs with information about the field. The publisher also keeps a Web site to update Internet links, acknowledging that these can be changed. There are e-books available for all titles.

Powell, Asher. *Cool Careers without College for People Who Love Coding.* 2018. 112p. **H**

Beco, Alice. *Cool Careers without College for People Who Love Houses.* 2017. 112p. **H**

Pelos, Rebecca. *Cool Careers without College for People Who Love Planning and Organizing.* 2017. 112p. **H**

Klein, Rebecca T. *Cool Careers without College for People Who Love Reading and Research.* 2017. 112p. **H**

Pelos, Rebecca. *Cool Careers without College for People Who Love Shopping.* 2017. 112p. **H**

Hammelef, Danielle.

Behind-the-Scenes Pro Sports Careers. <u>Behind the Glamour.</u> 2017. 64p. **M**

Sports are a great draw, strong enough that athletes may aspire to a professional career from an early age, though even the most talented would likely agree about the precarious nature of this type of profession. Instead, this volume in the <u>Behind the Glamour</u> series introduces a number of jobs that allow their practitioners to work around sports, supporting players and informing viewers about the games that they love. From the trainers and nutritionists who keep players in shape to sportscasters and officials who deal with games as they happen to facility managers who deal with upkeep, readers will find a wide variety of options not only for the sports-minded individual, but also for those with transferrable skills that would be applicable beyond the athletic arena. Each career profile includes a summary, a list of suggestions for how to get started, preferred skills, base salary, and educational requirements.

Keywords: Career planning • Careers • Sports

Henneberg, Susan.

Behind-the-Scenes Fashion Careers. <u>Behind the Glamour.</u> 2017. 64p. **M**

Most people who aspire to careers in the fashion world are thinking of the designers who create couture and the models who wear them. There are very few of these auspicious positions given the size of the business, but that doesn't mean there aren't plenty of choices for people looking to work in the business. This book presents a number of jobs for people interested in fashion, as well as information on what the job entails, potential educational requirements, a salary range, and median salary. Examples of careers include a display designer for potential merchandisers, a makeup artist, and a fashion photographer. This book looks at careers outside the normal nine-to-five office job while pointing out that these jobs will require schooling and courses and have wide salary ranges. Teens are encouraged to start planning with summer programs and internships.

Keywords: Career planning • Careers • Fashion

Kravetz, Stacy.

She's So Boss: The Girl Entrepreneur's Guide to Imagining, Creating, and Kicking Ass. 2017. 160p. **H**

This is an introduction to entrepreneurship rooted in practical examples and written with an encouraging tone. Specific cases are used to illustrate how to define a startup or how to take advantage of social media for marketing. Kravetz points out the importance of not devaluing the ideas of others and lists a number of prominent women bosses and their projects for inspiration; she also includes their thoughts on fear, failure, and not trying. The appendix lists resources for starting a business and includes links to programs available in North America.

Keywords: Business • Entrepreneurship • Startups

Consider Starting with . . .

> Demetrios, Heather, ed. *Dear Heartbreak: YA Authors and Teens on the Dark Side of Love.*

> Jensen, Kelly, ed. *(Don't) Call Me Crazy: 33 Voices Start the Conversation About Mental Health.*

> Kay, Katty and Claire Shipman. *The Confidence Code for Girls: Taking Risks, Messing Up, and Becoming Your Amazingly Imperfect, Totally Powerful Self.*

Fiction Read-Alikes

- **Anderson, Laurie Halse.** *Speak.* With the Printz honor award novel available in a 20th anniversary edition or in an adapted version as a graphic novel, readers are able to share in a realistic and powerful portrayal of one girl dealing with the aftermath of her attack. While Melinda Sordino is ostracized by her classmates in her first year of high school, it is generally believed that she brought it on herself by calling in the cops to a party and getting several people arrested. Nobody is going to believe anything else, and she's certainly not saying differently. It isn't until much later that she is able to speak up for herself by telling what happened and why she did what she did.

- **Waller, Sharon Biggs.** *Girls on the Verge.* Seventeen-year-old Camille is horrified when she finds out she is pregnant from her first and only sexual encounter. Determined not to give up her future for a baby with a boy she never spoke to again, she decides to get an abortion, even though in her home state of Texas in 2014 there are only 19 abortion clinics. Two of her friends agree to help, one because she believes in the right to choose, and one just because she is Camille's friend. Camille's journey, in which she faces several people who feel they know what is best for her, presents a timely and realistic view of teenage pregnancy, women's rights, and the right to choose today.

- **Del Rosario, Juleah.** *500 Words or Less.* Del Rosario's timely verse novel is centered on seniors so obsessed with obtaining admission into their Ivy League college of choice they are willing to pay Nic Chen to write their admission papers, even though she is either ostracized or denigrated by the members of her class as the girl who cheats. Nic, taking money from each classmate, feels increasingly guilty with each additional paper. She also reflects on her own mistake with the boy she loves. This slightly maudlin subplot with Nic, her ex-boyfriend, and their best friend looks at the difference between genders in dealing with relationships. Nic's essays, meaningful through the conviction of her delivery, provide a look at several of her classmates and the way they deal with issues relatable to teenagers today.

- **Giles, Lamar, ed.** *Fresh Ink: An Anthology.* The stories in this anthology are meant to provide readers windows and doorways into the lives of contemporary teens. Written by some of YA's best-known authors and produced in partnership with We Need Diverse Books™, readers will find protagonists dealing with issues of race, gender, and urban life, such as immigration status and police shootings. Also featured is "Catch, Pull, Drive," an essay from Schuyler Bailar, the first out transgender swimmer in NCAA's Division I.

- **Lyttle, Alex.** *From Ant to Eagle.* While Cal hasn't always had the smoothest relationship with his brother, he is fairly confident that it is an older brother's job to come up with ways to test a younger brother, if only to keep him busy. In his case, he comes up with tasks that he calls missions. When Sammy finishes a mission, he moves up a level from Ant, where he started, on his way to Eagle, where Cal is. Cal succeeds in keeping Sammy busy but doesn't anticipate the plan's adverse effects, like Sammy trying to get the 100 baskets needed for the Badger level managing to overtax himself on the first day of school and landing in the hospital. They are both very familiar with the hospital, as Sammy has acute myeloid leukemia (AML), a virulent form of leukemia, which has already spread to his brain. Cal's relationship with the other patients on Sammy's ward is meaningful and touching, as Cal deals with the progression of Sammy's illness and his own feelings about it.

- **Stone, Nic.** *Odd One Out.* Courtney Cooper and Jupiter Sanchez have been best friends forever, with straight-cis Courtney longing for Jupe and gay Jupe oblivious. Their relationship changes when a new girl, Rae Chen, appears in school, and they end up becoming somewhat of a threesome, especially when Jupe develops feelings for Rae, and Rae may have feelings for Jupe. Or Coop. Or both of them? Relationships can be very difficult when you're trying to figure out who you are, who you care for, and what it means to care for someone. This is a complex, funny and poignant look at friendships, gender, and sexuality.

References

Csikszentmihaly, Mihalyi. "Adolescence," *Encyclopaedia Britannica*, accessed July 9, 2019, https://www.britannica.com/science/adolescence.

"Teen Health," Caring for Kids Web site, Canadian Paediatric Society, accessed July 9, 2019, https://www.caringforkids.cps.ca/handouts/teenhealth-index.

Chapter 9

How To

Definition

Merriam-Webster defines "do-it-yourself" as the act of making something on one's own initiative, without help or professional assistance, dating the first recorded usage to 1952.[1] Do-it-yourself (DIY) continues to be a mainstay of popular culture, with blogs, Web sites, magazines, reality shows, and cable networks devoted to homes, gardens, fashion, food, cooking, style, technology, and other areas where people can learn how to create or remake something with little or no outside help.

Appeal

Books in this chapter provide more than a learning opportunity. Making and finishing any creative project is enormously satisfying, far beyond any tangible result. Handicrafts make great gifts, and the mastery of any skill can have applicable benefits in other areas and will long outlast the item produced.

The appeal of the books in this area is broad and far reaching from age to gender to skill. The particular attraction of this genre for reluctant readers is shown by their frequent selection for YALSA's Quick Picks for Reluctant Readers list.

Chapter Organization

This chapter is organized into sections by activity. Readers not looking for a specific kind of activity will find a variety under "General Crafts." Following that are sections that look at specific topics. Readers wanting a makeover will enjoy the "Beauty and Style" section. Titles for those interested in artistic pursuits follow in "Art and Design" and "Drawing." Readers looking for more active hobbies will find titles in "Cooking," "Technology," and "Survival Skills."

General Crafts

The books in this section frequently contain more than one kind of craft, with the title having an overarching theme. Crafters may choose to try something because of the material they will be working with, as with the environmentally themed *Craft-a-Day Book*, which uses recycled materials, or they may be more interested in the method or the finished product, as with Jamie Harrington's *The Unofficial Guide to Crafting the World of Harry Potter*.

Cornell, Kari.

The Craft-a-Day Book: 30 Projects to Make with Recycled Materials. 2018. 168p. 🄷

Cornell presents 10 unassuming and unusual projects, aimed at crafters with an eye for refurbishing and reusing materials. Each project is assigned a difficulty level of easy, intermediate, or advanced. Appropriate for many of her techniques, the accompanying designs have a somewhat folksy feeling, as illustrated by the mood-setting lights, striped beanie, or sockadelic mitts. The projects include sewing, felting, and the use of tools that may be unfamiliar to first-time crafters, such as the drill, pom-pom maker, and paper punch. Cornell starts each project by mentioning her inspiration before providing the necessary items and instructions. Photographs show her finished work and sidebars offer suggestions for embellishments, further creative tips, or guides for specific techniques necessary for the item. Readers looking to transform worn-out favorites or learn how to make new ones will find this an interesting option.

Keywords: Crafts • Recycled materials

Fields, Stella.

Lazy Crafternoon. 2016. 128p. 🄹 🄷

Stella Fields offers the concept of a "crafternoon," a gathering of interested crafters, preferably with snacks, in order to create projects. While this doesn't need to be a group event, she does note that it is a pleasure to have a number of people crafting together; in addition to having the benefit of company, it gives the opportunity to pool ideas and supplies. Suggestions in this book are divided into four sections. Supplies are explained as being available from local stores, with pictures and descriptions of the two most common. Two of the sections include projects that will likely provide greater appeal to crafters: the jewelry and wearable items in the accessories section, and the useful items in the school supplies section, where the added decorative touches may provide the possibility of greater use than either the home or party decorations. While the final section with ideas for get-togethers may serve as more of an inspiration than an actual menu, the pictures of all of the final crafts will provide any interested crafter with a wide variety of concepts for future undertakings.

Keywords: Crafts • Decoupage

Grandin, Temple.

Calling All Minds: How to Think and Create Like an Inventor. 2018. 240p. **M J**

This is a craft book that multitasks, as each project is accompanied by historical and scientific information about inventions as appropriate, whether sidebars for successful inventions or Grandin's reminiscences. The book's introduction informs readers that the author's lifelong tendency to take things apart and put them back together contributed to her inclination to make new ones. Here she is doing more than providing a simple craft book. In order to stir creativity, she gives students information and the basic principles about several subjects along with themed projects, all of which gives readers the opportunity to follow in her creative footsteps. Projects vary in complexity, occasionally within the same category, offering both a simple and a complex paper airplane in "Things That Fly." She does offer a word of warning for the projects that require power tools, which may be beyond the means and abilities of some readers; some projects also include suggestions for places where difficulties may arise.

Keywords: Crafts • Inventions

Harrington, Jamie.

The Unofficial Guide to Crafting the World of Harry Potter: 30 Magical Crafts for Witches and Wizards, from Pencil Wands to Tie-Dye T-Shirts. 2016. 292p. **M J**

Harry Potter has inspired a wide and devoted fandom, from the movie adaptations to the international theme parks, where one may be sorted into the most appropriate house. Knowing one's house preference means that the first craft in this guide for all Potterphiles, or "Potterheads," as they are called by Harrington, will at least make it easier to choose the colors to tie-dye a house shirt. The instructions for this craft, as with all the others in the book, start by stating what will be needed and provide color photos for the main steps. The text is straightforward and includes tips from the author, such as notes on how to contain mess. Her final words include a suggestion to wash a finished tie-dye shirt twice without other items in order to set the dye, as well as notes on how to personalize the project. She does indicate with any craft when help from another person or adult is advised. The crafts are fairly sparkly and decorative, with even the Nimbus Two Thousand, Dementor, and Slytherin items being transformed into, respectively, a hairpin, soap, and a photo frame. Fans interested in the series will find several things to wear, take to school, or decorate their rooms. Harrington also suggests quite rightly that a number of them would make great gifts for like-minded friends.

Keywords: Crafts • Decorations • Harry Potter • Jewelry

Lam, Che.

Learn How to Knit with 50 Squares: For Beginners and Up; A Unique Approach to Learning to Knit. 2016. 144p. **J H A/YA**

Beginning knitters, enamored of the idea of producing a finished project, may undertake a project without a full understanding of just how complex it can be to turn a heel in a sock, reduce (or add) stitches correctly for sleeves, or sew all of the parts together. Putting all of these together into one learning experience can potentially be overwhelming. This book is a viable alternative, intended to help newcomers learn how to cast on and then start from the most basic stitches before progressing to more complicated stitches one at a time. Projects are then added to allow knitters, once comfortable with their needles, to start practicing their newfound skills. Preparatory information about tools and materials is found at the beginning, along with information about how to read patterns, hold the yarn and needles, and obtain a proper gauge.

Keywords: Knitting • Techniques

Mollie Makes Papercraft: From Origami to Greeting Cards and Gift Wrap; 20 Paper Projects for You to Make. 2017. 160p. **H**

This craft book presents a number of projects that capitalize on paper's unique properties. As such, while they can be time-intensive and fairly detailed, and require an amount of care, they use inexpensive materials and provide unique finished designs worth serving as ornamentation for a room or as a gift. Ranging from napkin rings and garlands to scrapbook pictures, shadow boxes, and paper cuts, the projects utilize a wide variety of techniques. Each is laid out with an explanation, the needed materials, tools, techniques, and finished size before a step-by-step methodology accompanied by photographs. The final third of the book is devoted to explaining the various techniques used in the projects. Readers interested in creating anything from this book will find this section to be a great introduction not only to the tools and materials used in papercraft, but to the techniques used. Sections are included for embellishment techniques, origami, quilling, papier mâché, and scrapbooking.

Keywords: Crafts • Origami • Papercrafts

Beauty and Style

It is a generally acknowledged fact that the average female is likely to suffer from low self-esteem. Guidance from professionals about the makeup and hairstyle that will best suit a particular person will be gratefully received. That sort of advice, along with how to create a canvas for the makeup and what kind of clothing will best suit each body type, is found in the two subcategories, "Beauty" and "Style."

Beauty

Books in this section offer advice and treatments for how to make oneself look better. Fashion and makeup guides for teenagers are colorful and direct, and provide straightforward instructions that allow at-home treatments, styling, and makeovers that cost less than salon treatments, with the added luxury of allowing for practice time and multiple options.

Andrus, Aubre.

Botanical Beauty: 80 Essential Recipes for Natural Spa Products. 2017. 160p. **H**

Aubre Andrus, former lifestyle editor for *American Girl* magazine, presents recipes for a wide variety of treatments, offering them as a simple and appealing alternative to chemical-laden and expensive store-bought products, either for gifts or an at-home spa experience. Andrus begins with comprehensive advice to prepare readers to handle any of the included recipes, such as where to find packaging and ingredients they are not likely to have in their pantry. An explanation is offered for the inclusion of specialty ingredients and the benefits that may be derived from each, followed by tips for how to safely use, store, and clean up after the most unfamiliar and hardest to use. A further note about allergies should quell any potential fears. The recipes are divided into sections that cover the parts of the body, with products intended for hands and feet separated from those for the face, body, and hair. Each recipe gives directions, ingredients, and steps for preparation, packaging, and an approximate shelf life, along with several photographs that show the finished product in a manner sure to appeal.

Keywords: Bath products • Grooming • Hair care • Skin care • Spa products

Butcher, Christina.

Braids, Buns and Twists! Step-by-Step Tutorials for 82 Fabulous Hairstyles. 2013. 160p. **M** **J**

This is an ideal book for people with either medium or long hair who are looking for new ways to wear their hair. They will find a wide variety of hairstyles, from simple variations on the ponytail to increasingly complicated styles—such as a heart-shaped angel braid that would initially need assistance to be done correctly. The illustrated instructions for each style are assigned a difficulty level and come with suggestions for optimal hair length, any implements that would be needed, and tips. Anyone looking for a change after a long time with the same hairstyle or a way to modify their look while growing out a cut will appreciate the possible choices offered here. **QP**

Keywords: Braids • Buns • Grooming • Hairstyles • Ponytails

Carmindy.

 Bloom: A Girl's Guide to Growing Up Gorgeous. 2014. 160p. **M J**

The makeup artist from TLC's *What Not to Wear* applies her knowledge to teenage skin and sensibilities, from how to develop a great canvas by keeping good skin care practices to choosing the right kind of makeup to show off each feature rather than hiding perceived flaws. Carmindy also provides advice for issues that might be seen as obstacles, such as acne or glasses, and gives application tips and styles for special occasions such as the first day of school or an interview. **QP**

Keywords: Makeup • Skin care

Harris, Samantha.

Curls, Curls, Curls: Your Go-To Guide for Rocking Curly Hair—Plus Tutorials for 60 Fabulous Looks. 2016. 192p. **M J A/YA**

This is a book that any girl with curly hair will appreciate, as it goes far beyond the 60 hairstyles provided. The hairstyles alone are enough to make this an appealing guide for any girl wondering what to do with curly hair, which can be difficult to tame. Instead, Harris starts by identifying the different types of curls and offering quick tips for how best to handle them. She also presents a thorough discussion of hair care, treatments, and an assortment of products including shampoos, conditioners, oils, and tools for styling and accessorizing. Once these have been covered, Harris introduces how to care for your hair, including a washing and drying routine, hair treatments, and recommendations for maintaining curls between washings, segueing into the styles. These are divided into ponytails, buns and knots, and braids and twists. Each style starts by indicating the length of hair for which it is best suited, any suggested accessories, the difficulty level, whether assistance will be needed, a description including similar styles from the book, and pictures with several examples, each of which shows the style with different types of curl. The "How to Do It" feature provides both a numerical checklist and accompanying illustrations. Each is followed by a tip meant to embellish or improve the style. As the products and treatments are natural and include recommendations for things to avoid, rather than specific brands, this is a title that is not keyed to market trends.

Keywords: Hairstyles • Techniques

Rodgers, Catherine.

 DIY Nail Art: Easy, Step-by-Step Instructions for 75 Creative Nail Art Designs. 2013. 160p. **M J**

While having nice-looking nails is the best part of any manicure, that shouldn't stop anyone from having pretty hands all the time. That is the thought behind this book, written by the creator of the YouTube channel Totally Cool Nails. Her designs are presented with large, full-color close-ups of a hand with the finished design, and then with step-by-step pictures, also with a picture of real nails. All of the pictures are of the same left hand, likely to demonstrate that these designs are possible to do on oneself. She explains in an introduction that, along with a suggested preparation and finish, including a quality base and topcoat, some tools will be required for these designs. She explains what they are and suggests purchasing them from Amazon .com or at a beauty supply store. **QP**

Keywords: Beauty • Manicures

Rissman, Rebecca.

DIY Fearless Fashion.

The titles in this series give readers step-by-step directions, accompanied by numerous photographs, for a plethora of styles that run the gamut from fun to funky, with wild and crazy designs added in where appropriate. Each volume begins with general tips and preparations, including a list of supplies to have on hand. The instructions for the designs specify what will be needed, lay out the steps, and provide several colorful and enticing pictures that show exactly what the finished style will look like. Style tips are also provided to help the reader avoid any possible missteps and ensure a smooth finish. With these entertaining titles, fashionistas looking for a change will find a number of options to try something new without breaking the bank.

> *Fierce Fashions: Accessories and Styles That Pop.* 2018. 48p. **J** **H**
>
> *Freaky Nail Art with Attitude.* 2018. 48p. **J** **H**
>
> *Hair-Raising Hairstyles That Make a Statement.* 2018. 48p. **J** **H**
>
> *Makeup Magic with Glam and Gore Beauty.* 2018. 48p. **J** **H**

Strebe, Jenny.

100 Perfect Hair Days: Step-by-Steps for Pretty Waves, Braids, Curls, Buns, and More! 2016. 192p. **M** **J**

An expert stylist shows how to tame long locks into the smoothest of looks, with step-by-step illustrated instructions for 100 hairstyles. She also notes which type of hair—curly, wavy, straight, thick, or fine—will best suit the hairdo in question, whether a ponytail, braid, or bun. A supplementary chapter offers information about hair care, products, and tools to help transform your mane into your shining glory.

Keywords: Hair care • Hairdos • Hairstyles

Style

The titles here show readers how to put together a wardrobe and accessories to create a great look for any body type. Books are included that show how to remake clothes and introduce sewing techniques and projects geared to introduce new items into a wardrobe.

Dadon, Jess, and Stef Dadon.

#howtwolive: 36 Seriously Cool How-To Projects on Style, Nail Art, Blogging, and More. 2016. 128p. **M J**

Sisters, bloggers, and BFFs Jess and Stef Dadon translate the style and ideas from their Instagram account into a series of projects. The projects are intended to be fun while offering crafters a new accessory, a wardrobe tip, a recipe, or a new skill. Each project includes the necessary items, lays out the required steps, and offers additional tips to add even more to the final version. This is a fun book, with unusual suggestions unlikely to be found in other books, such as ways to wear prints, a list of magical food combos, and how to get a celeb to notice you on social media.

Keywords: Crafts • Fashion • Projects

The Fashion Book: Create Your Own Cool Looks from the Story of Style. 2014. 160p. **M J**

This thorough, fun, and highly illustrated retrospective on the history of fashion starts with a look at the most beautiful costumes of the ancients and works through all historical periods, providing information about what was worn by the stylish, and how each look can be replicated. Fashionistas will learn that despite all the changes from outer skirts and powdered wigs, some things have remained staples in wardrobes for centuries, like girdles and leather. Full-page spreads showing how these have been adapted are fun and fascinating, as are the introductions to fashion icons from Audrey Hepburn to Kate Moss. Resources include a glossary of terms and a directory of the designers who have influenced current fashions.

Keywords: Clothing • Fashion

Now Try: There is no denying that throughout history people in the public eye have a direct impact on other people. Whether because of their position in society, their talent, or their perceived power, the influence of many of these people on the world around them is reflected in their personal style. In *Bad Girls of Fashion: Style Rebels from Cleopatra to Lady Gaga*, Jennifer Croll presents a detailed biography of fashion icons, what makes them unique, how their styles were received at the time, and the influence they had. Examples of powerful and fashion-forward ladies and their daring changes include Marie Antoinette's riding costumes, chosen for comfort over fashion, and Coco Chanel's designs, which were developed using the clean and simple lines of men's clothing that were her preference. Readers will find that the inspiration of these icons, as well as other well-known people profiled in sidebars, has been profound and long reaching, making this a fun and interesting title. In a second book, *Bad Boys of Fashion: Style Rebels and Renegades Through the Ages*, Croll looks into the closets of some of the many men who have stood out from the pack and their own fashion trademarks, from Nelson Mandela's Madiba shirts to the Mao suit and Kurt Cobain's grunge fashions.

How to Sew: With Over 80 Techniques and 20 Easy Projects. 2018. 160p. **H**

This may be considered *Mollie Makes* magazine's introduction to hand and machine sewing. To provide a thorough overview of the craft, the book is divided into two parts. The first half of the book is composed of 20 projects. Each one starts with a short introduction to the finished project, which notes its potential use, and whether it is particularly appropriate for a beginner. This is followed by the needed materials, finished size, techniques that will be used, and things to know before beginning, such as where to acquire materials. The method for each project is laid out in steps, with any required templates included as photocopiable reproductions at the rear of the book. Steps that are not easily explained are illustrated with photographs, as are finished projects. The second half of the book contains a course for novices in sewing techniques. Readers will find information on every basic they need to create a garment, including sewing equipment, hand and machine stitches, seams and hems, buttons and zips, and trims and bindings. This is an all-purpose and practical guide that also provides fun and useful projects for practice.

Keywords: Sewing

McGraw, Sally.

Find Your Style: Boost Your Body Image through Fashion Confidence. 2017. 88p. **M J**

This is a readable introduction to how to build and use a wardrobe to help inspire confidence, or, as stated more succinctly, one that shows that clothes can be used as tools. In six chapters girls are shown why the media gives inappropriate and potentially damaging messages about body shapes, how to figure out their body type, and how to assemble an outfit and where to shop for it. The book includes a final discussion on why developing their own sense of style matters.

Keywords: Clothes • Clothing • Fashion

Moses, Susan.

The Art of Dressing Curves: The Best-Kept Secrets of a Fashion Stylist. 2016. 88p. **H AYA**

While it is a known fact that a majority of the North American population is considered plus-sized, celebrity fashion stylist Susan Moses points out in her introduction that whatever a woman's size, the most important thing is for her to know and be comfortable with her shape, and to find the clothes that will best accentuate it. She then presents readers with a thorough introduction to determining their own body type, and discusses the types of clothing that will best feature each type, starting with shapewear and finishing with accessories. Readers will want to have a cloth measuring tape ready, and will find this a comforting, validating guide to building and maintaining a wardrobe that will fit, flatter, and present a wide variety of looks. This is a highly illustrated book that includes annotated lists of retailers and bloggers.

Keywords: Clothes • Clothing • Fashion • Style

Myer, Sarah.

Create a Costume! **Maker Comics**. 2019. 128p. **M J**

This volume in the **Maker Comics** graphic series finds friends Bea and Parker, having decided to go to Comic Con, debating what costumes to wear. They come up with several different ideas, including sailors, a witch and wizard, animal mascots, and space heroes. The various permutations allow them to find items in their closet that can be repurposed. The characters demonstrate how to cut, sew, use tools correctly, and look for and add accents, all while saving money by reusing materials. Steps are illustrated carefully, while the text reiterates the safest way to perform each task and provides possible embellishments. This title would also double as an acceptable introductory guide to sewing, with introductions to the sewing machine, and tasks such as adding a collar, hand sewing, and papier mâché.

Keywords: Costumes • Sewing

Rissman, Rebecca.

Fashion Hacks: Your Fashion Failures Solved! **Beauty Hacks**. 2016. 48p. **M**

Using ingredients and tools found without a trip to a specialty store, Rissman provides ways to deal with everyday issues and misfortunes that can seem like a tragedy at the time. Whether it's a method for dealing with that brand-new perfect pair of shoes that turns out to be just a bit too small or providing ways to give old clothes a new life, the simple and practical solutions here can help readers save money and time, and keep their wardrobe up-to-date and full of their favorite items. When tips for purchasing, patching, cleaning, and restoring in order to make the wearer feel confident and comfortable aren't enough, the author also includes suggestions for downsizing or donating.

Keywords: Accessories • Clothing

Art and Design

Readers who enjoy advertising or appreciate any good layout will be able to understand why after reading this clever book. Readers who enjoy this title may also enjoy the titles about art appreciation in the "Art and Artists" category of chapter 10.

Kidd, Chip.

🎗 *Go! A Kidd's Guide to Graphic Design.* 2014. 160p. **M** **J**

Well-known graphic designer Chip Kidd explains the elements of design, including form, line, color, scale, and typography, adding examples from his body of work, such as movie posters or book covers. This is a fully illustrated and captivating title that culminates with 10 projects to encourage readers to both have fun and make use of their new knowledge while serving as an introductory course to graphic design. **AENYA**

Keywords: Graphic design

Drawing

Drawing remains a popular and high-circulating subject. In addition to titles that help develop artistic techniques, books that show how to draw particular genres and character types have become increasingly prevalent. Given that the step-by-step nature of the instructions may make the books look more like workbooks, they are likely to be written in and paperbacks may wear out in library collections. This category includes titles in both a general "Techniques" section and more specific offerings for "Manga and Anime."

Techniques

Crilley, Mark.

The Drawing Lesson: A Graphic Novel that Teaches You How to Draw. 2016. 144p. **M** **J**

When a boy named David is denied the chance to buy a secondhand art book, he decides the artist sketching in the park will be a suitable alternative source for a drawing lesson. The artist, Becky, agrees and starts with a basic tutorial, teaching David to draw what he sees. The book's graphic format allows readers to follow along with David's tutorials. Lessons progress through more complicated techniques, including shading, light and shadow, negative space, proportions, and creating a composition. The story provides humor in Becky and David's interactions and crafts a relationship between the two of them that helps carry the reader through the book. Projects are suggested for readers as they reach each new skill.

Keywords: Art • Drawing • Techniques

1

2

3

4

5

6

7

8

9

10

11

Hart, Christopher.

Drawing Superheroes Step by Step: The Complete Guide for the Aspiring Comic Book Artist. Drawing with Christopher Hart. 2016. 144p. **M** **J**

Knowing that most comics have heroes and foils, Hart starts this guide to drawing with the most basic and important part of the superhero's body: his head, along with an appropriate steely gaze. From there, the aspiring artist will be shown a heroine's head and how to fill in features before moving down the body, and will then learn how to move and position the figure. Only then will supporting characters and tools be added as options. Once the basics have been covered, all of the characters can then be added into frames. A splash page is used for effect, and thumbnails can be used to create storyboards for the whole story. Even placement of speech bubbles is covered after all of the characters have been placed, which is discussed in a section on settings. This is a tool for anyone interested in learning how to create a comic from scratch or looking for more information about any part of the graphical process.

Keywords: Art • Comics • Drawing • Superheroes • Techniques

Locke, Christopher.

Draw Like This! How Anyone Can See the World Like an Artist—and Capture It on Paper. 2016. 192p. **M** **J**

This is a drawing book for people who are interested in learning about elements of design, starting from the absolute basics of ink blots, sketching, and doodles. This fun and interactive book succeeds as an instructional tool by explaining concepts such as perspective and then demonstrating them with easily understandable examples, giving an example for practice to make sure the lesson has been understood. While this is an amusing book that is appropriate for any student looking for help in becoming a more competent artist, it may not last long in a library collection, as each of the concepts is summarized by an enticing write-in exercise.

Keywords: Art • Drawing • Techniques

Jennings, Simon.

The Complete Artist's Manual: The Definitive Guide to Painting and Drawing. 2014. 395p. **H** **A/YA**

This is a fascinating encyclopedic compendium for anyone interested in painting. Not written for the casual reader or someone looking for basic information, this is a volume for someone interested in art who wants to become proficient with painting. Detailed breakdowns and instructions are included in almost every area, including the drawing surface and how to best prepare it, drawing and painting media, a painting course, color and composition, painting techniques, suggestions for choosing subjects, and suggestions for the space in which the reader will be painting.

Keywords: Art • Drawing • Painting

Sautter, Aaron.

How to Draw Batman and His Friends and Foes. 2015. 32p. **M**

Taken as more of an inspirational guide for people interested in drawing superheroes than an instructional text for novices, this guide works well. An introductory page suggests gathering paper, pencils, a dark marker to go over lines of a finished drawing, and abundant erasers for all projects until that point. The rest of the book comprises 12 different projects. Each drawing is set out in four steps, which progress too quickly for beginners to follow easily but which are accompanied by information about the subject that readers will enjoy. Ideas for how to embellish the sketch add additional possibilities.

Keywords: Comics • Drawing • Superheroes

Manga and Anime

Manga and anime are types of Japanese illustration. The books in this category are intended specifically to help readers learn how to draw them.

Hart, Christopher.

Anatomy 101. **Christopher Hart's Draw Manga Now**! 2013. 144p. **M** **J**

Why an anatomy book specifically for manga? This book, divided into the parts of the body starting with the head, makes it amply clear: the eyes of a manga character are much larger than in a typical illustration and placed lower on the face. Hart indicates proper placement of the much smaller mouth toward the pointed chin, given that both male and female characters have almost no nose. From a detailed skeleton, each part of the body is broken down into easy-to-follow steps that will allow readers to practice and build skills in drawing characters, with several different examples given. One potential downside is the possibility of students and readers using the pages of the books for practice.

Keywords: Anatomy • Drawing • Manga • Techniques

Hart, Christopher.

The Master Guide to Drawing Anime: How to Draw Original Characters from Simple Templates. **Master Guide to Drawing Anime**. 2015. 144p. **H**

This volume in Christopher Hart's **Master Guide to Drawing Anime** series is intended as a guide to drawing anime's most popular character types:

schoolgirls, schoolboys, preteens, vengeful bad guys, humorous personalities, and fantasy figures. Wanting the artist able to draw their own original characters, Hart provides direction in these categories, starting with proportions and templates for drawing a schoolgirl's head and adding templates for eye color before adding in proportions for the body and offering suggestions for outfits. Finally, Hart shows options for several conditions and scenarios, such as silliness or gossiping girls. These are repeated as appropriate for the other character types, with accessories added in as options for the fantasy characters. Hart adds notes for key character traits and lines to watch when starting drawings.

Keywords: Anime • Characters • Drawing

Hart, Christopher.

Top Ten Essentials. **Christopher Hart's Draw Manga Now!** 2013. 144p. **M** **J**

This is a condensed guide to what Christopher Hart describes as the fundamental elements of manga. They are presented in turn, starting with the foundation of all manga characters: the eyes, including several examples with differing expressions. After this, student artists build through other manga essentials before being given illustrated steps in how to draw several archetypal manga characters. A final section allows students to practice their drawing; for books included in libraries, a link connects to extended e-book content to allow for repeated practice and extend the life of library copies.

Keywords: Art • Drawing • Manga • Techniques

Li, Yishan.

How to Draw: Manga in Simple Steps. 2017. 144p. **H** **A/YA**

This book from the In Simple Steps series shows readers how to draw manga by following a series of illustrations. Each character is developed from lines to geometric shapes, then a basic outline and further shape and color are added. This simple process is the brainchild of professional comic artist Yishan Li. The five books include a wide variety of character types, including: boys, girls, myths and legends, chibis, and animals.

Keywords: Art • Drawing • Manga

Cooking

Cooking is an activity that interests many teens. While it becomes a necessity for some as they gain independence, for others it is an acquired skill or something that has gained more prevalence on television. Cookbooks from Food Network chefs Emily and Lyla Allen and Eliana de Las Casas provide inspiration for any reader interested in getting into the kitchen. The popularity of this subgenre is attested to by the ongoing publication in this area, which continues to include a wide range of cuisines and updated editions.

Adams Media

The Quick and Easy College Cookbook: 300 Healthy, Low-Cost Meals that Fit Your Budget and Schedule. **2016. 304p. H**

This is a practical, thorough introductory cookbook that provides a plethora of recipes for each meal. It includes sandwiches, salads, soups, and pasta and rice dishes, and breaks down main courses into chapters for different proteins and vegetarian/vegan entrees. A primer for students thinking about stocking their dorm room kitchen covers many topics: the necessary (or just nice) appliances, cooking tips, meal planning, pantry staples, time-saving suggestions, shopping tips, and the dreaded freshman 15. This serves as a quick and basic introduction for novice chefs, who will also find metric conversion tables and a glossary of cooking terms.

Keywords: Cooking • Recipes

Allen, Emily, and Lyla Allen.

The Teen Kitchen: Recipes We Love to Cook. **2019. 192p. M J**

Having started their *Kitchen Twins* blog at the age of nine, high schoolers Emily and Lyla Allen attained a wider audience through appearances on the Food Network. This is a very appealing cookbook, with recipes that take advantage of the twins' experience gained from working with professional chefs. In addition to the tips offered with the individual dishes, including suggestions for alternate ingredients or techniques, the directions include serving and storage, with notes on how long any leftovers will last. As the sisters are vegetarians, information is included on food swaps, making the recipes useful for interested cooks with many dietary needs. Integrated into the book are full-page color photographs and fun articles about creating new recipes, taking pictures of food, and suggestions for ways to share food with friends.

Keywords: Cooking • Recipes

The Complete Cookbook for Young Chefs: 100+ Recipes that You'll Love to Cook and Eat! **2018. 208p. M J**

What sets this cookbook apart is that, in addition to its recipes, it is the closest thing to a primer for readers interested in learning how to use implements and ingredients. The beginning of the book provides a glossary of cooking terms, along with what is essentially a picture dictionary of tools and a guide to the instructions and symbols used in the rest of the book. The recipes are divided into sections common to most cookbooks, beginning with breakfast and following through to dessert, with additional sections that provide dishes to feed the family, snacks, and some simple choices for a solo meal. Each recipe includes the needed ingredients and tools along with the steps and features a sidebar with options for how to adapt it. It is the instructions that make this book stand out: photographs that accompany the text explain why steps are necessary and how to do them. Readers will turn into cooks able to deal competently with ingredients as varied as fish, quinoa, and nuts, with techniques including shredding, roasting, and toasting.

Keywords: Cooking • Recipes • Techniques

Capps, Tyler.

 Cooking Comically: Recipes So Easy You'll Actually Make Them. 2013. 86p. **H** **A/YA**

Novice chefs looking for guidance will appreciate Capps's offerings, which are laid out with pictures of the ingredients, each step in the process, and an occasional pithy aside. Humorous twists are added throughout the book, down to the graph indicating the recipe's level of difficulty. Originally published on his Web site, CookingComically.com, the book is divided into sections for each meal, as well as appetizers and sides. The recipes are presented with a combination of photographs and accompanying lettering, setting out the steps in comic format. An illustrated figure provides a somewhat snarky narration. A full shopping list for each dish is provided, along with some notes from the author about his preferences that also include suggestions for adaptations. **QP**

Keywords: Cooking • Recipes

de Las Casas, Eliana.

Teen Chef Cooks: 80 Scrumptious, Family-Friendly Recipes. 2019. 160p. **J** **H**

The most recent cookbook from de Las Casas, a *Chopped Teen* Grand Champion, is guaranteed to provide readers looking to move on to more inspired dishes with plenty of options. Eighty recipes are laid out by seasons in order to have the best chance of finding the highlighted ingredients locally. A list of in-season produce is featured at the front of the book. While there are no metric measurements or equivalents given, the recipes, each of which is accompanied by a note from the chef along with clear instructions and an indication of size, prep and cooking time, will have something to offer every palate. The full-page photographs provide a visual vindication of the meals' allure.

Keywords: Cooking • Recipes

Deering, Alison.

Sandwiches! More than You've Ever Wanted to Know about Making and Eating America's Favorite Food. 2017. 144p. **M**

This fun guide provides hungry eaters with everything they want to know about what and how to assemble things to eat. In five sections, they will find more than 50 choices, from a PB and J to wraps to successively more complicated choices, with each section requiring more ingredients, tools, and a longer preparation time.

There is information provided with each recipe, like a timeline showing the history of the grilled cheese or facts about breakfast sandwiches. This is a fun, highly illustrated introductory cookbook for novice chefs.

Keywords: Cooking • Sandwiches • Techniques

Goodman, Clio, with Adeena Sussman.

Puddin': Luscious and Unforgettable Puddings, Parfaits, Cakes, Pudding Cakes, Pies, and Pops. 2013. 160p. **H** **A/YA**

This is an homage to the creamy, rich goodness at the heart of a pudding. The recipes presented by Clio Goodman, the chef-owner of New York City's Puddin' eatery, are presented in a straightforward manner; they don't include photographs or metric measurements as aids, relying instead on their descriptions to act as a lure. This is more than likely to work, as both the introductory and more fanciful puddings are not only delicious but include suggestions for pairings, toppings, and sauces, the recipes for which are also included in the book, and they themselves are also combined or incorporated to help create the parfaits, cakes, pies, and pops. This is a dessert book for a wide audience, as these are all gluten-free desserts, and Goodman does include suggestions for people looking for low-fat or vegan alternatives. The recipes for accompaniments are also offered up as cookies, bars, or possibilities for snacks on their own. Given that several of the pudding variations use a number of the same ingredients, this would be a good title to recommend to a reader looking for options to practice. Who doesn't like dessert?

Keywords: Cooking • Desserts • Pudding • Techniques

Kelley, Amber.

Cook with Amber: Fun, Fresh Recipes to Get You in the Kitchen. 2018. 208p. **M** **J**

Kelley, best known for being chosen as the winner of the Food Network's *Star Kids*, presents a cookbook that anyone responsible for coming up with their own meals will appreciate. The recipes, in addition to having been chosen because of their proven appeal, have several categories that are geared toward inclusion in lunches. A section on dinner dishes that can be turned into lunches is followed by dinners that will provide enough leftovers to be able to be packed up. Suitable snacks, breakfasts to start the day, and suggestions for meals to feed the family or cook for parties are also included. Kelley doesn't omit looking out for the cook, either; the book includes some homemade remedies for the hair and face. Beginners will find this a useful volume, as it starts with a glossary to explain some cooking terms they will likely come across in this and other cookbooks.

Keywords: Cooking • Recipes • Techniques

Kim, Heather.

 Sweet Revenge: Passive-Aggressive Desserts for Your Exes and Enemies. 2018. 208p. **H**

Heather Kim dishes up a wide variety of sweet treats, offering up ways to recover from heartbreak and anger: killing with kindness those who did you wrong or eating your feelings, to name two. Either way lets you cream, beat, and whip, with delicious-tasting results. Recipes are organized into five main sections and include cookies and cupcakes, bars and balls, breads and pastries, and a final section with candies, bars, and more. Each of the recipe sections is given a pithy title that plays on the relationship theme, such as "Nobody's Butter Cup" (pretzel peanut butter cups). The recipes' instructions include additional notes to guide novice chefs who may not be familiar with terms or might wonder why certain ingredients have been chosen. In the butter cup recipe Kim notes why semisweet chips should be used and explains what it means to pipe chocolate. A conversion tool is provided, as well as additional information about ingredients, tools, and techniques. Photographs and the author's commentary, which compares relationships to cooking, make for engaging filler. **QP**

Keywords: Cooking • Desserts • Recipes

Koch, Falynn.

Bake Like a Pro! <u>Maker Comics</u>. 2019. 128p. **M** **J**

Sage, a young wizard, is initially disappointed with the assignment for her apprenticeship, only to find out that the knowledge and methods that differentiate baking from cooking really are magical. After Sage fails an initial trial by using a spell to rectify a failed attempt at baking a pound cake, the baking master to whom she is assigned, along with all of the talking ingredients, give her lessons in the science behind making some delicious creations. As she is shown the various methods, she learns the effects they can have on ingredients. Readers are given a comprehensible explanation of gluten, as well as the effect of adding too much or too little flour or eggs to cookie batter. Integrated into the text and listed at the back are several recipes, including pound cake, pizza dough, and lemon meringue pie. Helpful tips and a conversion table are also included.

Keywords: Baking • Graphic nonfiction • Recipes

Raab, Evelyn.

Clueless in the Kitchen: Cooking for Beginners. 2017. 204p. **M** **J**

Evelyn Raab begins her latest introductory cookbook with a few short sections giving advice to people who have little to no experience in the kitchen. The first offers a few pieces of salient advice, from following the recipe exactly to not letting mistakes destroy the experience. This is followed by a guide for the necessary and nice-to-have cookware, utensils, spices, and staples. An explanation of where to store food, accompanied by food handling tips and basic strategies for navigating the average supermarket layout will help with budgeting and sanitation, all before the 11 sections of recipes covering appetizers to desserts. Most recipes include variations, and each section has a sidebar or additional information to inform the reader about how to embellish a recipe or help them with it—the proper way to cut up a chicken, for example.

Keywords: Cooking • Recipes

Smith, Remmi.

The Healthy Teen Cookbook: Around the World in 80 Fantastic Recipes. 2018. 180p. **M** **J**

Teen chef Remmi Smith, who at the age of 16 has already been a competitor on *Chopped*, introduces curious teen cooks to the tastes of 39 different countries in her third cookbook. Organized geographically rather than by meal type, each recipe is presented with ingredients, directions, the expected prep and cooking time, a color photograph of the finished dish, and a note from the author giving her impression of the dish, the ingredients, or the cooking technique. Smith includes quotations from well-known chefs and information about countries and continents, providing readers and aspiring chefs with additional information about both cooking and the countries that have provided and inspired the dishes. In order to make this book more appealing to novice chefs, recipes have had steps streamlined and the number of ingredients limited, and it is indicated if items need to be chopped, sliced, or diced, which helps in guiding preparation.

Keywords: Cooking • Recipes

The Really Hungry Vegetarian Student Cookbook: How to Eat Well on a Budget. 2018. 144p. **AYA**

Intended as a guide for students learning how to live on their own, this is a book that gives novice chefs the chance to add vegetarian dishes to their repertoire. An interesting Kitchen Know-How section provides information that will be a boon to beginning chefs, including essential equipment, ingredients, food and microwave safety, food tips, and nutritional information, as well as a section on vegetarian know-how. The recipes are broken into eight sections, beginning with breakfasts and lunches, moving through several versions of meals and appetizers, and finishing with desserts. Each recipe includes a list of ingredients with the measurements in metric and imperial before listing the clearly laid-out steps. There is a full-page photograph with each recipe, each of which also indicates the approximate serving size.

Keywords: Cooking • Recipes • Vegetarian cooking

Technology

Technology offers multiple opportunities for creative outlets. Books on this topic offer projects in a number of areas, often while developing skills that are desirable in the job market, as pointed out in Reshma Saujani's *Girls Who Code*.

Cope, Peter.

*The Smartphone Photography Guide: Shoot * Edit * Experiment * Share*. 2018. 266p. **H** **A/YA**

As Peter Cope acknowledges, the photo capabilities of the smartphone may not be on par with those of cameras, but improvements in the quality of these devices make it prudent to learn how best to utilize them. This guide will help people interested in taking advantage of the basic tools available on any device, starting with a section on how to best use a smartphone's camera to improve pictures, from resizing photos, to holding the camera steady, to how best to frame the picture's subject. This is followed by more in-depth lessons on how to use the camera's features, tools, and apps. The book also includes a series of suggestions for themed shots with examples demonstrating how they were created, such as high- and low-light shots and action shots.

Keywords: Photography • Smartphones

The Editors of Popular Science.

The Popular Science *Hacker's Manual*. 2019. 248p. **J** **H**

This guide, from the editors of *Popular Science* magazine, will either entice or scare off prospective tinkerers. It starts with projects that may be finished quickly, designed for novices using items they are likely to have on hand, and finishes with more ambitious projects that require specialty items and tools. The book also includes plans for some of the archival items featured from the magazine's history. A basic, illustrated guide to the techniques necessary for completing the projects is provided as part of the introduction. The book also covers creating a soldering kit and basic soldering, circuit components and building a component, choosing a microcontroller, programming an Arduino, and basic woodworking and metalworking tools and instructions for important things to do with them. Projects are divided into four categories: Geek Tools, Home Improvements, Gadget Upgrades, and Things that Go. Each category contains jobs at levels from beginner to expert. Every project is illustrated, with the necessary materials and steps clearly laid out. The addition of "YOU BUILT WHAT?!" sidebars detailing stories of amazing and outlandish creations from over the years has the potential to spur creativity in future endeavors.

Keywords: Electronics • Industrial arts • Woodworking

Saujani, Reshma.

Girls Who Code: Learn to Code and Save the World. 2017. 168p. **M J**

Realizing that the future of the job market is in technology, and shocked at a dearth of girls in computer classes, Reshma Saujani founded the nonprofit organization Girls Who Code as a means of closing the gender gap in technology. An introduction demonstrates that the future is in computer science by showing what coding involves and delving into its history, which not only includes a surprising number of women but also demonstrates how exponentially knowledge and equipment have improved in a short period of time. Each step in developing a program is outlined from start to finish, including the tools for coding, coming up with an idea, choosing the appropriate language to use, and following through in order to ensure a finished item that will fill a need. A section about debugging reassures all future and novice coders that mistakes do happen. This is followed by sections for a number of areas in which codes are found, including video games, art and design, robots, Web sites, mobile apps, and security. Each includes a sample project from Girls Who Code, with explanations from the project designers about how and why they created it. A thorough glossary concludes the book, and readers interested in learning more or starting their own projects will find further resources on the project's Web site.

Keywords: Coding • Computer programming • Computer technology • Gaming

Survival Skills

Because it is undeniable that we are living in a dangerous world, titles in this area are offered to provide readers with the tools to survive everyday hazards, plan for an emergency, or learn skills that can help with outdoor activities and adventuring.

Johnson, Richard.

The Ultimate Survival Manual, Canadian Edition: Urban Adventure, Wilderness Survival, Disaster Preparedness. 2013. 256p. **H A/YA**

It must be acknowledged that there are many things that can go wrong outside the cocoon of one's own home. However, the 333 tips provided by the editors of *Outdoor Life* magazine start by prepping would-be adventurers for any eventuality by making an at-home survival kit the very first item on any checklist—whether training for an arctic mission or emulating Indiana Jones or Jason Bourne. This guide has a fun, easy-to-read layout that makes it easy to dip into, while providing basic instructions in several areas that range from practical first aid to more complicated wilderness and disaster scenarios. While not all skills—such as the ability to differentiate among bear species to avoid an attack—will apply equally to all readers, they all provide a measure of entertainment. The condensed narrative on pages filled with colorful illustrations will captivate any reader with interest in this subject, likely leading them to further titles in the subject area.

Keywords: Outdoor skills • Recreation • Survival • Wilderness

Miles, Justin.

Ultimate Explorer Guide for Kids. 2015. 96p. **M** **J**

Who better than a real-world traveler to prepare future explorers? Author Justin Miles makes sure that any intrepid would-be voyagers will know what they are getting into before they set off for any kind of expedition. It is important to know what to expect and how to deal with polar and desert climes, as the expedition equipment needed, the wildlife encountered, and the potential illnesses endured go far beyond what might happen when camping out in a national park. Practical skills such as knowing what survival equipment to keep in a backpack and how to tie a decent knot, acknowledged as essential skills in the days of unexpected storms and surprise evacuations, are also included. This makes for a combination of useful and exciting reading.

Keywords: Outdoor skills • Survival skills

Miles, Justin.

Ultimate Mapping Guide for Kids. 2016. 96p. **M**

Finding your way is a very useful survival skill, not only in the wilderness but in almost any situation. Reading a map is something that every person may have to do at some point, whether traveling to a new city or navigating an unfamiliar transit system. This useful, packed little guide starts by explaining different types of maps and their parts, allowing potential travelers to understand their uses and how to construct them. Miles starts with basics and works into more complicated concepts, providing examples and projects for each, such as an illustrated backyard for scale and the suggestion of recreating the reader's own. Along with the explanation of tinting and contouring for mountains, explorers are presented with a wide variety of material on how to survive, thrive, and have fun in the countryside. Readers will learn what equipment is essential, how to take care of the wilderness, how to use a compass and different ways to improvise and use one in a pinch, how to navigate, how to plan a route, and how to geocache. Miles even provides information about more modern technology, including a primer on the GPS. The book also includes a checklist for planning an expedition, a glossary, and a list of Web sites for further information about maps and navigation.

Keywords: Geocaching • Mapping • Navigation

Consider Starting with . . .

These titles are suggested as an introduction for readers new to the genre.

Cope, Peter. *The Smartphone Photography Guide: Shoot * Edit * Experiment * Share.*

Kelley, Amber. *Cook with Amber: Fun, Fresh Recipes to Get You in the Kitchen.*

Kidd, Chip. *Go! A Kidd's Guide to Graphic Design.*

Lam, Che. *Learn How to Knit with 50 Squares: For Beginners and Up; A Unique Approach to Learning to Knit.*

How to Sew: With Over 80 Techniques and 20 Easy Projects.

Fiction Read-Alikes

- **Mainwaring, Anna. *Rebel with a Cupcake.*** Jesobel (Jess) Jones loves to cook and eat what she wants and doesn't understand why food is "the enemy." But when Clothes Day at school starts with an altercation that splits her leggings all the way down and ends up in a showdown with her nemesis calling her fat, she starts wondering if she is. She considers losing weight, in typical teenage fashion, by following her sister's example of not eating, in order to gain the attention of the cutest boy, who pays her attention after she becomes a viral sensation. Later she realizes that it is more important to pay attention to what is beneath the surface. While adults know that it takes longer than a month to lose weight and realize that body issues may last a lifetime, younger readers may find this an amusing book about a girl who likes to cook and eat, and who comes to learn that it is okay to do so at any age.

- **Juby, Susan. *The Fashion Committee.*** Fashion is the driving force in Charlie Dean's life. John Thomas-Smith spends his time metalworking. In their school the arts program has been cut, and their only hope is to win a scholarship to the arts program at Green Pastures High School. When it is announced that the annual contest will be a fashion contest, Charlie figures that her time has come, while John resolves to do whatever he needs to in order to get a chance at a better education. Told in alternating points of view, these two characters give a well-rounded look at what it means to appreciate the beauty in what you have, what you make, and the style you choose to present.

- **Shrum, Brianna. *The Art of French ~~Cooking~~ Kissing*.** Seventeen-year-old Carter Lane has one goal in life: to become a chef. She has a chance to win a scholarship to a cooking school, but to win it she will need to participate in a grueling, intense, *Top Chef*–like competition with 11 of the other top high school culinary students from across the country. From the day she arrives, one of the other students, Reid Yamada, starts a battle he didn't see coming when he plays a prank on her in their first challenge. Soon they find themselves in an escalating culinary war they seem unable to stop. Just when it seems they have reached an impasse, they are assigned to the same team, and they will need to work together if they are to progress any further in the competition. Carter begins to wonder if there is more to her feelings about Reid than a desire to beat him.

Reference

"do-it-yourself," *Merriam-Webster*, accessed July 1, 2019, https://www.merriam -webster.com/dictionary/do-it-yourself.

Chapter **10**

The Arts

Definition

This chapter covers books about the arts, including artists, art history, art appreciation, music, dance, literature, and film and television.

Appeal

The arts provide a natural outlet for self-expression. Even with the understanding that any art is a product of the artist, the result is very appealing and may speak directly to its reader or audience. Titles that demonstrate a shared experience or help a person better understand how to express themselves can be very attractive. Readers who feel that they are not talented in one area, such as dance, drawing, or writing, may enjoy reading the advice of authors on how to explore another area or how to better appreciate existing artwork that already speaks to them.

Chapter Organization

The first section, "Art and Artists," is intended to introduce readers to various visual arts, artists, and works. This is followed by two other performing arts categories, "Music and Dance" and "Film and Television." "Literature and Language" is divided into two subsections, "Grammar and Writing" and "Books and Authors," with information on how to improve writing and suggestions on books to choose, thoughts about books, and biographies about authors. "Poetry" is divided into "About Poetry and Poets," with collections, anthologies, and information about poetical forms, and "Verse Biographies and Memoirs," in which authors explore lives using poetry. The chapter concludes with "Folklore, Myths, and Legends."

Art and Artists

Artists are some of the most visionary people in society, helping to create works that influence, move, and affect viewers, frequently for little recognition or validation during the artists' lifetimes. The books in this subcategory include books about art appreciation, art history, and artists. Readers interested in learning how to draw will find titles in chapter 9.

Art That Changed the World: Transformative Art Movements and the Paintings that Inspired Them. 2013. 400p. **H** **A/YA**

A compendium of art introduces the great art movements and the artists associated with them. From Ice Age cave paintings to modern pop art and abstraction, each section is presented in historical context. The many examples in each section speak to the importance of the artists and their art and help illustrate the characteristics of the movement. This work will appeal to both the serious art student and the casual reader interested in learning more about a particular artist.

Keywords: Art • Artists

Brooks, Susie.

Inside Art Movements. **J** **H**

Cubism. 2020. 48p.

Brooks uses cubist pioneers Georges Braque and Pablo Picasso to help readers understand how cubism differed from impressionism, which came before. Brooks uses examples to show how each artist's style developed. Brooks helps show the elements that influenced the individual style of the painters, demonstrates how they continued to evolve, and then presents a painting that allows the reader to differentiate between the two. The salon cubists continued to adapt the movement, bringing it into the mainstream with public exhibits and adaptation into sculpture. In the early 20th century cubism was taken up by female artists as well as internationally, although its representations during World War I were regarded with suspicion and the movement foundered. Supplementary information includes a glossary and further reading.

Keywords: Art • Artists • Braque, Georges • Cubism • Gris, Juan • Picasso, Pablo

Impressionism. 2020. 48p.

The artists referred to as "impressionists" in the original exhibition were meant to take the moniker as an insult, according to Brooks, as real art at the time was meant to be realistic, and their work was not considered worthy. Instead, the many artists belonging to the movement of the mid-19th century started to paint outdoors, use distinctive brushstrokes, and take advantage of light and inspiration from modern life in their work. Works show how impressionists like

Manet, Monet, Degas, and Renoir incorporated the changes and culture of the modern society into their works, including the advent and popularity of photography, ballet, and the presence of nature.

Keywords: Degas, Edgar • Impressionism • Manet, Édouard • Monet, Claude

Pop Art. 2020. 48p.

In the 1950s and 1960s there was a rebound from the gloom and austerity that accompanied the war years of the 1940s. People not only had money to spend but popular culture in those decades was brighter and faster. Artists, too, rebounded from the conceptual, often difficult to understand works of the abstract expressionists that preceded them. Instead, in both the United States and the United Kingdom a movement arose that borrowed instantly recognizable images from advertising, films, and magazines, and used techniques such as silk-screening, collage, and airbrushing to make their work look mass-produced. Examples of works from pop artists like Andy Warhol and Roy Lichtenstein demonstrate concepts in the movement, such as the belief that everything is beautiful, an ability to salute and laugh at American culture, and Warhol's prescient acknowledgement of the fleeting nature of fame.

Keywords: Art • Artists • Lichtenstein, Roy • Pop art • Warhol, Andy

Romanticism. 2020. 48p.

Romanticism began in the late 18th century as a European literary movement incorporating drama and emotions as a reaction against the Enlightenment's focus on reason and order. Artists, too, began to imbue their paintings with passion. Artists were inspired by current events, literature, nature, and their own personal lives. Examples demonstrate that Francisco Goya, whose own life, like his native country of Spain, was tragic, had a style that became darker and more intense as he got older. The rise of landscape art is shown through examples from John Constable and J. M. W. Turner. The book also introduces readers to other important artists and how they explored the world around them, painting portraits, animals, and catastrophes. The influence and legacy of the artists are discussed as well.

Keywords: Art • Artists • Constable, John • Goya, Francisco • Turner, J. M. W.

The Renaissance. 2020. 48p.

This volume of <u>Inside Art Movements</u> looks at the Renaissance in Europe from the early 15th through the mid-16th centuries. During this period artists began to make incredibly realistic paintings, frequently using classical motifs. Important painters of the period rose to prominence in Italy, where the church had previously used stylized, ornate art to teach the populace about Christianity. While this did demonstrate the importance and wealth of the Church, the works were not reflective of the world or the subjects. Examples show how painters such as Lorenzetti began to use perspective, leading the painters of the movement to discover the vanishing point and master its use. Advances in reproducing the human form also translated well into sculpture; some of the best-known art from the period was produced by Botticelli and Michelangelo. Artists of the Renaissance used a workshop system, training other artists in order to finish their commissions, which were frequently subsidized by wealthy patrons. The many examples of the artists' works help readers understand the development of their styles and the lasting and profound effect they had on art and artists that followed them.

Keywords: Art • Artists • Michelangelo • Renaissance

Surrealism. 2020. 48p.

Surrealist art, like the literary movement that preceded it, is an attempt by the artist to express subconscious impulses rather than any conscious or rational thought. Surrealist artists did this in different ways. Salvador Dali produced paintings in a realistic fashion with fantastical subjects that looked as though they came from a dream, while others, like Joan Miró and Max Ernst, used techniques originally created by the Dadaists. Surrealists incorporated objects into their art in a way that they believed could only come from the subconscious, portraying them as if brought forth from their dreams or their nightmares, eventually translating these strange visions into large-scale designs, furniture, and clothing. Women were also influenced by surrealism and involved in it, with Frida Kahlo's portraits remaining a vivid reminder of the period. Many surrealists, avowed socialists, were greatly affected by the politics of the day; many were required to abandon Paris and their body of work in favor of the United States to escape invading Nazi troops. Final sections provide a close-up look at Magritte and some of his iconic works, along with a discussion of surrealism's global spread and legacy, and a timeline of important moments.

Keywords: Art • Artists • Dali, Salvador • Ernst, Max • Kahlo, Frida • Miró, Joan • Surrealism

Brown, Matt.

Everything You Know About Art is Wrong. 2018. 160p. 🄷 ᴀʏᴀ

This novel introduction to art is presented in a particularly unique format, presenting declarations about art and then challenging them in order to both inform and educate. Brown points out that he learned the value of being wrong from an early age. He offers readers the opportunity to learn lessons in several areas, including the world of art, painting, sculpture, architecture, and other art forms. Each supposition, whether stating that art is useless and a waste of money or that Kandinsky invented abstract art, allows for a wide-ranging discussion from the author. Readers will feel comfortable either reading straight through or browsing. A final chapter listing some of art's most amusing conspiracy theories is an amusement not to be missed.

Keywords: Art • Artists

Crilley, Mark.

Manga Art: Inspiration and Techniques from an Expert Illustrator. 2017. 176p. **H** **A/YA**

Crilley, a well-known illustrator and art instructor, presents a gallery style book of his artwork. Each item is accompanied by a narrative that discusses his inspiration for the art and the materials he used to create it. The illustrations are divided into five themes, each of which begins with a short introduction meant to inspire readers into picking up their pencils, whether to create manga characters, find out about Japan, learn about science fiction, incorporate concepts, or imitate another artist's style. The format allows for a slightly less comprehensive presentation than a book designed to teach drawing, but this volume is just as inspiring. Many of the final pictures are accompanied by one or two sketches that show the characters or scenes developing their final form. This not only helps to illustrate the text but also provides examples for artists interested in how Crilley works, which might lead them back to his instructional books.

Keywords: Art • Drawing • Manga • Techniques

Eye on Art.

The Eye on Art series goes far beyond serving as a basic vehicle for biographical information about the artists represented in its volumes. Even the volumes that focus on just one artist go beyond acting as a biography, providing the reader with information about the artist and the time in which they lived. The books use numerous examples of their works to help explain the artists' techniques, the schools in which they worked, how they were influenced, how they became involved in the art world, the artists with whom they worked, and the influence they had on the world around them and the artists who came after them. Titles that discuss types of art are useful for spurring discussions, particularly where there has been debate about whether the format is a kind of art and in the demonstration of art's enduring value. The titles include lists of further resources with both books and Web sites.

Bartolotta, Kenneth L. *Anime: Japanese Animation Comes to America.* 2017. 104p. **J** **H**

Collins, Anna. *Graffiti: Vandalism or Art?* 2017. 104. **J** **H**

Dellaccio, Tanya. *The Art of Architecture.* 2017. 112p. **J** **H**

Dellaccio, Tanya. *Computer Animation: Telling Stories with Visual Art.* 2017. 112p. **J** **H**

Haynes, Danielle. *Claude Monet: Founder of French Impressionism.* 2019. 112p. **J** **H**

10

11

Huoh, Ruth. *Fashion Design: Clothing as Art.* 2017. 104p. **J H**

Orr, Tamra. *Leonardo da Vinci: Renaissance Genius.* 2019. 104p. **J H**

Oswald, Vanessa. *The Great Surrealists: Dreamers and Artists.* 2019. 112p. **J H**

Reynolds, Donna. *Graphic Design: Putting Art and Words Together.* 2017. 112p. **J H**

Vink, Amanda. *Postmodern Artists: Creators of a Cultural Movement.* 2019. 104p. **J H**

Grolleau, Fabien, and Jérémie Royer.

Audubon: On the Wings of the World. 2017. 184p. **M J**

This beautifully illustrated graphic novel is a lovely tribute to the artist whose determination to draw all of the birds indigenous to the United States led him to leave behind all the accepted trappings of his daily life, including his home, job, wife, and family. That he did so in the early 19th century with only an ill-prepared assistant, a rifle, and the artist's materials that were his most prized possession and yet left behind a legacy known generations later is a story worthy of note.

Keywords: Artists • Audubon, John James • Birds

Hockney, David, and Martin Gayford.

A History of Pictures for Children: From Cave Paintings to Computer Drawings. 2018. 128p. **M J**

David Hockney and Martin Gayford present an introduction to art, artists, and techniques through a timeline of pictures and accompanying commentary, starting with cave drawings. Readers are presented with pertinent notes about each piece, allowing them to learn what to look for in the picture, what its influences were, and what it inspired. Van Gogh's use of bright colors, for example, inspired later artists to use intense colors. Later chapters discuss marks, light and shadow, scenes, tools, and moving pictures. To demonstrate how many methods of creating pictures have been developed, an additional timeline of inventions is included, reflecting the wide range of materials that has been added to the artist's repertoire, from the stone tools and pigments used in cave painting to the computers and smartphones that can create a limitless variety of digital images today.

Keywords: Art • Art history

Parker, Kate T.

Strong is the New Pretty: A Celebration of Girls Being Themselves. 2017. 262p. **M J**

Kate Parker points out in her introduction that as a child she finally felt that she had the hairstyle that fit her when she got rid of her long hair in favor of a shorter one that suited her sports-playing lifestyle. Now, as a professional photographer, she has assembled a collection of photographs of girls of different ages, sizes, and colors. While they are all doing different things, they have one thing in common: they are all beautiful, confident young women, captured in lovely photographs and gathered in chapters that are headed by Parker's notes about what makes a strong girl.

Keywords: Photographs • Photography

Quintero, Isabel, and Zeke Peña.

🏅 *Photographic: The Life of Graciela Iturbide*. 2018. 98p. **J H**

Iturbide's work is at the center of this involving story, presented in a graphic format that avoids a straightforward linear biographical style, instead integrating Iturbide's photographs and words with chapters of her life intentionally chosen to show her journey and development as an artist. Quintero and Peña concentrate on Iturbide's time in Mexico during the 1970s photographing indigenous culture, resulting in a book that complements the photographer's grayscale photographs with a text that both highlights and gives them context while leaving the reader room to discover and interpret them. **BG-HB**

Keywords: Graphic nonfiction • Iturbide, Graciela • Photographer

Salva, Rubio.

Monet: Itinerant of Light. 2017. 112p. **H A/YA**

Monet, waiting to see if cataract surgery will adversely affect his vision, thinks back on his life, the development of his painting style, and all of the artists he worked with over the years. Readers may be surprised to the extent that Monet suffered, in terms of the years of rejection, poverty, and depression he endured, while devoting himself single-mindedly to his art at the expense of maintaining any normality with his family. Readers interested in the artist will find it a fascinating story. This beautiful graphic novel incorporates the paintings of several of the impressionists who appear in the book, adding copies of the originals and explanations of how and where they appear as a supplement at the end.

Keywords: Artists • Impressionism • Monet

Music and Dance

While the books in this subcategory will be of interest to lovers of music and dance, they will provide readers with much more. Readers pondering a dance class, for example, will find *The Ballet Book* gives them practical information about just what it would be like to start to learn ballet. Every other biography here provides not only information about the dancer or musician but also about the time in which they lived and how it influenced their work, serving a dual purpose and appealing to readers who enjoy history as well as those who like music.

Bagieu, Pénélope.

California Dreamin': Cass Elliot Before the Mamas and the Papas. 2017. 242p. **M** **J**

Long before Cass Elliot, born Ellen Cohen, became a member of one of the best-known folk groups of the 1960s, she was a child in Baltimore with a dream of becoming a singer. Bagieu's graphic biography depicts Elliot's life from the point of view of people who knew her, showing her early childhood with a family of music lovers, recognizing that even then she had a gift. While her determination to become a star remained a constant in her life, so too did a struggle with her weight, and the ongoing contradiction between the societal pressure for her to present a more acceptable outward appearance and her obvious and utterly captivating talent and presence. The book tracks her journey up to the point where she and the members of the group are perched on the point of stardom.

Keywords: Elliot, Cass • Folk singers • Graphic biography

Bowes, Deborah.

The Ballet Book: The Young Performer's Guide to Classical Dance. 2018. 144p. **M** **J**

This updated edition from Canada's National Ballet School (NBS) will be of interest to anyone thinking of taking a dance class or learning about the ballet. Potential dancers will find out what to look for in a dance studio before being given a thorough explanation of what they will learn in ballet, from first position to kinds of dance and ways to keep healthy. All of these are accompanied by color photographs of NBS students. The book then moves on to moments in famous ballets and ballet performances, providing an introduction to the story along with a quotation that introduces to the reader why each was chosen.

Keywords: Ballet

Curlee, Lynn.

The Great Nijinsky: God of Dance. 2019. 120p. **M** **J**

Vaslav Nijinsky was heralded as many things in the early 20th century, not the least of which was that as the star of the Ballets Russes he was widely acknowledged as the best dancer in the world. His flame burned brightly and burned out quickly; during his short professional career he starred in and choreographed ballets that not only influenced but changed the course of dance, enthralling the public onstage as a performer but leaving them unable to appreciate his own artistic vision. Nijinsky dedicated his life to his art, amazing his audiences and critics with his ability to turn himself into his characters, though unable to speak or interact with his public off stage. His life after his retirement from dance was marked by his severe mental decline and institutionalization. Curlee's book provides summaries of ballets and roles for which Nijinsky is remembered, along with portraits of him with his partners in their title roles.

Keywords: Ballet • Ballets Russes • Nijinsky, Vaslav

Howard, Mark, and Chris Howard.

Listen Up! Recording Music with Bob Dylan, Neil Young, U2, REM, The Tragically Hip, Red Hot Chili Peppers, Tom Waits. 2019. 230p. **A/YA**

Music producer Mark Howard notes that he has always loved, and been involved with, the music scene. He studied the drums, turned his basement into a studio, and worked at mixing music while still a teenager in Hamilton, Ontario. In the following years he worked with and learned from some of the most iconic acts in the music business. Here he provides a detailed, immersive account of his experiences working with artists and producers from Brian Eno to Bob Dylan. His narrative is incredibly descriptive, giving readers a sense of being in the room with the artists while providing significant technical information about how the albums were actually put together. Even readers without any musical background may end up skimming over this material in favor of following his experiences and getting to know more about the artists. Anyone interested in the technical aspects of music recording will find this book well worth their time.

Keywords: Howard, Mark • Music • Musicians • Rock musicians

Pinkney, Andrea Davis.

Rhythm Ride: A Road Trip through the Motown Sound. 2015. 176p. **M J**

This book introduces an iconic and recognizable musical movement that can be traced back to one man, Berry Gordy, the creator and driving force behind Motown. This fascinating look at what became more than just a company introduces not only the musicians associated with Motown but also their effects on the music industry and on society, including the civil rights movement and the Vietnam War. The included timeline is particularly helpful, given the number of hits produced by the artists referenced.

Keywords: Berry, Gordy • Motown • Music • Musicians

Silvey, Anita.

Let Your Voice Be Heard: The Life and Times of Pete Seeger. 2016. 112p. **M**

Pete Seeger's career and legacy as the United States' foremost folk singer of the 20th century was strongly influenced by two major factors: a stint in the merchant marines and his marriage to his wife, Toshi Ohta. The former, because Seeger's lifelong inclination toward peace could not outweigh his dislike for Hitler and all for which he stood, and the latter, because of her treatment as a Japanese American during World War II and her support of

Seeger during his lifetime. While Seeger was one of the most popular recording artists of his time, the incorporation of his own antiwar beliefs into his song lyrics led him to be named a communist and questioned by the House Un-American Activities Committee (HUAC). Decades later, Seeger was publicly recognized and welcomed as a performer at Barack Obama's inauguration.

Keywords: Folk singers • Seeger, Pete

Tiwary, Vivek J.

 The Fifth Beatle: The Brian Epstein Story. 2013. 144p. **H**

Brian Epstein had no management experience when he first saw the Beatles play, but that didn't keep him from believing in their future. His determination and guidance led them to the top of the charts in the UK, the United States, and elsewhere overseas, proving, as he said when they were playing in a Liverpool cellar, that they would become bigger than Elvis. This graphic novel portrays how Epstein managed this, along with several other jobs, while hiding his personal life at a time when homosexuality was a crime in Britain and anti-Semitism was common. This book, which has been added to the Rock and Roll Hall of Fame, is a memorable portrayal of the too-short life of the complex man who helped create one of the greatest acts of the 20th century. **GGNT**

Keywords: Beatles • Epstein, Brian • Graphic memoir • Musicians

Now Try: There is no denying the glamour and appeal of the top-selling musical group of all time. Readers interested in more information about the formation and importance of the boys from Liverpool will find it in Martin W. Sandler's *How the Beatles Changed the World.* Starting with their 1964 performance on *The Ed Sullivan Show,* which remains the highest-viewed telecast ever, Sandler ably demonstrates the group's subsequent impact on the music industry and a number of other areas, including popular culture, fashion, and the wider world, as they experimented in the arenas of activism and religion over the years and the public reacted to their personal and professional interactions and rifts.

Film and Television

Movies and television remain two of our most popular forms of entertainment, even as they transition to streaming and the Internet. Books in this subgenre look at fame, celebrities, and iconic titles. Rather than simply examining a single movie or television show, books here examine stars and series that have had long careers and remained popular for decades; future generations are likely to be familiar with them, ensuring a longer shelf life.

Burr, Ty.

Gods Like Us: On Movie Stardom and Modern Fame. 2012. 413p. **AYA**

Film critic Ty Burr presents a comprehensive look at what made (and makes) a celebrity. A precis of the careers of the foremost stars helps to explain just what it was about them that captivated audiences, separating them from the other actors of the day. Burr starts with the first silent film stars and works though movie and television stars, connecting them to the important events of the day. Stardom as a concept is also applied to singers such as Elvis and the Beatles, who revolutionized their industry. A running discussion of the public's fascination with gossip and its direct effect on a celebrity's bankability is illuminating.

Keywords: Celebrities • Fame • Movies • Television

Hidalgo, Pablo.

Star Wars: The Force Awakens; The Visual Dictionary. 2015. 80p. **M**

This is a fascinating compendium for anyone interested in the film or the larger Star Wars world. Noting that *Star Wars: The Force Awakens* takes place 30 years after the events of *The Empire Strikes Back*, Hidalgo presents a large, double-page spread that introduces the New Empire, in which the characters inhabiting this movie live. The characters, human and otherwise, follow. Each of them is shown in at least one spread that features multiple pictures, which allows for enough space to provide a character sketch that includes information such as background, personality traits, fighting skills, and details about equipment and weaponry. Outposts and locations are also mentioned and provide an opportunity to mention minor and background characters. These books provide an example of the kind of scope that goes into story development, character, and costume design in this kind of movie.

Keywords: Movies • *Star Wars*

Now Try: Fans of the Star Wars oeuvre recognize that the worldbuilding that began in a galaxy far, far, away with George Lucas's first film trilogy has now expanded into several other formats, including animation, print, and games. Many of the fascinating, fierce, and diverse characters that have helped propel those stories are explored by Amy Ratcliffe in *Star Wars: Women of the Galaxy*. Readers will find portraits of 75 characters from all walks of life, including heroes, warriors, and administrators, who have made an impression on the author. Each is accompanied by an artist's portrait and a character summary, and features comments from the actor and the creator.

Weitzman, Elizabeth.

Renegade Women in Film and TV. 2019. 120p. **M J**

While women have long found places to shine in both film and television, this book points out that they are still so outnumbered that their successes deserve to be celebrated. Featured are profiles of women who led the way for others in Hollywood, such as Rita Moreno, who went from her Academy Award–winning performance as Anita in *West Side Story* to winning an Emmy, a Grammy, and a Tony, making her one of the only living EGOT performers. Strong women have found a place both in front of and behind the camera, including people who have spent their lives telling stories that have had lasting effects on the lives of girls and women. Susan Harris's first experience with this phenomenon was writing a two-part episode of *Maude* in 1972 in which the titular character decides to have an abortion; the episode debuted months before *Roe v. Wade*. Supplements to the profiles include short interviews with 10 of the women included and a suggested viewing list for readers previously unfamiliar with the subjects. This last is a valuable addition, as their work is well worth the time even if some of the actors, newscasters, and directors are no longer household names; the descriptions are as enticing as the biographies themselves.

Keywords: Actors • Directors • Filmmakers • Screenwriters

Literature and Language

This subgenre is divided into two categories, "Grammar and Writing" and "Books and Authors." They include titles for readers who enjoy reading, books, writing, or words, or are interested in improving their writing without it seeming like work. Titles also contain recommendations for books and information about books and authors.

Grammar and Writing

Books in this subcategory look at writing in all its forms and provide advice on how to improve. They are written in a way meant to encourage creativity and foster a love of writing rather than seeming like homework. They are not write-ins and are suitable for including in a library collection.

Carter, Ally.

Dear Ally, How Do You Write a Book? 2019. 336p. **M** **J**

One might assume that this is a frank, serious guide to the nuts and bolts of writing a novel, starting with an acknowledgment that the whole process is long, involved and takes considerable pain and effort from a seasoned professional. This book, however, is one that speaks directly to teens through an author whose work they admire. Carter also writes to other young adult novelists and asks them questions so that readers interested in the subject have the benefit of their experience as well. It deserves to be reiterated that this is not an introduction to grammar but to the craft of creating a book. The questions cover many topics that will help a novice writer understand how to get started with their first work: planning the plot and storyboarding, determining the length of the manuscript, worldbuilding, crafting characters, and developing plotlines. Readers may also enjoy the authors' thoughts about the creative process, including how to get started, find and refine ideas, and work out a writing process. Readers will find reassurance in the knowledge that even the most prolific and esteemed authors recommend reading, rewriting, editing, and writing multiple drafts—and rejection is not uncommon. The authors also answer questions about publishing.

Keywords: Authorship • Publishing • Writers • Writing

Now Try: Readers that might not be ready for the in-depth treatment provided in Carter's work but who are still interested in the creative process will find an interesting take in Austin Kleon's *Steal Like an Artist: 10 Things Nobody Told You About Being Creative*. Author/artist Kleon presents 10 ideas readers can use as prompts to spur and guide their creativity, illustrating them not only with his own artwork and stories from his life, but with quotations from artists from a wide variety of fields. Kleon has produced a book with the things he wished somebody had told him when he was starting out.

Fletcher, Ralph.

Guy-Write: What Every Guy Writer Needs to Know. 2012. 192p. **M J**

This useful book is, first and foremost, a guide to writing in all forms. Each contributor mentions having a notebook, and Fletcher begins by suggesting to all readers that they write how, what, and when they want, before tackling the first of the enticing and appealing kinds of writing: humor. Fletcher tackles this as he does all the others, by incorporating several examples, including some from children, to better illustrate what does and does not work. He then moves onto incorporating disgusting things, using a vomit-filled episode from Jon Scieszka and an interview adding several of Scieszka's writing tips. This format is used for horror, fantasy, sports, and incorporating emotion. Later chapters speak to the value of the author's notebook, reading, and writing tips. The authors who provide the tips are all well known and highly regarded, and the books on the recommended reading list are classic titles, suggested either by Fletcher or the other authors as titles used as mentor texts. Their advice will work for either gender, making this a book a worthy read for someone interested in writing.

Keywords: Authorship • Writers • Writing

Higgins, Nadia.

The Whole Truth: Writing Fearless Nonfiction. 2015. 64p. **M**

This writing guide breaks down its task into several parts, providing explanations, examples, and prompts in order to spur interested authors to put pen to paper. Higgins starts with instructions on picking out and describing details from a scene before discussing how to make the details vivid, as Paul Zindel did in his memoir *The Pigman and Me*. More detailed writing techniques for memoir and narrative nonfiction include how to use storytelling, craft scenes, and write dialogue, making the details vivid. Higgins then mentions several forms of writing that will be useful beyond the scope of the book, notably writing persuasive text and writing a review; he also talks about changing voice. This is a very useful book for anybody interested in writing nonfiction, as it offers a wide variety of practice exercises, as well as further reading, suggested Web sites, and a number of new titles to choose from.

Keywords: Nonfiction • Writing

Petras, Ross, and Kathryn Petras.

That Doesn't Mean What You Think It Means: The 150 Most Commonly Misused Words and Their Tangled Histories. 2018. 208p. **H**

Presented in alphabetical order, Ross and Kathryn Petras offer examples of some of English's most incorrectly used words. Acknowledging that even they have had occasion to make mistakes, they have chosen a wide variety of the most frequently found errors, demonstrating just how widespread these misunderstandings are. Each example begins with a quotation demonstrating the word used incorrectly. The authors then explain how to correctly use the word; they also provide its history. At the end of the section a short definition is offered. It's particularly helpful that, when two or three words are frequently confused, they are included in the same piece, allowing the authors to clarify the reason for the misinterpretation and add tips for how to avoid it in the future. This may help with affecting change for a greater effect.

Keywords: Grammar • Linguistics • Writing

Petras, Ross, and Kathryn Petras.

You're Saying It Wrong: A Pronunciation Guide to the 150 Most Commonly Mispronounced Words and Their Tangled Histories of Misuse. 2016. 192p. **H**

Word lovers, grammar geeks, and budding authors alike will enjoy this compilation of difficult and obscure words that provides the reader with a preferred (pre-FURRED) pronunciation guide and each word's etymology. Many of the entries include a logical explanation for why many mispronunciations occur. In order to further help readers become erudite and informed orators, additional tables provide the pronunciations of potentially difficult tricky names of authors, designers, composers, and British names.

Keywords: Pronunciations • Speaking

Salas, Laura Purdie.

Catch Your Breath: Writing Poignant Poetry. 2014. 64p. **M**

In order to encourage interested writers, Laura Purdie Salas begins her book with the suggestion that reading and writing poetry are the best ways to become a poet. She also notes that it is not required to like every form of poetry, which may comfort some readers. The basic introductions to the various forms of poetry are informative and accompanied by examples that help differentiate, say, a haiku from a cinquain. They also provide information that clarifies why rhymes aren't as easy as one might think. Readers might even be tempted by the prompts that follow each entry, which may also help to explain tricky concepts, such as meter and rhythm.

Keywords: Composition • Creative writing • Poetry

Books and Authors

The titles in this section allow readers to find out more about their favorite books, authors, and genres, and get the chance to discover potential new ones. Readers who enjoy being pointed toward the authors' recommendations may look for similar titles under the "Film and Television" category as well.

Allen, Jessica.

The Great American Read: The Book of Books; Explore America's 100 Best-Loved Novels. 2018. 288p. **H** **A/YA**

In this illustrated companion volume to the PBS series *The Great American Read*, readers will have the opportunity to find out just why the 100 titles and series contained within were chosen as the best-loved books in America. A foreword by Meredith Vieira invites book lovers to use the list as an opportunity to become acquainted with the wide variety of titles, which includes an assortment broad enough to suit any reader, from classics to contemporary titles, and genres from literary fiction to science fiction and horror. The discussion of each title includes a summary, a researched introduction to the author, and the influence of the author's work. Readers will also enjoy segments that look at how several works intersect, such as the best female or male characters, settings, and adaptations. Each of these sections may also lead readers to try one or more of the discussed titles.

Keywords: Authors • Books

Hinds, Gareth.

Macbeth. 2015. 152p. **J** **H**

Readers both familiar with and new to the Bard will find this play kept largely intact, with the line breaks removed, allowing for smoother reading which translates particularly well into a graphic format. The illustrations allow Hinds to show the emotions on the characters' faces, highlighting well-known speeches and Macbeth's descent into madness. Endnotes include historical information and the author's notes about the text and individual pages.

Keywords: Graphic nonfiction • Macbeth

Judge, Lita.

Mary's Monster: Love, Madness, and How Mary Shelley Created Frankenstein. 2018. 312p. **M** **J**

> Judge's biography of Mary Wollstonecraft Shelley is presented in a verse format over more than 300 black and white illustrations. The sparseness of the poems and the shading of the illustrations suits the darkness of the subject matter, as Mary's life descends from difficulty to depression to outright tragedy. From the loss of her first child at the age of 19, to expulsion from her family after running away with her lover, the married Percy Bysshe Shelley, to facing several suicides and deaths among contemporaries, she accumulated more than enough material in her own life to spawn the monster still recognized 200 years later as one of literature's greatest creations.

> **Keywords:** Authors • Frankenstein • Shelley, Mary • Shelley, Percy Bysshe

> **Now Try:** Readers interested in a more thorough introduction to Mary Shelley will find it in Catherine Reef's *Mary Shelley: The Strange True Tale of Frankenstein's Creator*. Mary Shelley's life was not easy: condemned for loving a married man, suffering the loss of children, husband, and friends, and living in a time when her greatest accomplishment didn't earn her any significant praise or financial recompense. In addition to a thorough timeline of the lives, loves, tribulations, and tragedies of Mary and her husband, Percy Bysshe Shelley, Reef also integrates events that are not as well known; Shelley registered the birth of a baby girl in 1819 whose parentage is still in question, for example, and at least one of Shelley's works wasn't published until over a century after her death.

Kröger, Lisa, and Melanie R. Anderson.

Monster, She Wrote: The Women Who Pioneered Horror and Speculative Fiction. **H** **A/YA**

> *Monster, She Wrote* presents a timeline of the gothic novels of the late 1800s. Each biographical portrait introduces the reader to the author and provides further information about her contributions to the genre, such as writing the first science fiction novel, flaunting societal expectations, or writing cautionary tales about terrible men. Each offers a reading list with suggestions for which of the author's works to try. The summaries are written in a succinct style that is as informative as it is amusing, moving briskly through the decades as the authors incorporate ghosts and the occult. The summaries also describe the evolution of formats such as pulp magazines and mass market paperbacks. A concluding chapter looks at where these genres and the authors working in them are today, making this a fascinating book for readers who enjoy this style.

> **Keywords:** Authors • Gothic literature • Horror • Speculative fiction

Marcus, Leonard S., ed.

Comics Confidential: Thirteen Graphic Novelists Talk Story, Craft, and Life Outside the Box. 2016. 192p. **M** **J**

Fans of the 13 talents interviewed by Leonard Marcus in this book will not be surprised when most of them mention that they were greatly influenced by Art Spiegelman's *Maus* as a seminal work. It was Spiegelman's Pulitzer Prize for *Maus* that first gave the graphic novel as an art form the recognition it deserved. The interviews with the authors and illustrators in this book provide a basic introduction to their work while giving them an opportunity to say how they got started with graphic novels. As Harry Bliss started out as a cartoonist for the New Yorker and Matt Phelan was a bookseller who didn't know how to draw, this wasn't always an obvious journey. Interested readers will also learn more about each of the subjects as they answer questions such as what influences their work, what they find difficult to draw, and what their books are about. At the end of each interview is an original panel by the subject interpreting "City." There is enough information provided that readers being introduced to new authors will be able to decide which books they would like to try.

Keywords: Artists • Graphic novelists • Illustrators

Popova, Maria, and Claudia Bedrick, eds.

A Velocity of Being: Letters to a Young Reader. 2017. 280p. **M J**

The short pieces contained in *A Velocity of Being* can be described as love letters to books and reading. They are written by a wide variety of personalities who are as likely to be as well-known to the readers' parents as to the readers themselves, including Shonda Rhymes, David Byrne of the Talking Heads, actor Lena Dunham, Neil Gaiman, and Jacqueline Woodson. The contributors talk about what books have meant to them and provide poignant, pithy, or funny tales that will appeal to book lovers and may resonate with anyone hesitant to pick up a book. An additional draw are the illustrations added to each story, tailored to match that story's theme by artists from Mo Willems to Shaun Tan.

Keywords: Books • Reading

Rosenberg, Liz.

House of Dreams: The Life of L. M. Montgomery. 2018. 352p. **M J**

While L. M. Montgomery has fans all over the world, most of them know her best as the creator of the beloved character Anne of Green Gables and associate her with an idyllic home life in Prince Edward Island, Canada. Rosenberg allows readers a much closer look at Montgomery; she grew up a devoted bibliophile who escaped into books and used her writing as an outlet for the depression and anxiety she struggled with all her life. Seeing this icon as a person who battled, perhaps unsuccessfully, a debilitating mental disorder while still managing to create a body of work that has a substantial legacy, serves as a reminder of what a remarkable woman she was.

Keywords: Authors • Montgomery, L. M.

Poetry

Divided by sounds, meaning, and rhythm, poetry includes a wide variety of topics and forms. Readers are provided an introduction to poetry and well-known poets in Susan Dalzell's *Poetry 101: From Shakespeare and Rupi Kaur to Iambic Pentameter and Blank Verse, Everything You Need to Know about Poetry.* Both the writing and the reading of poetry can be very appealing to teenagers.

Poetry is divided into two subsections. "About Poetry and Poets" includes works that provide a background for poetic forms, intended to give readers an introduction to and greater understanding of poetry and collections of poems. This is followed by "Verse Biographies and Memoirs," titles that explore lives using poetry.

About Poetry and Poets

This section lists works that help readers understand poetry and poetic forms, as well as collections and anthologies.

Bulion, Leslie.

Random Body Parts: Gross Anatomy Riddles in Verse. 2015. 48p. **M**

This is a slight and humorous book of poems, with each double-page spread referencing a different body part accompanied by a suitably silly illustration. This book can be used in many ways, as the poems are not only presented in many different forms, but refer to Shakespeare, allowing the notes section to explain an epigram and the use of lines from Shakespeare's plays and poetry. While the body parts get harder to guess as the book progresses from stomach to auricle, the accompanying text boxes with scientific information are both informative and amusing. A glossary for the parts of the body, with anatomically correct illustrations of the organs in their proper place, done in the same style as the book's other drawings, completes this entertaining volume.

Keywords: Anatomy • Poems • Poetic forms • Poetry

Dalzell Susan.

Poetry 101: From Shakespeare and Rupi Kaur to Iambic Pentameter and Blank Verse, Everything You Need to Know About Poetry. 2018. 256p. **H** **A/YA**

The introduction to this novel and fascinating guide to poetic forms and poets goes far beyond an average introduction. Beginning with a suggestion for how to read a poem, the book progresses through a timeline from the Ancient Greeks to the present day, discussing the periods and the important poets in turn. This allows Dalzell to concentrate on the forms associated with poets and poetic movements, discussing sonnets with Shakespeare, and the romantic poets together. Readers will learn about the parts and variations of each form, and well-known examples are provided. Students new to poetry may also be interested in supplemental information, such as helpful terms, characteristics, and an explanation of the form's appeal.

Keywords: Poetic forms • Poetry • Poets

Grimes, Nikki.

One Last Word: Wisdom from the Harlem Renaissance. 2017. 128p. **M J**

Grimes introduces a wide variety of poets from the Harlem Renaissance to a new generation of readers and then uses their poems in a poetic form called "the Golden Shovel" that expands upon them by integrating them into a new poem. This is a difficult feat, but one to be congratulated, as it celebrates the original poem and gets the reader to look at it in a whole new light. A foreword with information about the Harlem Renaissance and original artwork from well-known illustrators such as R. Gregory Christie, Brian Pinkney, James Ransome, and Javaka Steptoe help to frame the works in the book. This title would find a home in both school and public library settings and appeal to readers interested in poetry.

Keywords: Harlem Renaissance • Poems • Poetry

Heppermann, Christine.

Poisoned Apples: Poems for You, My Pretty. 2014. 107p. **M J**

This collection uses retellings of fairy tales, myths, and legends in short, caustic poems to comment on issues and difficulties faced by girls, including body image, sexuality, and beauty. Spare, biting lines and allusions are particularly effective in this regard, as seen in a poem about Rumplestiltskin, when a girl goes from "a house of bricks, / point guard on the JV team" to "a house of sticks."

Keywords: Poems • Poetry

Nye, Naomi Shihab.

Voices in the Air: Poems for Listeners. 2018. 208p. **M J**

This book offers a series of free verse poems presented by Nye, as expressed in her introduction, in a form that allows for enjoyment, contemplation, and moments without distraction. The 95 poems in this collection present thoughts about and tributes to a series of creative, inspirational, and eclectic people, from Bruce Springsteen and Langston Hughes to Nye's father and the "mysterious wanderer" known as Peace Pilgrim. Poems may be read in their sections or individually, as quiet poems are integrated with musings on current political and societal difficulties. Biographical portraits of the people mentioned are included for readers who may not be familiar with them.

Keywords: Poems • Poetry

Reynolds, Jason.

For Every One. 2018. 112p. **M** **J**

In one long epistolary poem, originally delivered at the Kennedy Center for the unveiling of the Martin Luther King Jr. Memorial, Jason Reynolds speaks to every reader, describing a future in which they can and should go for their dreams. Divided into three parts, he speaks of a past in which he didn't know or wasn't sure of what he should hope for or should be doing, and the now in which he finds himself. He also speaks to the necessity of having a dream and the importance of taking the first step, putting in the time, and dealing with the issues that arise, because otherwise there is no chance of achieving the dream. In a voice that will speak to every reader and works well in spoken word, Reynolds's spare text will have a wide appeal and speaks to taking chances.

Keywords: Personal growth • Poems • Poetry

Verse Biographies and Memoirs

Using poetry as a vehicle to present a life story continues to be a format that captivates both authors and readers. Readers who enjoy reading about people may also enjoy the biographies and memoirs in chapters 3 and 4.

Anderson, Laurie Halse.

Shout. 2019. 304p. **H**

Anderson presents a verse memoir that introduces readers to the events that inspired her novel *Speak*. Divided into three parts, the first section includes explanations of her own sexual abuse, a strained situation at home, a struggle with drugs, and the things that finally helped her, including participating in sports, finding books, and a stint as an exchange student. In the aftermath of *Speak*'s publication, she saw others being subject to the same kind of scrutiny as her character, and witnessed the countless boys unaware of consent. Her books became the targets of censorship campaigns in the #MeToo era, yet she went on to write more books and speak out about abuse. A final section looks back at her parents and family.

Keywords: Anderson, Laurie Halse • Poetry • Verse memoir

Engle, Margarita.

 *Enchanted Air: Two Cultures, Two Wings; A Memoir.* 2015. 208p. **M** **J**

Cuban American author Margarita Engle presents a verse memoir about her first 14 years, recounting her memories of early idyllic visits to the island of Cuba, filled with lush flowers and her beloved *abuela*. These memories present an ongoing contrast to her day-to-day life in America: she feels that she doesn't fit in, as current events have her contemporaries watching her with suspicion for events she doesn't understand. As an American citizen during the Cuban Missile Crisis with both a

Cuban mother and family in Cuba, Engle experiences fear for her family, prejudice solely because of her background, and ongoing difficulties in the situation's aftermath. Her experiences are relatable for immigrants today and for any teenager who has felt themselves unable to fit in for reasons beyond their control or understanding. **AENYA Pura Belpré**

Keywords: Cuba • Engle, Margarita • Poetry • Poets • Verse memoir

Engle, Margarita.

Soaring Earth: A Companion Memoir to Enchanted Air. 2019. 176p. **M J**

The national young people's poet laureate writes about her high school in Los Angeles and her first year at Berkeley in the 1960s, where she finds an atmosphere that is light years away from her peaceful Cuban childhood, and which turns her away from education and poetry. Protests against the Vietnam War continue, and while she remains dedicated to peace, some things never change, including the prejudice she faces over misconceptions about the Cuban Revolution. Her lifelong love of books, which serves as both an ongoing escape and refuge, eventually helps to bring her back to college where she finds both her words and a new direction.

Keywords: Engle, Margaritas • Poetry • Poet • Verse memoir

Engle, Margarita.

The Lightning Dreamer: Cuba's Greatest Abolitionist. 2013. 192p. **M J**

Engle gifts readers with the story of Gertrudis Gómez de Avellaneda, known as Tula, in this fictionalized verse novel. Engle extrapolates the details of Tula's life from her published work, presenting a 14-year-old with strong feelings against both Cuba's slavery and the patriarchy that would have her married quickly to plump up her family's coffers. Tula loves to read and longs to write, despite her mother and grandfather's belief that a girl's only education should be in the kitchen. Inspired by a book of poetry she finds in the convent library, she inspires and entertains her family's housekeeper and the orphans she loves by writing plays that comment on the racial inequalities she sees around her. **Pura Belpré**

Keywords: Engle, Margarita • Poetry • Verse memoir

Grimes, Nikki.

Ordinary Hazards: A Memoir. 2019. 336p. **H**

Grimes recounts the story of her life through beautifully composed poems. Grimes had an absentee father and a schizophrenic mother and was placed at a young age in a separate foster home from her elder sister. Only slowly did she come to find herself contented with the family with whom she had been placed, finding there not only love but also other comforts for difficult times, including, for the first time, writing. Short prose passages from her journal are interspersed with the poems in which Grimes relates the ups and downs of her teenage years, as she deals with her immediate family, their crises, and events that are painful, moving, and, above all, inspiring to read.

Keywords: Grimes, Nikki • Poetry • Verse memoir

Pinkney, Andrea Davis and Brian Pinkney.

Martin Rising: Requiem for a King. 2018. 128p. **M J**

Andrea Davis Pinkney tells the story of Martin Luther King Jr.'s final months as a series of three "docu-poems" divided into daylight, darkness, and dawn. The verse may be savored or spoken and, as indicated in the author's note, may also be performed as a play. Concentrating on the time Dr. King worked to organize the Memphis sanitation workers, Pinkney's poems balance the activist with the man, the known and revered leader with the remembered and loved father. Complemented by her husband's artwork, this book allows both Pinkney's and King's words to speak for them, though both the author and illustrator do include their own thoughts, as well as a timeline and sources.

Keywords: King, Martin Luther, Jr. • Poetry • Verse biography

Woodson, Jacqueline.

 Brown Girl Dreaming. 2014. 336p. **M J**

When Jackie Woodson entered the world in Columbus, Ohio, in 1963, it was a place where her parents, with her father wanting a namesake and her mother unwilling to foist a masculine name on her daughter, reflected in a small way the fomenting changes of the wider world. Jackie and her siblings would be moved by her mother to her grandparents' house in South Carolina, and later to Brooklyn, where they needed to navigate the differences between living in the South and the North and adjust to a smaller community and city. Jackie had been expected to fit in with the rules of the house where she lived, which meant becoming a Jehovah's Witness in her grandmother's house, differentiating her further from children in her new school. The poems from the 2018–2019 ambassador for young people's literature, presented in the third person, show a young girl trying to find a place in her family and the world, against the backdrop of the civil rights movement. **CSK NBA Newbery**

Keywords: Verse memoir • Woodson, Jacqueline

Folklore, Myths, and Legends

The titles in this section contain traditional tales and myths and retellings of traditional myths or legends. They have either been adapted for younger readers or into a different format in order to make them more accessible, as in the case of George O'Connor's ongoing <u>Olympians</u> series.

Crossley-Holland, Kevin.

Norse Myths: Tales of Odin, Thor, and Loki. 2017. 240p. **M J**

The combination of Crossley-Holland's masterful writing and the enticement of understanding the stories behind the Viking gods that star in Rick Riordan's <u>Magnus Chase</u> series provides an almost irresistible allure. Books about Norse mythology are both uncommon and frequently unsatisfactory, providing explanations that can be difficult to follow. This book is intended for a younger audience, providing introductions to Loki, Odin, and Thor that have been clarified enough to make them easy to follow while leaving the structure and the details of the stories intact.

Keywords: Loki • Norse mythology • Odin • Thor

Gaiman, Neil.

Norse Mythology. 2017. 304p. **H A/YA**

Rather than an encyclopedic volume, presenting short introductions to the best-known characters associated with the Norse myths and tales, Gaiman presents a beautifully composed narrative nonfiction book that will draw readers in as he recounts the stories from the before times to Ragnarok, bringing about an end and a new beginning. It is Gaiman's love for, and intimate acquaintance with, the material that allows him to present the stories in a fluid and appealing manner, maintaining the feel of the original while giving it a modern sensibility. Gaiman's approach helps readers feel as if they know Odin, the leader of the gods, and Loki, the trickster, as well as the many others who surround them and play a part in their journey.

Keywords: Loki • Norse mythology • Odin • Thor

O'Connor, George.

Olympians.

Apollo: The Brilliant One. 2016. 80p. **M J**

The story of Phoebus Apollo, the "'most Greek' of the Greek gods," is told by the nine muses, who each share a story about him directly with the readers. Apollo, son of Leto and Zeus and half-sister of Artemis, the goddess of the hunt, is known for many things, notably a trail of romantic relationships that ended poorly for the other party, and his son, Asklepios, the great healer and founder of modern medicine. His story is told with charm and in a straightforward manner that does not skip any of the more brutish details, including his skinning of Marsyas. Readers wanting more information will find endnotes, discussion questions, and a bibliography with suggested books and Web sites.

Keywords: Apollo • Artemis • Asklepios • Graphic nonfiction • Zeus

Aphrodite: Goddess of Love. 2013. 80p. **M** **J**

While the best-known image of Aphrodite is that of the most beautiful of the Greek goddesses rising from the sea foam, this graphic guide reminds readers that she is a child of Eros, the power of love. While Zeus tries to forestall any threats to his own power by placing her in a loveless marriage, she will end up as part of a contest that will change the course of history. This is a novel launch into any unit with Helen, Paris, and the Trojan War.

Keywords: Ares • Graphic nonfiction • Zeus

Ares: Bringer of War. 2015. 80p. **M** **J**

Ares, to whom battle is everything, is shown watching over the most bloody and unreasonable of the challenges of the Trojan War in this volume of George O'Connor's <u>Olympians</u> series. It is entirely appropriate that the duel to be fought between Paris and Menelaus, which has been instigated by Ares's goading Paris into choosing Hera, Athena, or Aphrodite as the most beautiful, will be watched by all of the gods and goddesses of Olympus. With most of them having a child fighting on one side or the other, they do not hesitate to weigh in on the conflict, although only Ares is eager for battle for its own sake. It is that which most exemplifies his character. In a book that sheds light on many of the gods while telling the story of this final battle, Ares is shown to be the most staunch, single-minded, and destructive of the pantheon.

Keywords: Ares • Graphic nonfiction • Trojan War • Zeus

Artemis: Wild Goddess of the Hunt. 2017. 80p. **M** **J**

The story of Artemis begins with her mother Leto and the indignities heaped upon her by Hera, angered by the unfaithfulness of her husband, Zeus, in fathering Artemis and her twin, Apollo. After the newborn Artemis successfully serves as midwife to her mother for Apollo's birth, the three are invited to live on Mount Olympus, where Artemis pleases her father and is given the gifts she desires, which will make her the goddess of the hunt and allow her never to marry. She will go on to develop hunting skills without equal, which she will use to help protect all women as well as people unable to help themselves.

Keywords: Artemis • Graphic nonfiction • Zeus

Hermes: Tales of the Trickster. 2018. 80p. **M** **J**

A traveler shares stories of Hermes, a god so clever that his exploits amuse rather than anger the other Olympians, with Argus Panoptes, the all-seeing giant, in this volume of <u>Olympians</u>. The son of Zeus and Maia, one of the Pleiades, Hermes begins a lifetime of tricks from the day he is born. This graphic novel highlights both his intelligence and his guile, with a format that capitalizes on his legend by starting with funnier stories—such as the infant Hermes charming everyone except Apollo—and moving on to more dramatic scenes with his son Pan and the monster Typhon. A conclusion showing the entire episode to have been a frame story will draw readers into wanting to find out more.

Keywords: Graphic nonfiction • Hermes • Pan • Zeus

Hephaistos. **2019. 80p. M J**

Hephaistos is born to Hera, cast out because she feels he looks unworthy, and raised on the Island of Lemnos by Thetis and Eurynome. There he develops his gifts, making wondrous treasures that he bestows upon the gods. He earns his place among them, although he prefers to keep a home below, with his forge. O'Connor tells the story of the ugliest of the gods, who not only makes the most beautiful things but is himself married to Aphrodite. In the final volume of Olympians, also told as a frame story, readers will revisit the gods they have come to know through the series as Hephaistos tells his story to Prometheus, who is bound to the Caucasus mountains. His trials and the methods through which he continues to gain his revenge, or at least stand up for himself, mark him as worthy of his place among the Olympians. The title concludes with an author's note and information about Hephaistos, Prometheus, and Pandora, as well as suggested discussion questions.

Keywords: Graphic nonfiction • Hephaistos • Pandora • Prometheus

Consider Starting with . . .

Anderson, Laurie Halse. *Shout.*

Carter, Ally. *Dear Ally, How Do You Write a Book?*

Gaiman, Neil. *Norse Mythology.*

Popova, Maria, and Claudia Bedrick, eds. *A Velocity of Being: Letters to a Young Reader.*

Woodson, Jacqueline. *Brown Girl Dreaming.*

Fiction Read-Alikes

- **Alexander, Kwame, and Mary Rand Hess.** *Swing.* In Alexander's latest poetical offering, after a third time failing to make it through the tryouts for the baseball team, seventeen-year-old Noah decides to take a different road for this year of high school. Encouraged by his baseball-loving friend, Walt, he decides that this will finally be the year he tells his best friend, Sam, that he loves her. Noah composes collages for Sam, artworks inspired by letters he finds in a purse he buys for his mother's birthday, but it isn't until Walt delivers the first piece that Sam's anonymous admirer seems to bring new possibilities to their relationship. All seems well until, like life and the jazz music that Noah loves, the high notes turn all too often to the sharp.

- **Manga Classics.** Readers daunted by an assigned title or left out by the abridging of the movie version may find UDON Entertainment's manga adaptations a great introduction to Shakespeare, Dickens, or Austen. The titles include faithful adaptations of *A Midsummer Night's Dream, Hamlet, Macbeth, Pride and Prejudice,* and *Great Expectations.* The artwork adds depth to the characters and settings, helping to provide context and meaning to these complex and involving works, while the graphic formats keep the stories moving along at a brisk pace.

- **Santoni, Manuela.** *Jane Austen: Her Heart Did Whisper.* Santoni explores the early life of the author in a fictionalized biography, mixing what is known of both Austen's family life and the time in which she lived with a portrayal of the popular speculation about an early relationship, referred to in letters that were not destroyed at the author's behest after her death. While the world in which Austen lived became fodder for her writings, Jane herself chose to remain single, against all norms and conventions of the day. While dealing with her writing and society's constraints, she meets and forms a connection with a man named Tom Lefroy, here shown as the great love of her life. Readers interested in Austen and her works will find the notes provide further insight.

Chapter 11

Social Justice and the World

Definition

This chapter provides readers with books about popular culture, the media, social concerns and issues, and religions. These titles give readers a greater understanding of the world in which they are living.

Appeal

The books in this subgenre provide readers with background on both sides of topics in the news, giving them the opportunity to make up their own minds about issues relevant to their own lives, as well as fostering debate and introducing them to other belief systems. Readers encouraged by the students at Marjory Stoneman Douglas High School who want to become involved in a campaign of their own will find titles that demonstrate how others have made significant changes and that offer ways to mobilize efforts to make a difference in the world. These titles have a wide appeal, speaking to students and readers beyond the immediate vicinity. The areas under discussion, whether YouTube, a particular religion, or an environmental cleanup, pass beyond borders and have a wider implication. They may also reach a broader age range, as younger readers can volunteer long before they are able to vote, while older readers are more likely to become and remain personally involved.

Chapter Organization

The initial section, "Popular Media and Culture," provides readers with titles that examine different forms of media, including television and social media. This is followed by "Religion," which offers readers overviews of the most prevalent faiths from around the world. "Social Concerns and Issues" and "Activism and Awareness" finish the chapter.

Popular Media and Culture

The titles in this category look at the development of various forms of media and the effect they have had on popular culture. Readers well familiar with the ubiquity of television may not understand the impact it had in its infancy, while YouTube's astounding growth may surprise even the most jaded user. Readers interested in this area may be attracted to the story of Meridith Rojas, creator of DigiTour, the number one social media tour.

Allocca, Kevin.

Videocracy: How YouTube is Changing the World . . . with Double Rainbows, Singing Foxes, and Other Trends We Just Can't Stop Watching. 2018. 352p. **H** **A/YA**

Kevin Allocca explores the history of YouTube in order to discuss how it has become the single biggest repository of cultural data in human history. Since its inception in 2006, it went from having no users to 30 million users monthly in its first year. Now its billion users make it one of the most watched sites on the Internet, with hundreds of hours of video uploaded every minute. How it works and how it is used is both complicated and fascinating. Allocca provides a timeline of popular culture through what is now one of the most ubiquitous methods used to capture and access it. Allocca explains different metrics for measuring popularity, and offers timelines that help explain YouTube's growth from a single video clip to specialized content offerings like specialty channels and TED Talks. Readers unfamiliar with the videos mentioned in the book will be certain to keep their copy handy when browsing for something to watch.

Keywords: Videos • YouTube

Captured Television History

The advent of television news gave the viewing public not only the opportunity to have immediate access to the most important moments in history but the option to feel as though they had seen them live, as television networks replayed footage on nightly news over the following days and weeks. This close-up view, presented over and over to viewers in their own homes, introduced the events to viewers in a way that reading about them could not possibly have done. Additionally, over time, broadcasts would be able to reach a much larger audience, which at the time of each event represented a huge technological advance. The volumes here represent events that, because they were witnessed not only by the people present but by those that watched and debated them repeatedly to gain perspective about them, changed the culture in the days, weeks, and years that followed.

Burgan, Michael. *TV Launches 24-Hour News with CNN.* 2020. 64p. **M** **J**

Rissman, Rebecca. *TV Brings the Moon Landing to Earth.* 2020. 64p. **M** **J**

Rissman, Rebecca. *TV Displays Disaster as the Challenger Explodes.* 2020. 64p. **M** **J**

Smith-Llera, Danielle. *TV Exposes Brutality on the Selma March.* 2020. 64p. **M** **J**

Rojas, Meridith Valiando.

Selfie Made: Your Ultimate Guide to Social Media Stardom. 2018. 272p. **H**

Meridith Rojas had a personal goal to be a rock star, and, while not having quite the voice to make it past her audition with Clive Davis, she still successfully managed to end up in her preferred area of finding and managing talent at J Records before coming up with the idea of DigiTour. Her explanation of the company's first social media tour is used as a springboard to provide advice for anyone interested in starting a new venture. She also introduces a number of Internet stars to demonstrate how to best use social media. Rojas consistently uses herself as an example, posting pictures of herself at venues and with other social media personalities. Readers interested in DigiTour and its artists or looking to increase their social media presence will find this a very interesting book.

Keywords: DigiTour • Rojas, Meridith • Social media

Religion

In this section are books that introduce teens to faiths from around the world. Publishing in this area is generally infrequent, particularly in volumes dedicated to particular religions. As the content is slow to date, weeding should be done based on condition, as it may be difficult to find replacements.

de Heer, Margreet.

Religion: A Discovery in Comics. <u>Discovery in Comics</u>. 2015. 120p. **J**

In this entertaining volume, de Heer frames the book around writing it, incorporating her reflections as the daughter of ministers into her introductions to the world's five most commonly practiced religions. She also delves into a discussion of any religion as an organized system of beliefs, the antithetical and opposite reaction of atheism, and the extreme dedication of fundamentalists. Her introductions to the basic tenets, core, and books of each religion helps provide a bridge to understanding them. The format of this book will appeal to a wide readership, providing an additional look at women across all religions, as well as a look at some of the things people have been doing outside the mainstream.

Keywords: Buddhism • Christianity • Graphic nonfiction • Hinduism • Islam • Judaism • Religion

1

2

3

4

5

6

7

8

9

10

11

McFarlane, Marilyn.

Sacred Stories: Wisdom from World Religions. 2012. 192p. **M J**

This book provides stories central to seven of the most commonly practiced faiths in the world. Integrated into each section are sidebars that provide facts and the key tenets of the religions. From the introductory page readers will note the similarities among religions, like the use of some form of the Golden Rule, and will benefit from a greater understanding of traditions from around the world.

Keywords: Buddhism • Christianity • Hinduism • Islam • Judaism • Religion • Sacred Earth

Social Concerns and Issues

Books that examine the social and political issues of the world have become much more prevalent in the last few years. The titles in this section give teenagers a firsthand look at what it is like to live in a day and age where gun violence, the destruction of our environment, systemic racism, and misogyny are just a few of the legitimate concerns faced by teenagers on a daily basis. Readers may be interested in titles that explain the background and current status of these issues in terms of research and governmental actions, and will enjoy finding titles that provide examples of how teenagers have become involved.

Charleyboy, Lisa, and Mary Beth Leatherdale.

 #NotYourPrincess: Voices of Native American Women. 2017. 112p. **M J**

Native American women from across North America express their opinions in poems, essays, and art about what it is like to be indigenous. Thoughtful, incisive, and ranging from poignant and painful to hopeful, this book will engender discussion and leave a reader with much to ponder. **AENYA Norma Fleck**

Keywords: Essays • Native American • Poetry

Berne, Emma Carlson.

Guns and the #NeverAgain Movement: What Would It Take to End Mass Shootings? Informed! 2020. 64p. **M J H**

While possession of a gun in the United States is a right, not a privilege, mass shootings have become as frequent as they are tragic, with "active shooter" having entered the public lexicon as the person committing that crime. Berne gives context to the percentage of the world's mass shootings that take place in America, noting that Americans own 40 percent of the world's guns and also have some of the industrialized world's most unrestrictive gun laws. A timeline follows, leading up to a discussion of the current debate between gun control and gun rights advocates. The book gives information about the National Rifle Association (NRA), their position, and their lobbying power, as well as the advocacy efforts of the #NeverAgain movement started by the students from Marjory Stoneman Douglas High School. Information about what happens after gun violence, including the effects of PTSD, precedes suggestions for how to get involved. Readers pondering sides of the gun debate will find critical questions and a list of further resources.

Keywords: Gun violence • Mass shootings • National Rifle Association • Post traumatic stress disorder

Stanborough, Rebecca.

Sexual Harassment in the Age of #MeToo: Crossing the Line. **Informed!** 2020. 64p. **M** **J** **H**

While there has been an increase in the reporting of high-profile incidents in recent years, it remains necessary to educate the public about the different types of harassment, the difference between harassment and abuse, and why harassment is so prevalent in our culture. Abuse and harassment both happen regularly and contribute to a rape culture that has had lasting impacts on victims. In 2018, a Hollywood scandal and the founder of an organization to support female survivors set off a firestorm by asking survivors to share their stories on Twitter, and the #MeToo movement was born. Not all reaction has been positive. It is important to know your rights and to have discussions on how to change rape culture, behavior, and public policy. Suggestions for how to support victims and myths about rape are included, along with a list of further resources.

Keywords: Rape culture • Sexual abuse • Sexual harassment

Braun, Eric.

The Deep State Conspiracy: Does It Exist? **Informed!** 2020. 64p. **M** **J** **H**

One of Donald Trump's campaign promises was to remove the bad actors from Washington and, in so doing, "drain the swamp." After the 2016 election, after numerous conflicts and firings within his government, President Trump accused former President Obama of spying on him, and in 2017 the first narrative appeared about the shadow government known as the deep state, the idea of officials actively working against the president. How and where this narrative appeared leads into a discussion of whether such a thing exists, and if so, where, and when it may have appeared. The use of espionage in government is debated with several examples that may be as useful for students as they are relevant to an understanding of current events, providing backgrounds and timelines that include Watergate and Edward Snowden as case studies. Critical questions, further resources, and a glossary are provided.

Keywords: Deep state • Espionage • Nixon, Richard • Trump, Donald • Watergate

11

Smith-Llera, Danielle.

You Are Eating Plastic Every Day: What's in Our Food? <u>Informed!</u> 2020. 64p. **M** **J**

It is both eye-opening and terrifying to read of the extent of the proliferation of plastic into the environment. Putting aside the small amount of plastics that are recycled, and the large amount that is illegally sent to other countries and buried in landfills, there is still a vast amount to wind up in the world's oceans. How it gets there, and the ways that it breaks down into particles small enough to become part of the food chain, is laid out clearly, accompanied by photographs and sidebars with pertinent statistical information. While the extent of the problem is such that readers may be left feeling rather hopeless, the list of further resources and Web sites is a welcome addition to the suggestions of things to do for limiting use and recycling.

Keywords: Microplastics • Plastics • Pollution

Nevertheless, We Persisted: 48 Voices of Defiance, Strength and Courage. 2018. 320p. **M** **J**

In the foreword to this volume of stirring essays, Senator Amy Klobuchar remembers a moment on the Senate floor, when the words "nevertheless, she persisted" were first spoken about her colleague, Senator Elizabeth Warren. After trending on Twitter and inspiring women to tattoo this inspirational sentiment in Klobuchar's home state, she set out to find stories that embodied the deeper meaning implied by these words. The 48 essays in this volume are stories from activists, actors, athletes, artists, writers, and politicians. They share personal experiences from their youth, having faced loss, heartbreak, prejudice, bullying, and what might seem like overwhelming obstacles. These stories let readers know that there are different ways to persist, as standing up for what is right may be just as difficult when being told that as a transgender teen you should not be allowed to use the bathroom of your choice is a different kind of pain than dealing with the loss of a sibling to a gunman.

Keywords: Social activists

Jensen, Kelly, ed.

Here We Are: 44 Voices Write, Draw, and Speak about Feminism for the Real World. 2017. 240p. **M** **J**

Forty-four authors present their takes on feminism, providing readers with views that vary in both theme and format. The pieces are grouped loosely by themes such as "body and mind" and "culture and pop culture," and the authors contemplate things such as their bodies, sexuality, race, or mental health. They also discuss what feminism means and what it means to them. Others offer lists of various top "female" things, and interspersed throughout the book are

FAQs about feminism explaining key concepts like the Bechdel Test. An additional list of fiction, nonfiction, films, and Web sites is included.

Keywords: Feminism • Gender identity • Intersectionality

Johnson, Anna Maria.

Debunking Conspiracy Theories. <u>News Literacy</u>. 2019. 64p. **M** **J**

This quick and accessible volume explains what a conspiracy theory is and how it spreads, and provides examples to show how it is possible not only for incorrect information to remain in the public domain long past the time that the subject has been disproven, but for it to be considered valid and disseminated. How this happens is shown using both historical and current examples that demonstrate the possible outcomes. Readers are shown how it is now possible to research information more easily and efficiently in order to evaluate the veracity of claims, which is increasingly important given the speed with which any sort of information is spread on the Internet. Useful tips and strategies for evaluating information provide a valuable conclusion and discussion point for any student.

Keywords: Conspiracy theories • Media literacy • News literacy

Kuklin, Susan.

We Are Here to Stay: Voices of Undocumented Young Adults. 2019. 182p. **M** **J**

Nine undocumented immigrants share the stories of how they came to the United States and their lives after they came. From different countries and routes, from traveling legally on visitor visas to having been a trafficker's victim, the young people are now all in college and contributing members of society, having faced discrimination and difficulties assimilating to American society. Common among them is the desire for a greater education having been a key factor in their desire to come to the United States and the poignancy of their presentations. All identifiers such as names or photographs have been stripped from the text in the initial publication. Names are written with first initials and a dash, and photographs have been removed, leaving only an empty frame alongside the header. Readers looking for more information will find it in a timeline of immigration law and executive actions dating back to 1790, and a list of Web sites of interest for undocumented immigrants. It is an unfortunate truth, as pointed out in an included photo essay by Rev. John Fife, cofounder of No More Deaths, that historically there are several instances of refugees trying to escape death that have been met with walls and stronger borders.

Keywords: DACA • Dreamers • Immigrants • Undocumented immigrants

11

Nazario, Sonia.

Enrique's Journey (The Young Adult Adaptation): The True Story of a Boy Determined to Reunite with His Mother. 2013. 182p. **H**

Journalist Sonia Nazario first published the story of a 17-year-old Honduran teenager entering the United States illegally as a series of Pulitzer Prize–winning articles in the *Los Angeles Times*. In order to find out just how harrowing it was to make his journey, which involved crossing two borders illegally, she followed his footsteps herself, adding avoiding rape to the already perilous trip. This updated edition not only illuminates why so many mothers are willing to leave their children behind in the hope of earning a better life for them, but also just how damaging that can be for both mother and child emotionally. Using Enrique, his mother, Lourdes, and their family as a case study, readers may see how dangerous it is to be an illegal immigrant in the United States given the current political climate. It is also dangerous to be an ordinary citizen in Honduras, much less one as famous as Enrique, especially considering the country has one of the world's highest homicide rates. Nazario's source notes and the included statistics about migrants and immigrants are worthy of consideration and discussion.

Keywords: Emigration • Immigration

Activism and Awareness

There has been a recent increase in the number of published titles aimed at demonstrating that teenagers are able activists for any number of causes. This was likely due to an amplified discussion around the increasing importance of teenagers in the political process, which began before the 2018 midterm elections, in terms of debating lowering the voting age.[1] The books in this category introduce readers to a number of areas that will affect them, as well as teenagers who have become dedicated activists, allowing them to find out how they can become involved and providing various ways that they can make a difference.

Anderson, Carol, with Tonya Bolden.

One Person, No Vote: How Not All Voters Are Treated Equally. 2019. 288p. **M J H**

Anderson presents a thorough and detailed history of the many ways in which elections in the United States have been affected by voter suppression, including violations and subjugations of the voting laws, before presenting tales of outright chicanery which resulted in unfair voting practices and undemocratic elections. As horrifying as they are fascinating, the outlandish and appalling machinations that political parties have used to disenfranchise citizens in order to ensure their continued power will affect readers concerned about the state of the country in which they are living and working. Whether readers are left worried about the gerrymandering of their own districts, concerned about the fate of people unable to cast a ballot, or determined to become involved in the political process, this book will enlighten readers as to the importance of exercising their right to vote.

Keywords: Disenfranchisement • Elections • Racial discrimination • Voting Rights Act

Bowles, Stella, with Anne Laurel Carter.

My River: Cleaning Up the LaHave River. 2018. 96p. **M J**

Nova Scotia native Stella Bowles was 11 years old when she found out that the use of straight pipes, rather than septic systems, meant that sewage was being dumped into the river that was a main source for recreation and fishing for her community. She swung into action, developing a project to measure the levels of contamination and demonstrating that the dangers were at a level where immediate help was needed. Bowles and Carter summarize her process, including how she was going to actually do the project, ways to continue actions after the project and how to adapt it, and information about demonstrable change at the site. Readers will also learn about the mentorship program that Bowles started, which is illustrated by her showing a group how to test water. They will also follow the progress of her inquiry from its beginning as a simple testing for a science fair project, through its rise in national competitions and the support and monetary commitments it received from three levels of government.

Keywords: Contamination • Environmental action • LaHave River • Septic system

McGraw, Sally.

Living Simply: A Teen Guide to Minimalism. 2019. 112p. **M J**

McGraw presents a history of minimalism, pointing out that both recycling and upcycling were a necessary and accepted part of daily life until the 20th century. Not until after the austerity of the Great Depression and the world wars, coupled with the development of cheap, reusable materials, was it possible for rampant consumerism to make possible the abundance and the ever-increasing waste that leads to climate change. Chapters here introduce practical ways to keep from adding to either, by making conscious choices in what to eat, wear, buy, and maintain as a lifestyle. To help with this, readers are offered projects to remake items in order to avoid throwing them out and suggestions for where to purchase gently used clothing or how to correctly dispose of items. It isn't suggested that all methods will be foolproof or that they need to be followed by everybody, rather that all contributions will add up and help the planet, encouraging more people to help.

Keywords: Minimalism • Recycling • Upcycling

11

Paisley, Erinne.

Can Your Conversations Change the World? <u>PopActivism.</u> 2017. 160p. **M** **J**

Teen activist Erinne Paisley's focus in this volume of the <u>PopActivism</u> series is women's rights. Paisley uses the backlash to her paper prom dress, explained in other volumes of the series, to explain empowerment and the need to create equal opportunities. Paisley includes explanations for several different types of feminism, including the feminist waves, global feminism, intersectionality, and HeForShe. Paisley discusses equality, consent, and body image, presented in terms of popular culture. Each is accompanied by suggestions of how to get involved and stay involved in dialogues to change the status quo, whether looking up the elected representatives for the area, or looking up one of the suggested Web sites.

Keywords: Activism • Women's rights

Paisley, Erinne.

Can Your Outfit Change the World? <u>PopActivism.</u> 2017. 133p. **M** **J**

Erinne Paisley's prom dress was definitely the most unusual at her prom. She made her dress out of her old math homework and decorated it with a political statement inspired by her favorite activist, Malala Yousafzai, and sent the money she would have spent on buying a dress to Yousafzai's nonprofit organization. The questions that she was asked afterward about why she did this led her to wonder about the origins of her other clothing, including what it was made of, the working conditions of the people who made it, and what she was saying by wearing the clothes she did, whether she was supporting company logos, phrases, or labels. This book provides a number of ways to learn how to become globally conscious in terms of fashion. Paisley provides information about materials that are produced and designers and clothing manufacturers that do and don't follow ethical practices. Beyond the strictly environmental material is also a chapter that looks at how to question fashion messaging. Suggestions for how to get involved are shown through some fairly impressive examples, such as Erek Hansen's creation of Go Green Ohio, which supports green clothing campaigns.

Keywords: Activism • Clothing • Environmentalism • Fashion

Paisley, Erinne.

Can Your Smartphone Change the World? <u>PopActivism.</u> 2017. 133p. **M** **J**

When Erinne Paisley made a prom dress out of newspaper and turned it into a fundraising campaign, she didn't expect it to go viral, but the pictures of the event posted by her brother brought national attention. Paisley uses her book to give a background of her own volunteer history and an explanation of social justice, explaining the good that can be done by teenagers in the community.

In this volume of the <u>PopActivism</u> series she offers several examples of projects using different social media, including YouTube, Instagram, and Twitter, and encourages teenagers to become involved in ways that interest them. Younger students may be interested in volunteering, and older students may be better equipped to become involved in some of the groups mentioned in the resources.

Keywords: Activism • Social media

Rich, KaeLyn.

Girls Resist! A Guide to Activism, Leadership, and Starting a Revolution. 2018. 240p. 🔲

This book is a guide for the many ways in which girls interested in activism may become involved. An introduction notes why girls deserve to fight for things they believe in, noting that they have historically been seen as the weaker sex, and that by organizing they have power. Rich does note that an important part of resistance is being aware that existing gender norms enforce the idea of the gender binary, and suggests ways to address this, such as the use of inclusive language for means of address. Future activists will learn about what it takes to organize and plan campaigns, protests, and fundraising opportunities, as well as needed resources and tips for the implementation of the various events. Definitions are also provided for key ideas such as microaggressions and privilege, and future activists are encouraged to keep themselves going by practicing self-care.

Keywords: Activism

Sanders, Bernie.

Bernie Sanders Guide to Political Revolution: A Guide for the Next Generation. 2018. 240p. 🔲 🔲

In this book, 2016 and 2020 Democratic presidential candidate Bernie Sanders gives an introduction to the Democratic Party's platform. As he notes in the individual planks, young people are likely to be affected by any changes he proposes. Every area he looks at, whether taxes, education, health care, climate change, justice reform, or the government itself, is accompanied by a breakdown of the current situation in the United States, how it has changed and may be compared to other countries, and what can be changed. Definitions are included for key concepts. At the end of each chapter supplementary links are included for key reports, and additional information about the topic and volunteer groups are included under a "Mobilize" section. As of this writing, the Democratic and Republican nominees haven't yet been chosen; this title only mentions Donald Trump as having been the Republican opponent in the 2016 election. While Sanders's areas for reform are all valid discussion points as of the writing of this book, this is a book that will likely date rapidly depending on any legislative changes.

Keywords: Climate change • Democratic party • Economic reform

Stone, Tanya Lee.

Girl Rising: Changing the World One Girl at a Time. 2017. 208p. **M** **J**

Girl Rising is the name of a global campaign for girls' education and empowerment. This book was inspired by the documentary of the same name and presents the stories of girls around the world, giving statistics to show that girls are not given the same chance at schooling as boys, and how and why this gender disparity affects their future. The potential to stop serious and ongoing barriers, including poverty, early child marriage and sexual trafficking, offers not only a better future but also a steadier and more prosperous future for generations to come.

Keywords: Education • Empowerment • Gender disparity

Consider Starting with . . .

Bowles, Stella, with Anne Laurel Carter. *My River: Cleaning Up the LaHave River.*

Charleyboy, Lisa, and Mary Beth Leatherdale. *#NotYourPrincess: Voices of Native American Women.*

de Heer, Margreet. *Religion: A Discovery in Comics.*

Kuklin, Susan. *We Are Here to Stay: Voices of Undocumented Young Adults.*

Fiction Read-Alikes

- **Caletti, Deb.** *A Heart in a Body in the World.* Caletti's Printz honor–winning novel finds Annabelle, the victim of a tragedy that has left her completely hollowed out, deciding to leave her tragedy behind her in Seattle and run across the country to Washington, D.C. Accompanied by her grandpa Ed and backed by her brother and friends, who create a GoFundMe Web site in her name, she finds herself unable to outrun her demons or an unwitting media star, as her attempt to escape becomes a cause.

- **Oseman, Alice.** *Radio Silence.* Seventeen-year-old Frances Janvier is a student with one goal: getting into Cambridge. It is so important to her that she devotes pretty much all her time to it, giving up everything else except listening to and writing for her favorite podcast, *Universe City.* When she meets Alex Cast, it turns out that they have more in common than getting good grades. Can they make great radio?

References

Oosterhoff, Benjamin. "Should 16- and 17-Year-Olds Be Able to Vote?" *Psychology Today*, October 24, 2018, https://www.psychologytoday.com /ca/blog/civically-engaged/201810/should-16-and-17-year-olds-be-able -vote.

1

2

3

4

5

6

7

8

9

10

11

Appendix A

Nonfiction Readers' Advisory Resources for YA Librarians

Although there are few readers' advisory or reviewing resources devoted solely to young adult nonfiction, there are sources that can help with both readers' advisory and collection development.

Reference and Readers' Advisory Sources

Carstensen, Angela.

The Readers' Advisory Guide to Teen Literature. American Library Association, 2018.

Fraser, Elizabeth.

Reality Rules II: A Reader's Advisory Guide to Teen Nonfiction. Libraries Unlimited, 2012.

Pawuk, Michael, and David S. Serchay.

Graphic Novels: A Guide to Comic Books, Manga, and More. Genreflecting Advisory Series. ABC-CLIO, 2017.

Review Journals

Booklist. PO Box 607, Mt. Morris, IL 61054-7564. Phone: 1-888-350-0949. Web site: www.booklistonline.com.

Booklist is a critical collection development and review journal, which reviews more than 2,500 children's titles annually, with both a print and an online component. Booklistonline offers access to a database of more than 130,000 reviews. Monthly, Booklist includes a compilation of reviews from BlueInk Review, a fee-based review service of self-published books. Reviews indicate which of the adult reviews would have appeal for young adult readers, and Michael Cart's "Carte Blanche" feature offers cogent discussions of YA titles.

Horn Book. 7858 Industrial Parkway, Plain City OH 43064. Web site: www.hbook.com.

Horn Book's Web site includes subscription information for the long-running bimonthly magazine; the semiannual *Horn Book Guide*, which provides readers with 2,000 reviews; and access to 80,000 more through *Horn Book Online*. Additional enticements include Roger Sutton's blog and coverage of the Boston Globe–Horn Book awards.

School Library Journal. 160 Varick Street, 11th Floor, New York, NY 10013. Phone: 646-380-0700. Web site: www.slj.com.

Subscriptions to *School Library Journal* may be obtained through its Web site, which offers articles and some of the strongest, most interesting blogs around, such as the *Teen Librarian Toolbox*. Nonfiction titles may also be found in Booklist sections for school and public libraries.

Voice of Youth Advocates (VOYA). E L Kurdyla Publishing LLC, Bowie, MD. Web site: voyamagazine.com. Email: cs@voyamagazine.com.

VOYA includes nonfiction titles in each bimonthly magazine and occasional themed booklists. Its August issue also features a Nonfiction Honor list.

Web Sites

In addition to the strong sites developed by review journals, bloggers, book lovers, and library associations have interesting discussions about books in the months running up to the Youth Media Awards.

Cybils (Children's and Young Adult Bloggers' Literary Awards). http://www.cybils.com.

The Cybils are intended to recognize both literary quality and popularity. Among the eight current categories, with nominations open to the reading public, readers and librarians interested in nonfiction will find titles not only in the Nonfiction category (Elementary/Middle Grade and Young Adult levels), but also in Poetry and Graphic Novels.

The Hub. http://www.yalsa.ala.org/thehub/.

YALSA's The Hub is a one-stop shop "to find out about great teen reads," with content created by librarians and teens. This is also the current location to find out the nominees for several committees that work virtually, including Amazing Audiobooks, Best Fiction for Young Adults, Great Graphic Novels for Teens, and Popular Paperbacks.

Reading Rants. http://www.readingrants.org.

Jennifer Hubert Swan's blog contains well-written and thoughtful reviews of new titles that will appeal to a wide variety of readers.

Book Awards and Selection Lists

The increasing amount of quality nonfiction for young adults is well reflected in the recognition these books receive. The following is an explanation of the awards and book lists which consider and recognize achievements in nonfiction.

The YALSA Award for Excellence in Young Adult Nonfiction. http://www.ala .org/yalsa/nonfiction-award.

Awarded for the 10th time in 2019, this award honors the best in nonfiction published for an audience between the ages of 12 to 18. A short list of five titles is published annually in November and the full list of the committee's nominated titles is published after YALSA's media awards are announced at the ALA Midwinter meeting.

The Young Adult Library Services Association (YALSA) has several committees that work to find the best books for teens aged twelve to eighteen. http://www .ala.org/yalsa/book-media-lists.

The librarians who choose these books work throughout the year, selecting their final lists at the ALA Midwinter meeting. Lists include: (1) Quick Picks for Reluctant Young Adult Readers, pleasurable books for teens who do not like to read; (2) Popular Paperbacks for Young Adults, pleasurable reading in a variety of accessible themes and genres, and: (3) Great Graphic Novels for Teens. Additionally, every five years a team of public, secondary, and academic librarians develop a list of books intended to introduce readers to academic disciplines, under the title Outstanding Books for the College Bound, which is updated every five years.

The Michael L. Printz Award. http://www.ala.org/yalsa/printz.

Given annually by YALSA to the book that exemplifies literary excellence in young adult literature, as many as four Printz honor books may be chosen annually.

The Alex Award. http://www.ala.org/yalsa/alex-awards.

Sponsored by the Margaret A. Edwards Trust, after whom the award is named, the Alex award is given to the best 10 adult books for young adults. The committee also publishes its full list of nominated titles after the Youth Media Awards announcement at the ALA Midwinter meeting.

The Coretta Scott King Book Awards. http://www.ala.org/rt/emiert/cskbook awards.

> The work of the Coretta Scott King task force commemorates the life and works of Dr. Martin Luther King Jr. and honors Mrs. Coretta Scott King with the Coretta Scott King Award. These titles promote understanding of the cultures of all people and their realization of the American dream. The Coretta Scott King–John Steptoe New Talent Award, which celebrates the beginning of a career, are given to African American authors and illustrators for outstanding inspirational and educational contributions.

The International Literacy Association (ILA). https://www.literacyworldwide .org/get-resources/reading-lists/teachers-choices-reading-list.

> A professional organization for people involved in teaching reading to any age group, their annual Teachers' Choices include fiction and nonfiction books in primary, intermediate, and advanced reader categories. The goals of the project include choosing books that may be used across the curriculum and that will encourage young people to read more.

The Robert F. Sibert Informational Book Medal. http://www.ala.org/alsc /awardsgrants/bookmedia/sibertmedal.

> Awarded annually by the ALA's Association for Library Services to Children (ALSC) at its Midwinter meeting in January, the Sibert award is given to the author, author/illustrator, coauthor or author, and illustrator of the most distinguished informational book published in the United States during the preceding year. Honor books may also be awarded.

The Norma Fleck Award for Canadian Children's Nonfiction. http://bookcentre .ca/programs/awards/norma-fleck-award-for-canadian-childrens-non-fiction.

> Overseen by the Canadian Children's Book Centre, The Norma Fleck Award was established in 1999 to recognize the high quality of informational literature available to children and young adults.

The Boston Globe–Horn Book Award. https://www.hbook.com/?detailStory= boston-globe-horn-book-awards.

> Cosponsored by the *Boston Globe* and *Horn Book* magazine. Nonfiction is one of the three categories of the award, which is judged by three children's literature professionals.

The Lane Anderson Award. http://laneandersonaward.ca/.

> Honoring the best science writing in Canada in both a Young Adult and an Adult category, the award was established in 1987 and is administered by the Fitzhenry Family Foundation.

The National Book Award for Young People's Literature. https://www.national book.org/national-book-awards/.

> The National Book Award has been celebrating "the best in American literature" since 1950.

The Orbis Pictus Award. http://www2.ncte.org/awards/orbis-pictus-award-non fiction-for-children/.

> Chosen annually by the National Council of Teachers of English. Winners should appeal to a wide age range and be useful in K–8 classrooms.

The Yellow Cedar Award. http://www.accessola.org/web/OLA/Forest_of_Reading /About_the_Forest/Programs_for_Kids/OLA/Forest_of_Reading/Programs_For _School_Aged_Readers.aspx.

> Administered by the Ontario Library Association and a new introduction to their annual Forest of Reading awards as of 2020. A young reader's choice award intended to honor the best nonfiction books for readers in grades five through eight.

ALSC Recommended Titles. http://www.ala.org/alsc/awardsgrants/notalists/ncb.

> The Association for Library Service to Children (ALSC), which serves children up to the age of 14, makes its annual Notable Book Lists, as well as information about the Newbery Award and the Sibert Award, available on their Web site. The Robert F. Sibert Informational Book Medal is awarded annually to the author(s) and illustrator(s) of the most distinguished informational book for children.

Amelia Bloomer Book List. http://www.ala.org/awardsgrants/amelia-bloomer -book-list.

> The Feminist Task Force of the Social Responsibilities Round Table of the American Library Association creates an annual book list of the best feminist books for young readers, for children from birth through age 18. A list of the criteria used to choose the books is available on the task force's Web site.

Appendix B

Library Vendors and Wholesalers

These companies offer a wide variety of services to libraries, including selection, acquisitions, custom cataloging, and processing services.

United States

Baker & Taylor. www.baker-taylor.com/index.cfm.

Ingram Content Group. www.ingramcontent.com.
One Ingram Boulevard, La Vergne, TN, 37086.
Phone: 615-793-5000.

Junior Library Guild. www.juniorlibraryguild.com.
Phone: 800-491-0174.   Fax: 800-827-3080.

Mackin. mackin@mackin.com.
3505 County Road 42 West, Burnsville, MN 55306.
Phone: 800-245-9540.

Canada

Library Bound, Inc. www.librarybound.com.
Main office: 100 Bathurst Drive, Unit 2, Waterloo, ON N2V 1V6.
Phone: 519-885-3233. Toll Free Phone: 800-363-4728.
LBI West: 8370 Prince Edward Street, Vancouver, BC V5X 3R9.
Phone: 604-434-5242. Fax: 519-885-2662.

Library Services Centre. www.lsc.on.ca.

    131 Shoemaker Street, Kitchener, ON N2E 3B5. Phone: 519-746-4420.

    Phone: 1-800-26-3360 (Canada only). Fax: 519-746-4425.

Tinlids. tinlids.ca.

    130 Martin Ross Avenue, Toronto, ON M3J 2L4.

    Phone: 416-665-5663 or 1-800-461-9397.

    Fax: 416-665-0775 or 1-800-461-9405.

    Inquiries: info@tinlids.ca. Orders: orders@tinlids.ca.

United Library Services. www.uls.com.

    Head Office: 7140 Fairmount Drive SE, Calgary, AB T2H 0X4.

    Phone: 403-252-4426 / 1-888-342-5857 (Loc. 0). Fax: 403-258-3426.

    Email: info@uls.com

    BC Division: 101B - 3430 Brighton Avenue, Burnaby, BC V5A 3H4.

    Phone: 604-421-1154 / 1-877-853-1200. Fax: 604-421-2216 / 1-866-421-2216.

    Email: burnaby@uls.com.

Whitehots, Inc. www.whitehots.com.

    205 Industrial Parkway North, Unit #3, Aurora, ON L4G 4C4.

    E-mail: admin@whitehots.com.   Phone: 905-727-9188.

    Toll Free Phone: 1-800-567-9188.   Fax: 905-727-8756.

    Toll Free Fax: 1-888-563-0020.

Appendix C

Bibliography

Caring for Kids. "Teen Health." Accessed July 9, 2019. Available at https://www .caringforkids.cps.ca/handouts/teenhealth-index.

Carstensen, Angela. *The Readers' Advisory Guide to Teen Literature.* American Library Association, 2018.

Cart, Michael. "Just the Facts, Ma'am." Carte Blanche. *Booklist* 114, no.14 (March 15, 2018): 35.

Cords, Sarah Statz. *The Real Story: A Guide to Nonfiction Reading Interests.* Genreflecting Advisory Series. Westport, CT: Libraries Unlimited, 2006.

Csikszentmihalyi, Mihalyi. "Adolescence." Encyclopaedia Britannica. Accessed July 9, 2019. https://www.britannica.com/science/adolescence.

Fraser, Elizabeth. *Reality Rules II: A Guide to Teen Nonfiction Reading Interests.* Santa Barbara, CA: Libraries Unlimited, 2012.

Horning, K. T. *From Cover to Cover: Evaluating and Reviewing Children's Books.* New York: HarperCollins, 2010.

Hunt, Jonathan. "The Amorphous Genre." *Horn Book Magazine* 89, no. 3 (May/June 2013): 31–34.

Merriam-Webster. "do-it-yourself." Accessed July 1, 2019. https://www.merriam -webster.com/dictionary/do-it-yourself.

Milliot, Jim. "Print Unit Sales Increased 1.3% in 2018." *Publisher's Weekly* 266, no. 2 (January 4, 2019): 4

Mueller, Mary E. "History and History Makers: Give YAs the Whole Picture." School Library Journal 37, (November 1991).

Oosterhoff, Benjamin. "Should 16- and 17-Year-Olds Be Able to Vote?" *Psychology Today*, October 24, 2018. https://www.psychologytoday.com/ca/blog/civically-engaged/201810/should-16-and-17-year-olds-be-able-vote.

Summers, Kate. "Adult Reading Habits 'and Preferences in Relation to Gender Differences." *Reference and User Services Quarterly* 52, no. 3 (Spring 2019): 243.

Author / Title Index

Subject Index

About the Author

ELIZABETH (BETSY) FRASER is a selector at the Calgary Public Library in Alberta, Canada. She is author of *Reality Rules!: A Guide to Teen Nonfiction Reading Interests* and the 2016 winner of the YALSA/ABC-CLIO/Greenwood Service to Young Adults Outstanding Achievement Award.